A Horse Can't Buck in Sand

Accounts of Western Country Life in the Early 20th Century

Edited, with Introductions

by

David G. Clark

Let not ambition mock their useful toil,
Their homely joys, and destiny obscure;
Nor grandeur hear with a disdainful smile,
The short and simple annals of the poor.

Elegy Written in a Country Churchyard
Thomas Gray (1716-1771)

Contents

Preface

BELLVUE, COLORADO: Altitude 5149 feet (depending on where you stand, and the accuracy of your altimeter). Go west, though, and you climb. Up through Rist Canyon eventually you reach the top of Stove Prairie Hill. Keep on west, and you descend to Stove Prairie School. There you have a choice. Left to Masonville or Buckhorn Canyon, straight on, it's the old Jacob Flowers Road (but you probably don't have keys to the locks at the gates along the way). Most people turn right, and head down to the Cache La Poudre River. Just before hitting the pavement, off to the left, you may spot a large rock with a skull and crossbones: Rattlesnake Polly Brinkhoff's place was back in there.

I stand atop Bingham Hill and look down. Art Denham and Bill Lloyd, who used to grade the road up and over the hill and down into Bellvue, called it Bang 'em Hill. Even back then it was a lovely spot where lovers parked around sundown and stayed.

To the north is the Bellvue Dome, mentioned in some geology textbooks for its readable formation and history. On the east side of the dome is the pavement of U.S. 287, formerly known as the Overland Trail, a path of least resistance on west. Farther on, you go through The Glade, past House Rock (or Sign Rock, as it has become these days), and on up to Livermore, Virginia Dale, and finally, Laramie. Buffalo Bill used to saunter along that road, on his way home from Denver, after stopping over at Norma Salisbury's granddad's house. Jack Slade held up stages along that road, until he got bored with the easy pickings and left for his appointment with the hangman.

Over my shoulder, to the southeast, Fort Collins is on its way out here. Just across the road from the overlook are a couple of designer homes, two of the many that perch on the ridges to catch the light and view. They have the full comple-

ment of satellite dishes and SUVs. I wonder what the old-
timers would have thought of the money that is flooding into
Pleasant Valley.

In 1974, Alice and I started looking for a house in Fort
Collins. Prices in town were high, and the selection poor. The
real estate agent was getting tired of seeing us turn up our
noses at the new tract houses, so one day he told us about a
place out in the country a few miles northwest. That's how we
found Bellvue.

The house was definitely different. Bill, the agent, had
said it was built out of logs. But when we saw it, it was
shingled. Not just the roof, but the sides. Gray asphalt
shingles, top to bottom. The owners, Art and Edna Denham,
said they hadn't done it, but they understood it was an attempt
to insulate the place from the outside. We peeled back one
shingle, and sure enough there was a log behind. But we
agonized for days. Were the logs in good shape, or were they
rotted out? There was only one way to know. At last—we
were getting desperate, and the price was right—we went
ahead and bought it. Strolling through Bellvue, we would see
more shingles of the same style and color covering chicken
houses, woodsheds, and barns. Did some slick-talking roofing
salesman come through sometime after World War II and sign
up the whole town?

The first thing we did for our house was take off the
shingles. As an unemployed new college graduate, Alice did
most of that. One day she was prying away at shingles and
roofing nails with hammer and crowbar when she uncovered a
large brown bat, inches from her face and furious at being
awakened in the middle of the day. After that, I picked up a
larger share of the work. Almost miraculously, the logs were
in good shape. Over the years, as our children arrived, we
added to the house. The interior of the new part is modern,
but the old part is still out of plumb and rustic. We were told
it was built by the first licensed woman carpenter in Colorado.
Bessie Tamlin's son Vic, who finished the inside, was in the

South Pacific with the Marines in World War II. At Iwo Jima, he won the Bronze Star for carrying a wounded buddy to an aid station, even though Vic was badly wounded himself. He refused to accept it, saying any Marine would have done what he did. He was hit in one arm and shoulder, and the carpentry he did later shows it. But since we know why some of the joints don't fit, we don't care.

It took three or four years to get to know our neighbors. The Denhams lived next door, and we made friends with them right away. And with our neighbor across the way, Katie Davis. All three were in their seventies. Finally we were invited to join the Cache La Poudre Grange, and that was the sign we had been accepted. Most of our fellow Grangers were also in their seventies or beyond. In fact, many of Bellvue's residents were in that age range. Quite a few of them had lived their entire lives in the area.

Partly as a way of learning about our town, partly to get to know more of our neighbors, but mostly to document a generation that was rapidly passing from the scene, we decided to undertake an oral history project. The Colorado Humanities Program gave us money for tape, and the Fort Collins Public Library let us use its recorder. We spent a year interviewing three dozen people on what life had been like for them, and whatever they wanted to tell. The agenda was theirs. We put typescript copies of their interviews into the Oral History Center of the Library, and we produced a half-hour tape and slide show, *Bellvue Voices*, featuring some of the participants. All that work was finished in 1979. Alice and I went on to other things. We raised our two wonderful children, Sarah and Matt, and enjoyed my son Andy as he grew to adulthood, married, and started a family. Alice embarked on a career of her own as adult education director for her church, while my own work led to increasing responsibilities, first with the university and later with the Colorado State University System. Always, though, the *Bellvue Voices* kept tugging at me, and finally I found time to edit and compress some of the stories that had so attracted me.

Although as a group the people were not particularly self-reflective, their characters shine through their stories as they relate what gave them joy and misery. If they were interested in the big social issues of their day (and they certainly were affected by them), that interest did not remain strong in their old age. Mostly lacking in formal education (only a couple of the women had college educations), they were all well schooled in how to do things with their hands, and how to survive with next to none of the niceties. Perhaps fatalism is an over-riding attitude of octogenarians, but they seemed pretty matter of fact about their misfortunes: lost loved ones, injuries, natural disasters and all the rest. Somehow they conveyed the feeling that, rough as their lives were, they wouldn't really trade their experiences for an easier time. With one exception in the summer of 2004, they are gone now, and so is their way of life, but bits of their stories, told in their own voices, remain. For that we are grateful.

Acknowledgments

Many people assisted with this task, which has taken more than 25 years to bring to its ultimate completion. The original project, an oral history of old-timers in and around Bellvue, Colorado, was finished in 1979. That first section of the task was greatly aided and supported by the Cache La Poudre Grange No. 456; Robert Webb, Grange Master, and his wife, Edith; Charlene Tresner, local history librarian at the Fort Collins Public Library; Stella Sapp, Helen Burgess, and O.J. Burgess, who guided planning of the oral history project and suggested persons who should be interviewed; Kathlene Lemmon, executive director, and Connie C. Bowman, administrative assistant, of The Colorado Humanities Program, as it was then known, during 1978-79; James Downing, First National Bank of Fort Collins, and Lois Hunziker, fiscal agents who volunteered to track expenses related to the Colorado Humanities Program grant that purchased tapes and provided typing for the final copies; Alice Clark, who provided much inspiration and useful advice from start to finish, typed initial drafts of the interviews, and conducted several interviews herself; and numerous Fort Collins businesses who provided in-kind support with discounts on tape and other recording supplies; and The Coloradoan and Triangle Review, Fort Collins newspapers that helped publicize the public presentations.

The second component of the project benefited as well from Alice Clark's continuing support and encouragement. Andy Clark provided sketches of Bellvue scenes and tools that grace the interior pages. Sarah and Matt Clark, with their interest and questions about a time long gone helped in ways they probably did not suspect. Rheba Massey, local history coordinator of the Fort Collins Public Library, was very helpful in certifying dates. Rowene Danbom, good friend and former colleague, lent her sharp eye and keen mind to improving the manuscript.

Of course, the major assistance throughout these two decades was provided by the interviewees themselves. Without exception, they gave their time to an inquisitive visitor and allowed him to ask numerous questions about how they had gone about their lives. While space limitations have, regrettably, prevented me from including sections from every contributor, each has played an invaluable role in educating me regarding early 20th century life in Pleasant Valley and in the West. So, once again, I express my thanks to them.

David G. Clark

Summer 2004

Introduction

From Ansel Watrous' *History of Larimer County, Colorado*, 1911, 1976 edition (Fort Collins: Miller Manor Publications, Old Army Press), pp. 188-189:

Pleasant Valley is a beautiful park lying just back of the first ridge of hogbacks, six miles northwest of Fort Collins. It is penned in between the high hills of the Front Range on the west, the hogbacks on the north and east, and is crossed from west to east by the Cache la Poudre river, which debouches from the canyon at the extreme west end of the valley. It is about two miles long from east to west and varies in width from one-fourth of a mile to a mile. This beautiful valley early attracted the attention of the first settlers on the river and all the farm and pasture lands were squatted upon in 1858-59 and '60. One of the first settlers of which there is any record was G. R. Sanderson, who located on the farm owned by Mrs. Joshua H. Yeager. Sanderson built the first irrigating ditch that took water from the Cache la Poudre River, and it was the first ditch built in Larimer County, its priority being dated June, 1860. It was also the second irrigating ditch built in Northern Colorado, the first having been built just below Denver and took its water from the Platte. . . .

In the fall of 1872 Jacob Flowers and a man named Laidlaw came west from Wyandotte, Kansas, in search of a location for a colony, and after looking over the state quite thoroughly, decided that Pleasant Valley and the

Cache la Poudre valley afforded the best
opportunities for their project. They returned to Kansas soon after the holidays and
submitted such a flattering report that
twenty-five families decided to leave the
Sunflower State and journey westward.
Some of the colonists stopped in Greeley and
the remainder came on to Fort Collins in the
spring of 1873. . . . Mr. Flowers purchased of
Joseph Mason a farm in Pleasant Valley,
which he owned and occupied until his
death a few years ago."

In 1882 Flowers built his stone house and
platted the town of Bellvue. In 1908 there
were two stores, a meat market, wagon shop,
blacksmith shop. 131 votes polled that year
in the precinct. He also showed that fruit
could be grown in Northern Colorado.

That was how people saw the scene a hundred years ago.
However the West was won, it had been. Next came a generation between the old and new, with characteristics of each.
They were, as it turned out, a generation that made a bridge
between pioneer days and modern times. They had pioneer
attitudes of self-sufficiency and self-reliance. Often their best
friends and companions for long periods were their horses and
other animals, wild as well as domestic. Of the group, only a
few women went to college, they to prepare to teach. For most
of them, formal education ended when they grew big enough
to work full time. Their real education they received on the
range or farm, in the day-to-day dealings with people around
them. They weathered the Depression (you have to have
something to lose before you can lose it). Their knack of
making do with little material goods and few prospects stood
them well. But they were also of the 20th century, of the car
and train if not airplane. And they saw how, for all its useful-
ness, the car changed their sense of family and community by
providing instant escape from or to. Near the ends of their
lives, what stood out in their minds were the personal triumphs

or hardships (especially those): broken bones, eyes put out, deadly sickness endured with little or no medical help available or expected. Most of all, they treasured their experiences of their early years, well aware that the world in which they were born, grew to adulthood, and lived most of their lives had vanished forever.

The Voices

Helen Barnes Burgess   Born May 14, 1902, Yuma County, Colorado
Parents: William Matthew Barnes and Anna Elmira Barnes
Married: Oliver Jasper Burgess
Children: Alice, Ruth, Dean, Jerry
Died June 5, 1993

School teacher, wife, mother, local historian, seer of the bright side, and believer in God.

Oliver Jasper Burgess   Born May 20, 1889, Rist Canyon, Colorado
Parents: William Burton Burgess and Minerva Howard Burgess
Married: Helen Barnes Burgess
Died December 10, 1981

Truly a stoic, he accepted his share and never complained. Through German shelling in World War I, loss of an eye while cutting logs, cancer in his old age, he retained his good humor and zest for fiddling. He knew he would never get out of this world alive, and he didn't.

Rev. Clifford Conard
Born May 6, 1898, Rush Center, Kansas
Parents: Abner and Mary Bristow Conard
Married: Flora Spragg Shunn
Children: Gloria Conard, Chrystal Conard, Fountain Conard
Date of death not determined

Not successful as a farmer, he found the Lord, who did not always provide. Laboring in His fields was hard, but at least it was out of the sun.

Flora Spragg Shunn Conard   Born December 30, 1889,
Kirkwood, Nebraska
Parents: Abner and Florence Spragg
Married: Dan Shunn and later the Rev. Clifford Conard
Children: Dorothy Shunn, Vernon Shunn, Minnie Shunn
Died August 30, 1984

Blessed with a happy childhood, surrounded by older siblings, mother and father, she decided that family was the most important thing in life. Ever after she sought to maintain those early, close ties.

Mary Geneva Krieg Creed   Born May 14, 1909, Hamilton, Missouri
Parents: John and Anna Krieg
Married: Loyce "Shorty" Creed
Son: Lonnie
Died February 15, 1993

Bronco and trick horse rider in women's professional rodeo. Beginning at the age of 16 in 1925, when she won the bucking horse contest at Cheyenne's Frontier Days, she performed throughout North America and in England and Australia.

Loyce "Shorty" Creed   Born March 4, 1903, Kingfisher, Oklahoma
Parents: William Creed and Myrtle Pearsall Creed
Married: Mary Geneva Krieg Creed
Died July 13, 1992

Held the Madison Square Garden record for bulldogging for nearly two decades. Also rode broncs and bulls, and supplied riding stock to rodeos. Rode in towns and cities across the country, and abroad.

Katie Worthan Davis   Born January 12, 1902, Bolivar, Missouri
Parents: Edward and Mamie Worthan
Married: Theodore R. Davis
Daughter: Barbara
Died March 25, 1991

The closest thing she had to a honeymoon was riding the chuckwagon on a cattle drive, when the rattlesnakes were so thick they climbed up the wheels.

Nettie Swatman Davis   Born December 13, 1902, Great Bend, Kansas
Parents: Harry W. Swatman and Katherine Wells Swatman
Married: Hershel Albert Davis
Children: Helen, Alice
Died April 19, 1979

Her enduring memories were of family disasters — a mentally disturbed mother, a feeble-minded sister, a tornado that brought ruin — and unrelieved labor.

Arthur Denham Born March 17, 1906, McComb, Mississippi
Parents: Ernest Arthur Denham and Lora Lee Denham
Married: Edna McLennan Denham
Son: Lee Ervin Denham
Died August 28, 1986

Worked hard all his life, on ranches, in the mines and in road
maintenance. Frequently beaten with a lariat by his stepfather, he
left home at 14 and went on his own. He later forgave his tormen-
tor.

Edna Denham Born October 23, 1907, Albany, Wyoming
Parents: John and Rosell McLennan
Married: Arthur Denham
Died November 11, 1990

Warm-hearted and fun-loving, she feared horses and snakes, but
loved dogs and cats.

Elmer Foster Born March 10, 1902, Bellvue, Colorado
Parents: Hiram Porter Foster and Anna May Newlin Foster
Married: Freda Lavantia Huppe Foster
Children: Frieda Louise, Stanley Elmer, Marvin Wayne, Walker,
Thelma May
Died August 31, 1985

Born in and lived all his life in one house. As a youth, loved a good
fight, and according to more than one contemporary, got canned
from school for fighting.

Lilly Fry Hout Born November 8, 1911, McAlester, Oklahoma
Parents: William L. Fry and Sarah C. Fry
Married: Leland Hout
Children: Herbert, William, Jeannine, Lawrence, Betty
Died March 30, 2000

Incurably cheerful, to her life was a party to be savored, and she
stayed late.

Charles Howard Born September 19, 1890, North Park, Colorado
Parents: John A. Howard and Ruth Stogsdill Howard

Married: Miriam Leigh Howard
Died March 1982

Along toward twilight, he met the love of his life.

Paul Millington   Born April 11, 1898, Harmony, Colorado
Parents: Elmer E. and Rosa Pearson Millington
Died May 31, 1990

Grew up, worked, and spent his whole life in Bellvue. In all that
time, took two trips, one to Iowa and one to North Park, 100 miles
west. His friends thought that with an education he would have
been a banker or economist.

Laura Alexander Read   Born May 17, 1897, La Veta, Colorado
Parents: Charles and Stella Queen Alexander
Married: Ivan Read
Children: Ivan Jr., Mary
Died May 21, 1990

She was stubborn, and single-handed held off Death when it came
for her and her older sisters. Much, much later, it slipped back and,
while her back was turned, stole her husband.

Norma Baxter Salisbury   Born November 21, 1902, Fort
Collins, Colorado
Parents: Frank Eugene Baxter and Florence Emma Baxter
Married: Walter Salisbury
Children: Robert, Jim, Richard
Died April 17, 1994

She remembered her father as a generous, understanding and
forgiving businessman in the Depression's hard times.

Walter Salisbury   Born July 29, 1901, Rist Canyon, Colorado
Parents: Cassius Rice Salisbury and Hattie M.
Davis Salisbury
Married: Norma Baxter Salisbury
Died January 8, 1983

His Rist Canyon neighborhood was a refuge for moonshiners.

Ernest Sapp Born January 23, 1894, Greenville, Illinois
Parents: George Luther Sapp and Ella Opha Skeen Sapp
Married: Stella Willey Sapp
Children: Edna Sapp, Elmer Sapp, Betty Sapp
Died December 10, 1979

He lived in a sod house, endured the Dust Bowl, in his earlier years
loved homemade whisky, but found the Lord and wound up
married to a member of the Women's Christian Temperance Union.

Stella Willey Sapp Born March 8, 1895, Stanton County, Nebraska
Parents: Thomas Benton Willey and Rosetta Melinda Butler Willey
Married: Ernest Sapp
Children: Ardith Hampel, Hazel Hampel, Harry Hampel, Clayton
Hampel
Died January 10, 1992

Left to fend for herself and her children when her first husband
went back to South Dakota, she helped build B-17 Flying Fortresses in World War II.

Lora Ebert Shipp Born September 15, 1894, St. Claire County,
Illinois
Parent:s: Cornelius Joseph Ebert and Mary Eliza Frazier Ebert
Married: Walter Shipp
Children: William, Dick, Mary Margaret, Helen, Elsie
Died March 19, 1984

She helped Americanize Germans from Russia, though her husband
resisted her working outside the home.

Francis Albert "Ab" Tamlin Born May 12, 1895, Cherokoee, Oklahoma
Parents: William Tamlin and Minerva McCorkle Tamlin
Married: Cleta Leyerle Tamlin
Children: Larry, Russel, Phillip, Phyllis
Died April 23, 1984

Scourge of coyotes on the eastern plains, he wasn't all that easy on
water thieves, either.

Bessie Villars Tamlin Born December 17, 1893, Joplin, Missouri
Parents: George Benjamin Villars and Eliza Elena Villars

Married: Henry V. Tamlin
Children: Victor, John Jackson, Henry Albert,
Robert Charles, Richard Villars, Francis Lee,
Betty Elena
Died March 27, 1987

She went through life with a placid, helping disposition.

Pearl Thomson Yager Born January 6, 1908, Elk City, Kansas
Parents: Riley Clyde Thomson and Frances E. Thomson
Married: Clarence Yager
Children: Betty Jane, Joylene Frances, Billie Lou

There was nothing much she couldn't do, on the ranch or in the
house.

I.

From the Plains

Many of the people came from prairie lands in Texas, Oklahoma, Kansas, Missouri, South Dakota or Nebraska. Impelled by a desire to move west, they halted when confronted by winter and the rising foothills of the Rocky Mountains. When spring came, they gave up the trek west and settled willingly and permanently on the eastern plains.

Ab Tamlin

He was around 5'10" and stalk slender. His eyes were light blue, and his full head of hair iron grey. During daylight hours he was constantly tending his half-acre place, on which he kept a couple of horses, chickens, and some pigs. Root crops he planted in the dark of the moon, and he knew within a day or two when the last spring frost would come. If he wanted to sell a sick horse, and the prospective buyer was too dumb to ask or discover the truth on his own, he saw nothing wrong in making the deal. But when he gave his word you didn't need a paper copy.

Ab Tamlin's father took land in the 1889 Cherokee Strip land rush in Oklahoma and Ab was born on the homestead in 1895. From the way Ab described him, William Tamlin was shrewd, good-natured, a bit of a gambler, and inclined not to take life too seriously.

He come across on a boat when he was nine years old. Just a little feller. He got in with a circus outfit and worked. Played the violin. It was funny. He'd set it up facing you out there on his knee, you know, and he'd sit there all night.

And we left down there about 1900. I was five years old. They was headed for Washington. But it come a big snow and caught them at Stone City down there by Canon City and they stopped over there. At that time there wasn't much of a place to get a job so they pulled out here on Elbert County to a place. There was a great big—looked like a big round hill, kind of, but they had it all planted to potatoes. So we all got out there and we worked two or three weeks there, picking potatoes. I remember that I had to carry the sacks and scatter the sacks for them, you know. The snow stopped us, but Uncle Bob and Uncle Jake, they went on to Washington. They made it through. But we didn't make it, so we never did go, then. We homesteaded north of Callahan. Dad did.

The funny part of it was, you know, we had three wagons, but we had an old cow tied on behind, taking along, and we had a bunch of chickies and I had a couple of guineas. And we turned them guineas loose at night, you know, there. Just let them run around. The old hen, when she'd see us a-packing up and getting ready to go, she'd go get in the box. But I'd have to play cowboy and rope him. He wouldn't come. But he'd foller us like a dog. And I remember that. I know he scratched me on top of the head one time. I roped him with a rope and he flew up high and I stopped him and he come back fighting. He was a booger.

Dad was actually a horse trader. Boy, on that big sandy between Simla and Callahan, we had about 75 head of horses, down that draw. I remember whenever we got one in to ride, we never turned it out till it was rode. He wouldn't let us spoil one. We just stayed with it till we broke it. We had a ready-bought rodeo at our place on Saturdays and Sundays. They'd come from every place out there. But there was lots of good riders, then.

We learned to do it pretty quick. You know a horse can't buck very hard in sand. His feet'll go down in and when they hit sand, they'll go down in that far and stop you. I wasn't afraid of them. I generally wound up in the saddle and I could ride them in the sand draw. They never did bring one in there that I couldn't ride. But get out on that hard dirt, once in a while I'd go to the moon. And then we had one gentle horse. We'd tie the other one to it and hitch it to a big breaking cart we had there, and take off down the road. A lot of people thought, well, if you let them run when you broke them, they'd always want to run. But if you let him run and he wants to stop and you make him go on another mile before you stop, he learns to quit that right quick. So us kids all broke horses all the time. My oldest brother, he broke horses. He broke them to ride more than I did. We raised a lot of mules. I'd pick the horse for you to ride, you'd pick the one for me to ride, you know. And I knew which ones bucked the hardest and I'd always have a hard bucker for the other guy. And a mule. We had lots of them. Come a big rain in the big lagoon out there—a hole in the pasture, you know—we'd ride a mule right in there. If they ever stick their head down in the water and get water in their ears then they'd never stick their head down no more, while they was bucking. They'd just buck out there straight, like that, you know. Heck, you could ride them. Easy. But we never told all the kids that. But they all took their turn riding, or trying, if they couldn't ride. Wound up that I went around the sand draw and get on and I rode him for about an hour and then I had him broke pretty good.

We always had eight or 10 milk cows. And Mama had 200 or 300 chickens and raised our hogs and everything. She could go to town once a week in a lumber wagon. (It was) nine miles to where we'd go. She'd have a couple of cases of eggs, a couple of cans of cream, and she'd always come home with a big box of groceries. We had to make it that way. We didn't have no money, we traded it. But when Dad'd get one of them horses broke good, you know, if he was mean, why, we'd put the double-u on him and learn him to stand. One of them guys would come in and he wanted to know if he was broke. Dad'd holler for me to come down there. He says, "Get on him, Son, and ride him out." I'd just take the halter rope and jump on him. He was afraid to buck. He knew if he bucked with me, we'd take him in the sand draw and throw him. And that's the way we broke them. They come out of it pretty quick. But it didn't hurt them, you know, in that sand.

My daddy-in-law was a carpenter and he contracted all the time, you know. We built schoolhouses every nine miles. Over that whole big country there. It all settled up at once, you know. Just right in a year or two. We built schoolhouses every nine miles so they wouldn't have to go over three miles to school. I knew we was building schoolhouses for two or three years there. Now, we was down there not too long ago. They've took all of that out, you know. All of the little 320 acre guys, they're all gone, and it's into 10, or 12, 15 sections. Little cow ranches, now. And they went to raising wheat. It's good country there, now. But that's just the way we had to do. We had to get our cows and our hogs and all of that stuff and then we'd take it to town and sell it and buy our groceries and come back. I don't ever remember a time, when it come time for school, that Mama didn't go to town. She'd come home with all the clothes we needed. Was kind of rough sledding, but. . . . All the fun we had, we had to make it, you know.

Oh, we'd give a box social. A party. And a dance or something, you know. And we'd have ball games on Sunday. We had one of the best ball teams there was down there. We got smart on it, you know. We bet dollars every Saturday. We'd win. We'd win about four out of five. And that was a big joke, you know, that was. And then they got to having the Elbert Fair there. They had that big tent there, on my place, and I got a couple of big long railroad irons and rails. I used to drag the road with them. They was awful good drag, then, you know. You didn't have nothing like they got now. I drug that ground all around there, for that ball diamond. Sometimes there'd be such a crowd there, there'd be a complete circle around the diamond, way out in the field. Was nothing else to go to. They just come in there for every place. There were some hot arguments. I guess I played on short stop. I must have been there 30 years, wasn't it? Yeah. Thirty years, I stayed on short stop. I got so I liked to play.

We had one pitcher that was kind of lazy, you know. He was a good one. On these games, if he wanted to get the guys in there, he'd motion them in and he'd put that old ball where you wanted it. It'd come right down to your glove. We could put them double plays, too. Not quite so snappy as them professional guys, but we went down to Canon City and played tough guys in Canon City, there. In prison. We won the first game and they won the next one. They had their umpire. We didn't take no umpire, you know. We just let them go. Didn't want to start no fight in there with a fighter. And everything the pitcher throwed was a strike. I says, "Well, we can't win them and do that." So then they'd had their umpire one inning and we'd have ours the next inning. And we never had very many arguments. It always fell for me to get them straightened out when they got into something. Had my brother-in-law there, if they got like they wanted to fight too much. I had to hold up my part of it, but they'd come and get a hold of me and take me away and I wasn't hard to lead away. But it was just a good old country, all the way through.

Sometime in 1912, Ab met Cleta Leyerle.

Well, we just met at the dance, and she was a pretty good dancer, and I just thought, well, heck, I'll cabbage on to her. Went with her about—oh, a year and a half, and we decided to get married.

After he married, Ab picked up a relinquished homestead in 1915. He was 20 years old.

Somebody'd farmed it. They took it as a timber claim. And there wasn't a tree on it, see? He broke up 80 acres, put a big irrigating ditch down through there, and he planted some trees and things and he couldn't water them. They didn't grow. So he was going to lose it anyway, and I bought his relinquishment. And we moved right on and had a little old two-room sod shanty. There was a lot of them there, that way. Took some big planks, you know, and put a big blade like a grader blade just down like that, and across here, and if you wanted to sod that thick, we'd put enough weight on it to put it in the ground. Put four head of mules onto it, and it just went through there and just cut it, wherever we wanted. Then we went through with a spade, and cut them how long we wanted them, and hauled them. Chinked them all up. The gyp mines was oh, about four miles from there. We'd go over at that gyp mine and dig up some of that gyp. It was kind of a pinkish color. When it dried, it was pretty near as white as that paint. Plastered all over inside with that, and then mix that up like that paint and paint it. It just looked like paint.

Then we decided we wanted to put in a floor. So we got enough money ahead to buy enough 1 x 12's to make a 1 x 12 floor. Then I don't know. About the third year or fourth, we got a pretty good crop and I had enough beans and stuff to sell and her daddy built us a new house. It was a pretty good house. But I remember the times you could work 10 hours for

a dollar and a half. If he had the money he'd pay you. If he
didn't, you waited till he got it. And he always was honest.
Pretty honest. I had a pretty good corn sled. Cutting horse, you
know. For cutting corn. You'd set on a stool, catch that, and
get a big armload, and set it down in the shock. I got dollar
and a half an acre for doing that. And I'd cut and chop 10
acres every day. So I'd make 15 dollars. That's more than 30 or
40 today. We thought we was millionaires when we got the
check for that. I'd cut corn just as far away as I could get to it
and make wages. Well, sometimes I'd cut till it'd have frosted
head and all I'd have was what was in my hand. Have to quit.
Freeze up and blow away. But I cut lots of corn. That's the way
we got by. I left my corn sledding horses there and rode one of
the other saddle horses.

About 1918, let's see. . . . There was a buyer, Wilson,
from Benkelman, Nebraska. Come out there and he bought
150 head of white faces right there at the ranch by us, and then
he went on to Colorado Springs and that country down there.
He wanted to know if I wanted a job. I said, "Yeah," so I went
back to Benkelman. We was 32 days going from there down
through, with them cattle. But we had a thousand head when
we got there. Just string them out.

That was the luckiest guy that I ever seen. Now we got
down there just the other side of New Raymer and a guy had
one of them meadows that run up the hillside. Springs out
there, you know. The old grass was that high. He said, "Go
down and see if we can turn in there." The man laughed at me.
"Why," he says, "I couldn't do that." I says, "Well, it'll rain
tomorrow, and. . . ." I was just joshin' him along, you know. I
says, "It'll rain tomorrow and the grass'll be out and you get
just as much as you would anyhow. Besides, you'll have a 20
dollar bill. I'll give you 20 dollars to turn them cattle in there."
"I'm going to take you up, young feller," he said.

And that's the way we got them in there. Wilson was one
of them old guys. He had a long moustache, you know, and a
big old six-shooter strapped onto him. Never did see him go
anyplace unless that gun was strapped onto him. Well, he'd go

down and talk to them. We'd get in, he'd pay him 15, 20 dollars for that many, you know. They didn't have no money, and heck, that was big money for them. We never did get turned down.

Some days we'd only make eight hours. Some days we'd make 15. Eighteen's the most we ever did make. That was a pretty good run. But it was just lots of work, to keep that many strung out and keep them going. We went through St. Francis, Kansas. You know there's always be a few in the bunch that'll take the lead and go. He sent me up with them and he says, "Just don't go over two streets into town, and we'll string them through." And there's people climbing on top of houses and every place, you know, and I had them three going on down the line and calling the others, and here they come stringing down through there. They was strung out for two miles, three miles. But they would foller. But that's the only place that we had, oh, much trouble. They broke a time or two in there, but we just left them alone. Went and got two or three, and called the others up, and then they'd go along.

Oh, I got to farming big, you know, after I got so I wasn't afraid to making a dollar. I'd get a good working boy and he'd come there and stay and I'd give him 50 acres of beans. Didn't have no money. But he'd have money when he sold them beans. And I got two of them. I'd rent ground all around as far as I could get to, and we'd just farm it right along, three outfits. We'd just go into the field and finish it and go into the next one and finish it. Them guys on their beans, they made more cording than I did, you know, because I boarded them, had to give them the money to buy their dance ticket with, and one thing and another. But there was some awful good boys in the country along about then, you know. Them guys would do anything for me.

Rattlesnakes. Was lots of rattlesnakes. Oh, if you leave them alone, they won't bother you. They'll just crawl off. But if you stop and throw a rock at him, boy, he's ready for a fight. On my dad's place, at one turn in the crick down there, there was a lot of big old tall sagebrush, and he decided to cut that out. Grass would grow in better. He took one of them double-

bitted mattocks and cut that out, and I think the first year
when he cut that out, he killed 45 or 47. Right there in that
little spot.

But the colts. . . . We raised lots of horses, you know. He
was a horse trader. If you had a good horse, and say for
instance I had a couple old plugs, why, he'd make a pass at you,
you know. "Well, for that horse and 15 dollars, I'll trade with
you." "Nope." He says, "I'll throw in this other horse and you
give me 15 dollars." That's the way he'd get the money, see?
Nothing crooked about it, just. . . . He had enough horses, he'd
put in another horse and he'd get a good one. And then when
he'd start out again, or go down the line. . . . But he most
generally always traded for oh, 12, 15 head. Broke ones when
he went out. And when he come back, he'd have 50. And a
pocketful of money.

*Where buffalo herds 100 miles long had once grazed on lands the
Arapaho had considered theirs, Ab in the 1920s found both a hobby
and a source of income: coyote hunting. In his customized Model T,
he roared into and out of gullies and washes until he could get close
enough to release his dogs. His system paid off.*

I had greyhounds. I sent Ray Young 87, one winter.
Eighty-seven hides. If three got up, and man, you was after
them, and I had three dogs, you know. . . The door'd just lay
out over the wheel, but I wouldn't stop. I'd just slow down.
And they'd get out and I'd just keep a-going, and sometimes
the dog would just be right down there ready to grab him
before he knew he was after him. And if we jumped three, I'd
turn the two little white dogs on one. I had a little whippet-
greyhound. Black. And oh, that thing was fast. I'd turn him out
and you'd go with him, and then you'd watch and see whether
they'd catch him. I'd lay the automatic shotgun across my arm,
and I'd go on up and I'd get that other. We'd get three just like
that. But we couldn't get more than that, you know, cause we'd
have to watch and see where they went and then load them up
and go again.

Oh, I had the fastest Model T in the country. There couldn't nothing catch it. Well, some kid had it and he souped it all up, you know, to run races up Pike's Peak. I heard him standing there on a corner one day, and he was talking to a guy, and he said, "You know, if I'd have just put in another sack of sand," he says, "I'd have took that race." He said, "It'd skid and I'd have to slow up." And then he'd catch him and turn and skid and he couldn't make it. He says, "I want to sell it." I says, "Well." I walked over there, you know, and butted into their talk, and I says, "What do you want for it?" "Oh," he says, "I want 50 dollars. I need 50 dollars pretty bad." I says, "Wait right here and I'll be back in a minute." I just went over to the bank and got 50 dollars and bought it.

We took the head off of it. And put another one on it and had the radial head, you know—and four pipes shot right out the side. That sounded like an airplane was roaring. I guess all the time I had that, two years, I had two motors. It was hard on rods if you left it open too long. But you didn't have to. I'd get to them so quick, and I'd turn the dogs loose. I didn't go just a-hunting all the time. I'd have made more than I would have, farming. But you'd come in: "Let's go a-hunting." Away we'd go. That's the way I done. Then I had that little black hound. Everybody laughed at me. Said, "You can't make a greyhound kill coyotes, they won't fight." I said, "You just watch." And I'd take him. Go out in the open country, you know, and I'd shoot a jack rabbit and cripple him. He could still run. I could get out and catch him, and I'd turn them little hounds about so big, you know—turn them out and let them go catch him.

Then, they growed up that way. They caught everything I turned them on. They didn't know what they was supposed to do. So, come time to catch coyotes, I took my best dog. We'd always go in and one of the others would throw, and he'd get him by the throat and right now. And he'd kill them right quick. I didn't want them pups to get bit up very much, you know. So we jumped a pup coyote—the worst thing we could find. Their teeth are little and sharp, you know, and if they do bite, they just cut a hole. We turned them dogs loose and I turned the old dog with them and the pups ran up to him like that and they didn't know what to do, you know. And then he hit him, took him down, and they went right in and killed him. They never did let a coyote get away from them. I had that car and them three dogs and we went by Deer Trail, toward Limon. South and west of that, them big pastures.

One of them guys got a coyote hunt. Sixty-three cars of us in that coyote hunt, and I had this little car all souped up, you know, and fixed. And I had another motor on the bench over here all fixed up ready to put in there, you know. But I'd drive along 15, 20 miles an hour while I was looking for the coyote and quick as I seen him, I'd just go right to him like that. And oh, I-don't know how fast that thing would go. I never did have it opened up, only twice. And we got old Gus Buck. He was a guy on a ranch where we'd worked, where we caught the coyotes. That guy had got up the hunt. He had a little stock car. And you know them little Stars, when they come out, they was a snappy little car. They was a fast little thing.

He come down where I was, there, when he was about ready to start out and he says, "Ab," he says, "I'll get down the line here, six or eight cars," and he says, "I've got a fast car. I'll herd for you like bulldoggers catching a calf." And I just grinned, you know, and I thought, "Oh, boy, if you have to herd for me, I'm going home." There was seven coyotes caught and I got six of them. I got every one of them. They couldn't follow that car. Course, I had it on the axle, you know. I had about 2 strands of telephone wire tied onto it and just pulled-setting there, just pulled them tight. Had two of them. Front end was tied down and the back end was tied down. Then when you got in to ride, why, they come down about so far. You didn't notice them, but going up is what broke the springs.

If I'd have sold them dogs that day, I'd have got anything I wanted. They'd never seen anything like it. I played it wrong when I first started. I turned them all three at once. Loose, you know. Then I woke up. I ought to keep one of them in, and have him for the next race, you know. It was a kind of nice warm day, and darn that.... We come to a sand draw, and if I was going in to any place that was bad, I had to gear in the gear I wanted. And I was a-going, pretty rough and pretty bad. I went down across that sand draw and come up out of there and next guy that went in. . . . It was just too sharp at the bottom. If you didn't hit and jump to catch it, the back end would drag. If you went down easy, the front end would drag. But you hit it, you'd jump out of it.

So I turned the dogs loose and I didn't know what was down in there, you know. I didn't want them to get into the coyotes thick, and get whipped. So I said, "We're going to try it. You hang on." And I went down, and when I seen what it was, I just give it to it and hit, and bounce, and I bounced a-way up the other side. I went right on up out of there. Well then the other guys wanted to cross. I said, "You can't cross there." In good cars, you know. "Well, we want to try it." And I pulled about 15 of them up there. That was hard on that car, you know, the one I had. I put four strands of barbed wire down to it, tied it on. I said, "Now when you hit that sand, give it the gas and the bump will take you out." And I says, "You come right up out of there." I took about 150 them out of there.

We seen a bunch of antelope that day. I'll bet there was—on, there must have been 500. They claimed a car couldn't catch them, you know. "Aw, a car can't catch them." I says, "I can split that herd." And I just cut like that, and the antelopes? You know. . . .If he's out here running, you just slow up a little bit, he thinks he's out-running you, he'll go in front of you every time. Every time. And I slowed up and they thought they was going to go in front of me and then I just turned and went for them. Heck, I could go through it, and then come back through it any time I wanted to. They couldn't outrun that car. And them big pastures was pretty good running.

I got a price list right here now. A good coyote's worth 165 dollars. I think I got—oh, between 12 and 15 dollars. We started to Christmas dinner one time and the dogs run out and got in the car, you know. They wanted to go. And I said, "Well, put them in and bring out a heavy comfort," so we could wrap the kids up. I had the top off of it, you know. You had to fix a door tight so they couldn't get their legs in it. Slide right off of that wheel and I'd turn loose. A-going about 10 miles an hour. We just like to about—oh, a mile, getting down to where we was going to dinner, and here come two coyotes. They wanted to go across. I speeded her up. I tried to get her to shoot, and she wouldn't do it. So I got the gun out there and I done the shooting and I done the feeding the gas and the brake, and she drove, and boy, I put her down the road that day. Out-running them coyotes.

One of them was close enough to the road to kill when I went by him. I just pulled out there and got him and turned the dogs loose after the other one. He was a little bit too far. They run on over there and jumped onto the one I shot. So I had to go catch him then. But I turned them loose on a long turnout on him. I thought I'd just fool the old boy. You learn to go where you weren't supposed to. But if I turned them loose a half mile out there, they'd go catch him. Were upset twice. Never hurt nothing. You know them spindles in the Model T's? Spindle that held the axle in the wheel on the axle? They would break off once in a while. And that's what broke off. That's what upset me. But I had the wagon rods that they put in to hold the wagon bed together. I had one of them in the back end of that and then I had it tied crossways so it wouldn't shake up. Didn't want to put nothing on there that a dog would catch a leg on, you know. Why, he'd hang hisself. So we took that out, and took a coal chisel and twisted that in, and out of there, and put that down in there and bent it. And it was a little bit small.

We jumped one coyote. I just run out the way they was and they run up there and that was one of these old sod shanties. The door—they hadn't put the door up yet. They was laying down like that inside, and that coyote must have knew it. Cause he run in there and crawled behind that door in that old sod shanty. Old Sailer, he come in and he went in and got him.

Pulled him out. The other time, that spindle broke and that axle. . . . Like if you'd start it, plowing the ground, holding the handle, you know, it'd go deeper. The axle went in about that deep. We had a heck of a time getting that axle out. But we finally got her out. And that's when I put the long wagon rod in there and just bent it around. And I followed that coyote—oh, about two miles—and I said to that guy who was with me, I says, "Which is the worst, running along here about 40 miles an hour in these soap weeds or open it up and a half a mile and then get him?"

He says, "Open her up." He had his hand over his eyes and I went. That wheel was just flying like that, you know. Cause it wasn't trued up. She had the ladies' club you know, and we had a little old Model A sedan. She forgot to drain it. Froze up and just busted. She wanted to go to that doings and I had to take the other car. I had heard some guys talking down at the dance where there was a bunch of coyotes. He says, "I see them there every day." And I just figured it would be a good time to get into them, you know. They was ready to catch. Somebody'd get them. So in order for her to go to the—let me have that car, why, she went along with me, so I'd come home. So we went down. We got three of them.

A guy come down for me to take him to Limon and haul his cream in. His car wouldn't start. I says, "OK, I been wanting to get up that way anyhow." I says, "Wait'll I get my gun, and we'll kill a coyote or two on the road." He just laughed at me, you know. We got along there and just happened to look out a little old draw, just that far, and he was out of sight, see? See, I just seen him as he dropped over in that little draw. And I said, "Gee whiz," I says, "We're going to spill this cream and everything else in here when we get out to that coyote."

About that time, he just walked up on the bank and stood there. He was just about—oh, off just looking from here to the first river bridge, about 200 yards. I found him like that, you know, and I just pulled her up till he was down here under the barrel. Pulled the trigger and knocked him down.

And he got up and he stood there like that. And I started a-walking to him. I throwed in another shell and I started walking to him. I got down there to him and he was a-biting his teeth, like that, you know. I hit him. He was hurt. I just walked up there and gee whiz, I just hauled off and I kicked him one to start him. I wanted to give him a chance for his life. If he could get away, without me hitting him again, why, I'd try him again some day. He come under, like that, and I stuck the gun out, and he got the gun, instead of my leg, and boy, he just shaved his teeth off on that gun. I couldn't get back far enough away from him to shoot him. Finally I jumped back and I says, "Get back out of the way," and I shot him right there. Looked like I hit him with a double bitted ax. But he'd like to have bit that gun stock and everything else off of it.

I had one old blue hound. Everybody says, "Aw, you ain't got a dog that would kill a badger." I says, "You find one and come and get me, I'll bring my dogs and I'll let just one out. "Why," he says, "they can't kill them, Ab." I says, "He'll go in that culvert and bring that badger out or bring a coyote out." I called one of them Sailer, you know, he was fast. For four years he was my catcher.

We went up there and this coyote was out on the plains. Had a little sagebrush. The coyote just stick up about that high (above it). And you could see him a-going, you know. I'd always get old Sailer. Soon as you speeded up, I'd say, "Come on, Sailer," and gosh darn it he had his head out and oh, he wanted to go. He'd find him. And he'd find that coyote quick as he seen him. Then I'd slow down to about five, six miles an hour, and that coyote. . . . Well, we learned a lot of their tricks, you know. He'd jump up there and he'd start to run and he'd just look back like that and then he'd go on about 10, 15 jumps and he'd look back again. Then he wouldn't look back no more. He'd get about 50 yards, and we wouldn't turn out, till he made that third look. You could tell, you know, when he looked up. That was on long turn outs. I'd say, "Watch him. Sailer, now watch him!" And then he'd whine. Let me know he's seen him, you know. And he—oh, he'd want out so bad.

But then when the old coyote'd look up, and look back down to see where he was a-walking, I'd turn him loose. I've had him just right up there ready to take a-hold of him. The dogs won't run their best, you know. They just run along there, a pretty good hike, but when that old coyote looked back and seen them, oh, he footed another gear. But this little rat dog, I wanted to see what he'd do. So we got a hold of the other two and that guy held them. I had to stop to get him out, you know. They all wanted to go. I got him out and he went. It was just a young dog, but he caught the coyote, all right, but he was a-getting cut up awful bad. That big old coyote was just a-chewing him up. So I said, "Aw, let them all onto him for a while. They'll fix him." And about every 10th or 15th coyote, somewhere along the line there, I'd just let them have him, see? Just let him kill it. That's what they wanted to do. If I was going a-hunting, I'd get to them just as quick as I could, and get my foot on his neck and hit him in the head with a hammer. They'd have him down and done, but he could still bite you.

They're such big plains, I knew everybody there in a hundred mile square. I knew which ones to not hunt on, and which ones I could hunt on. If a coyote had went through the fence, I went through and got in, and fixed the fence. And if he caught me, we had to go.

There was one of the Gordons that had sheep. She says, "I lost 27 lambs last night." I says, "What killed them?" "Coyote." "Well," I says, "darned if I go over there after them. You'll shoot me. You said you would." "You come and get him." And we went over there and we looked and looked and looked and hunted and we couldn't find no coyote. See this was late in the spring, you know, a little bit, and hides wasn't no good. But we couldn't find no coyote.

The guy that was with me said, "Let's turn the little dog out. Let him catch him. Run him around for a little bit." I said, "Well, we'll run him right down to the house. He acted like he wanted to get in. I was afraid he'd get into something, you know. So I speeded up and I got between him and the house.

It was about a quarter of a mile over there. I got a hold of two big dogs. I stopped and got a hold of their collars. He didn't run that doggone thing 200 yards till he had him. That dog— he just look like a hawk flying. I hollered, and they come out, you know.

She says, "Well, I ain't got no money." They had lots of sheep. She says, "I'll give you a quart of whiskey." I said, "Well, I don't drink much whiskey. That's all right. We'll get him. . . ." We went 15 miles from her place and caught that one and it'd been shot in the hind leg right here. There was a big old, looked like a .45 just under the hide and it'd broke that leg. She put that whiskey in. I don't know how long we had that setting in the cupboard.

One year the grasshoppers came.

There was about three miles this way going, traveling. And wide. It was 30 miles wide. Like a swatch of hay cutting through the field, you know. Three feet wide, and they just kept going. That's how big a bunch there was on, then. They just cleaned that off slick as that floor. We's a-getting about— oh, I don't know, 25 or 26 gallon of cream a week, and a case or two of eggs. When that hit, they just took that grass and weeds and everything down to where we didn't get three gallon a week. It was just along about roasting-ear time. July. They was so thick around on the ground or on the fencepost, nothing couldn't light without lighting on hoppers. They'd just fly out like muddy water in the road when you'd drive a car down. They cleaned everything out.

Well, we got right on to them. They poisoned them. They hit about 10 acres of my field. Just come across one corner, just right there like that. We left the next year. Heck, I thought if they was going to take everything, they could have it.

We poisoned them. We got sawdust and banana oil. We got that in the back of the spring wagons. They had them little mixers. Took the back end of an old Model T, you know, and turned the gear up on the axle, and that turned the barrel, and that barrel had pie cuts in it like pie. You know, this here was coming around while that one was filling. And that'd throw it. Scatter it. We didn't have enough of them, they was so thick. We tried to get the whole length of it, you know. Well, if we didn't this morning, next morning we'd go where we left off. After sun-up, though, when that dried, they wouldn't eat it. But while it was damp, boy, they'd gobble it up and die.

I had a big lagoon there on my brother's place. Hay around it about three feet high. And I thought, well, I'll wait till we kill the grasshoppers and then I'll cut the hay. Didn't get much. Two or three ton, but we had to save it all. When we got through poisoning grasshoppers, they got sick and went down there after a drink and just as deep as that hay was, was grasshoppers piled up. You couldn't get within a mile of that, that stunk, yeah. But we got them. They'd go to a little hill, bore down and lay them eggs up there. They're smart. They'd get them up where the water wouldn't soak them out and kill them. And they tried to hatch them out the next spring. Just looked like a string of cattle coming out over the hill, you know. When they'd come up out of that ground, they'd turn black.

You could just look on the road while you was driving, you could see them. But we took the listers and listed pretty deep, and we'd throw that banana oil in there in hands full. Just go along, and throw it along, and that would kill all of them. Them little devils would eat it all. And that's the way we got rid of them. We poisoned them. Well, they traveled about— we checked them—oh, three, four miles a day. They'd clean that much off and just go on. Now, we took a spray. Had a big spray on the front of the car so it'd blow out white paint. We'd go along and blow that out over them, you know. Then the next day we'd go down here where we started and we'd look around and see how many of them white grasshoppers we had down there. They moved just about three, four miles a day.

You just took your hat off like that and threw it in the air, and where it lit, couldn't be less than 35 hoppers under it. Pretty thick.

Oh, we poisoned them little ones when they first started coming out. I got in on all of that. They wasn't hard to handle. You just see that, we just start listing around it. Fill up that lister full. It would fill up with dead hoppers in an hour. Just fill up, and they'd just crawl over it, you know. Then they'd crawl up. They had to have something to chew on, you know. And the banana oil was poisoned. That made them draw to it. Didn't have no way of throwing it out. The only way (was) to hand a lot of it. We just set in the back end of the wagon and throwed it like that. Sort of like they was broadcasting grain. And they'd go along there and pick up a little chunk of that sawdust, and eat it, and he was gone. Like flies to sugar. It sure worked. And they never have been back. We got them all. Them sons-of-a-guns is three inches long. Big ones. They put—I don't know what it was—boxes on the front of them cars, you know. On the bumper. It would hit down like hay, pick up the thing, and it had screen around it. They'd get out there and drive in a circle, or drive across the prairie, and when that filled up, that was turkey feed. Before they got to feeding poison to them. And they'd have 500 or 600 pounds of them hoppers in there. They just come out and picked them up with a—well, we sacked them up and throwed them over the side. . . . That was why *I* left, yeah.

Even after Ab left southeastern Colorado and moved to Bellvue, the memory of the grasshoppers remained strong.

When we got up here, it was funny. The kids over here, we was talking about the grasshoppers: "We got some in the car." And I wanted to see what kind they was, you know. And they was them big yellow ones about so big. They was like this popcorn with sugar on it, you know. They was parched and putting in baskets and the people was a-selling them! And they just et them like they was candy. But gosh darn, I turned my back on them. I didn't want none of them. And the store was just filled up with them. Lot of them would go in there and buy them a case. And I thought, "Well, you dizzy son-of-a-gun." They didn't have to. Just like that popcorn, you know.

Ab's last salaried job, one he took at 60 and held until he was 83, was as ditch rider for an irrigation company. Water's scarcity impelled the building at the end of the last century of complex collection systems ringing the peaks with drainage canals and high mountain reservoirs, from which water is sent down throughout the year. Ab's job was to make certain each shareowner received whatever amount of water the share is entitled to – but no more. The job is one of the world's oldest professions, going back 5,000 years to Mesopotamia and Egypt when the Tigris, Euphrates and Nile rivers came under at least partial subjugation. The concept is simple enough, but putting it into practice required him to be excavator (to clean out the ditch), engineer (to keep the water gates functioning), rationer (to figure and issue equal amounts from a constantly varying supply of water), and water law enforcement agent, as judge, jury and executioner (to catch and punish thieves).

And now, I've been there what? Twenty-three years, I think. Something like that. Now there's no more water than before, but there's 103 or 104 guys you have to turn the water out to. Saw an acre off, put a little bit of water to it. And that's what made you a headache. But it wasn't too bad, only just. . . . Well, I don't know how the heck they done it, but when they put them checks in to raise the water up to get it out on the ground, you know, they got some of them too low. When they got it down, it was down under the water. Then when something went wrong with it, you dig it out after the water got in the ditch. It's awful hard to get the collar around it, you know. It was down in the mud. But I never found very many guys that wanted to work down there in that mud. If I got anybody to come and help me, when they got their shoe soles wet, they crawled on the bank and I had to finish it.

If you didn't want your water, why, you'd call me, and I'd shut it off in the morning. Or I'd let him go and shut it off that night if he was done, to save me a trip down there. But it worked out pretty good.

After everybody had had their share, or whatever portion of it they wanted, the water is supposed to go back into the stream, for the downstream users.

It just goes on down to lower ground all the time, you see, and they got a ditch there, down to the outlet at the bottom. Drain it right out. There's a new guy on there this year. He put more in Long Pond—a whole lot—than he should have. He cut these here farmers back pretty short. Boy, they're pretty well after him. But . . . they can't do nothing. They cut down to 12 feet, and that ain't enough, but they stayed there. I don't know why this guy didn't go on up to 26 or 38 for three or four days and then cut back down, and you could get some place with a big head of water, you know. A little bit, you can't do nothing with hardly. And that's what they had. He gypped them. So I don't think he could get the job back if he wanted it.

The term "water war in the West" does not only apply to disputes between states, such as Colorado, Arizona and California, for water rights from large rivers such as the Colorado. Sometimes the war gets personal and local: neighbor against neighbor, down the ditch versus up the ditch, would-be user against over-user. Ab was usually involved at some stage. And, at age 83, he was still willing to get physical with people who tried to take more water than they were entitled to.

They'll shoot you. That's what they do. Oh, I had the sheriff out there and I had the boss out there, and he says, "You go ahead and run it." I says, "Well, I'll take it, and if I can't handle it, now—have too much trouble—you just get a man out here and put it on." Well, I had a little bit of trouble, but not too much. Heck, they wasn't going to hit an old man. Some of them would, all right, if they thought they could get away with it. But I never let none of them run over me.

And I was good to them. If water come in at 10 o'clock, I went down the line and made another trip and cut their water out to them. One place, one guy. . . . I got orders to cut the ditch back to 12 feet, and I cut it back, and went around the ditch, and he went out and shut his ditch off and went to town. And about noon, why here come the water again. Well, instead of letting it go into Long Pond, you know, I just went back down the ditch and this guy had his canvases there, where he was irrigating, you know, and I had irrigated the ground. I knew what to do.

But I didn't have to do it. Instead of letting him lose that water, I went down and put it back in his corn just like he had it, you know. Gee whiz, he just jumped on to me. "Well, now," he says, "what if that'd got over in my corn? Then I couldn't have cultivated. I couldn't have done nothing." I said, "Mister, I thought I was a-helping you out." I says, "Don't worry any more." But that's all the dadgum things I'll run around extra for. I says, "I made an extra trip down here to get that water for you so you wouldn't lose it." That's how I run it. But oh, he was patting me on the back when it cut down, you know. "I'd like to get some of that water that went down the ditch." I says, "No." I said, "We tried to keep that water back up here. I did." And I said, "You jumped onto me and I didn't like it." I says, "You just take it as it comes, now." He was ornery. That was one of the ornery ones.

They've got it doped out, how much a tree at the side of the ditch out there—how many gallon that would use in a year. The ditch company's got a 30 foot right-of-way at the side. They can cut every tree on it if they wanted to, see, to make a road so they can maintain it.

But now, there's several of them great big ones, you know, that big around, and they want me to saw them down and take them out. And I says, "I can't take them out. I ain't got no equipment to handle them." I said, "You'd have to saw a week there, with one of these little saws, and then you couldn't get in to get it down. Just saw a 'V' around it so far, and half of it would be a-standing, waiting for the wind to blow it down. Kill some stock or something.

No, most of the guys is pretty good. If you can settle it there, it's better than to go down there. "How long has this been a-running like that?" I didn't know nothing about it. I wouldn't short them. Sometimes they'd run that way. Maybe by the time I started around, something would happen down there, and I wouldn't get all the way around till after dinner sometimes on some of it. And here was the gate leaking to beat the band. Or they'd found a chicken drownded. Or they'd throwed them in there. There'd be chickens in one of them head gates hooked up in under there, drownded .

I just got to where if one of them was having an argument, I'd say, "Now, I come down to settle this. I got orders to give you your water, and if you can't settle it without trouble, I'll screw it shut, tight, and lock it, and when you settle this argument, you call me and I'll come down and open it." It was the best deal I had, was right there. I had to do some of them that way. Quick as you'd leave, I'd go up there and take it. Quick as I'd leave, you'd go take it. And you couldn't get no place.

Oh, heck, they'd fight you like a bulldog after a cat. One son-of-a-gun down there, it was old Jack _____. Ah, he's a booger. I just had all kinds of trouble with him. In fact, by gosh, I took the board down there one morning. They was going to change the ditch. It'll plug up. He'd feed right there on the bank, you know, and all the hay'd blow and everything. It'd blow in the ditch and fill it up. Have to clean it every year. Then he'd make fences across it. A corral, so you wouldn't have to get in the water. And aw, he was ornery. He wanted to buy a little right-of-way around the house, like that. Let him have that for a corral. Just turn the water around there. And he popped off. I'd had trouble with him, and I couldn't catch him. Only right up to the yard, you know, and I was going to work him over.

Harvey Johnson, Hy Stegner, Bosky, they was on the board. I took them down, and I says, "You guys handle him." I says, "There's only one way to handle him," and I says, "you hit him twice and then if he ain't down, run around and see what's

a-holding him up." I says, "That's the only way you can get
along with him."

"Oh, that don't get you no place, Ab." I says, "OK." He
went in the house when he seen us coming. They couldn't get
him out. It was my place to go get him, see? So I went down
there, and I yelled at him, and hollered. And "What d'ya
want?" I said, "There's some men out here wants to talk to
you." "I don't want to see them." "Well," I says, "You'd better
come now, Jack, because they're going to sue you," I said. "The
sheriff come and get you and you'll come out."

He come out and he got kind of smart. We didn't quite
get down to the head gate, and he says, "I'd just like to know
why," he says, "every time we're around a bunch of men, you
want to fight me." I says, "I never have whipped you, yet." And
I says, "And I want to, that's why." I walked over right where he
was and I says, "I'm going to take this fence out." Water gap.
For his water. Wasn't doing nobody no good, only him. All the
rest of us would all have to pay extra money to get that ditch
cleaned. And I said, "Jack, I'm not going to monkey with you."
I says, "I'll talk to you now."

And bang, I took him. I was going to stomp him. And
Bosky got a hold of me and he says, "Ab," he says, "he'll have
you arrested and it'll cost you all you got." I says, "Well, I just
as well kick him twice, then." He got up, and he behaved
himself. He was laying right at the side of the ditch. I could
have rolled him in it. I would have rolled him in it if I'd have
had to went in with him. He was bigger than I was quite a bit,
you know, and a younger man, but he just wasn't one of them
rough and tumble guys.

Bessie Villars Tamlin

Conditioned early in life to expect little and to receive it philosophically, Bessie Villars Tamlin accepted the worst knocks with something bordering on fatalism. By the time she was 86, when she gave this interview, she was at peace. What had happened had happened. She spoke of loved ones' deaths as dispassionately as she described canning vegetables.

She was born in Joplin, Missouri in 1893. Her father was of French extraction, and somewhere along the line, his family name had been shortened from "de Villars." He had been a music teacher for awhile before marriage, but then worked in lead and zinc mines at Joplin and afterward did farm work mostly. And carpentry work. He told Bessie that he had a thick head of hair when he and her mother married, but working in those mines, he lost his hair. All except just a ring around the sides of his head, because of the minerals.

My parents were George Benjamin Villars and Eliza Elena Villars. We lived in Joplin until I was 15 years old. I can always remember walking to my grandma's with my mother, in the summertime, and we lived in Missouri, and they had johnny jump-ups there. So I always had to stop and pick johnny jump-ups. My folks left Joplin and went to Coy, Missouri, and we stayed there. That isn't there anymore. Anderson was our address when we left there. And we left there in 1908, I believe. Then we went to Kansas. And we lived there, oh, I don't know just how long. Not very long.

I was 15 years old in 1908. I had five sisters. No brothers. I'm the oldest. And my sister Daisy, she's three years younger than I am. So that'd be 1896. And then my next sister was born in 1901, I think. Quinvilla Eleanor. She was named for my grandmother on my mother's side. And then the Eleanor was for my dad's mother. I was born December 17, 1893. My sister

Daisy was born May 26, 1896. And Quinvilla Eleanor was born December 12th, 1901. My third sister, Susan, was born July 12, 1904. And my sister Pearl was born March 5th, 1909. And my youngest sister, Pauline Bernice, was born July 25th, 1911.

It was that birth that took her mother's life.

And then we came to Colorado. Simla, Colorado. We came to Colorado, and my dad and Daisy and I came in a covered wagon. And rain, rain, rain, rain, rain. I thought I never saw so much rain in my life. One time we had to lay over two days, I think it was. Two or three days some place in Kansas. My dad run a big ranch there at Simla, east of Colorado Springs.

And then I have had three sisters adopted. After Mother died, I was here in Colorado, and the rest of them was in Oregon. And I couldn't go out there. And there was no one else old enough to take care of them. So then Dad had to adopt three of them out. Pauline and Susan and Pearl. They were strangers that adopted them. I had one sister I haven't seen since she was two and a half years old.

I went to school in Kansas. First I went to school in Missouri. The Lone Star School. Then when we came to Kansas, I went to school while we lived there. And then when we came to Simla, I went to school in Simla. I never finished the eighth grade. I got married. I didn't have any sense.

I loved school. One teacher. They were all small schools. Not like the schools they have now. And I think we got more out of them, then, than they do nowadays. In Missouri, we had an old maid for a teacher, and they had a pointer. You know, to point to things on the blackboard? She used the pointer and a ruler to crack their knuckles. I never got my knuckles cracked, and I don't think I ever got hit with a ruler. I tried to behave myself. But I've seen other kids get it.

Bessie met her future husband, Henry Victor Tamlin (Ab's brother), in Simla.

His father run a livery stable. And he worked for his father. And I was going to school, so I'd see him every day because we had to go past the livery stable to get to our school. So that's how I met him. He was three years older than I was. And he was born in 1890. September 2nd, 1890.

After we were married, he worked at the carpenter trade and he worked in stores. Mercantile stores and grocery stores, and things like that. And then in 1920, why we went to Colorado Springs, and he went to Barnes Business School. We wasn't there too awful long, till he come out and went to CSU. Only it was an agriculture college when he went and took his high school. He didn't get a high school diploma, either. So he took his high school there, and then in 1922, we moved to Laporte, and we run a vegetable garden and raised chickens and sold eggs and chickens and fryers.

I just worked in the garden and took care of the house and the kids. I have worked out some, but not very much. I got to crocheting and I sold a lot of that. There was a dry cleaners' in Fort Collins that had a great big window with a kind of a shelf in front of it, so she let us put our stuff down there. Several of us crocheted and put our stuff down there. I was probably 50.

I really learned to can, myself. I knew how to can like Mother did. But you know, after we got older, why, then they started canning differently. When Mother canned, why she just boiled stuff on the stove and put it in a jar, you know. Sterilized her jars, and put it in the jar and sealed it up. But then later, they started cold-packing. And so then I learned that through a home extension agent in Fort Collins. Mrs. Johnson. We had 4-H. And home economics class. And so my mother taught me to sew, but then there was lots of things that she didn't know how to do, like they did later. Then I had a 4-H club when Betty was about 10 years old, I guess. About '43 or '44, something like that. And I had to learn along with the girls, the way they sewed for the club, you know. But I learned a lot that way. I pieced my first quilt when I was seven years old. It

was a doll quilt. And I've been piecing quilts ever since. I
started a new top today. But anymore I just cut out squares and
sew them up on the machine. I don't do the fancy ones
anymore. I used to do those.

And we had about 20 acres, I think. And part of it was
pasture, and part of it, we raised chickens and pigs and cows
and calves. Just had milk cows. And then we always raised pigs
to butcher. Once in a while we sold one. He used to smoke the
pork. The north end of this tool shed out here—it's a tool
shed now—he had that for a smokehouse. He built a little hole
in the ground and dug it, and then put a pipe in that and then
put a cement floor around it. And then he built a fire in this
little hole on the outside, and then the smoke would go up in
the building and he had his meat hanging in there. I don't
know how long. He'd just smoke it a little bit each day. So it
wouldn't get too hot. It dried out some, but not bad. Just on
the outside. The inside was nice and moist. You put it in sugar
and salt and saltpeter, and I don't know what all he put in it,
and let it cure for a while. And then he hung it and let it drain,
and then he'd build that fire in the pit and let the smoke go in
the building.

Then, of course, I got high blood pressure and we had to
quit raising pigs to eat. We had white leghorns and white
rocks, and oh, different kinds. We had several different kinds
when we lived in Laporte. We didn't have very many chickens
when we lived up here. Just enough for our home use. And
sometimes we'd sell a few eggs. We raised all kinds of vegetables: carrots, parsnips, and beans—several different kinds
of beans and peas. One year down to Laporte he planted so
many peas, my sister-in-law and Bea, Victor's wife; we canned
70 pints of peas apiece. And you know how much work there
was to that. Just shelling them, for one thing. And we could go
to the town and borrow the county's pressure cooker. And I
think that was before—maybe it was afterwards, that we
started borrowing that. But we had peas a-coming out our ears.
We never had such a year for peas as that year. We never did
raise so many, before or afterwards.

My sister-in-law and Bea and I canned together, off and
on. And then they moved up to Roach, up in there, in the
timber. My sister-in-law did. And then Vic and Bea, they lived
back here in this little house that Mr. Denham tore down. And
then her and I canned together for years. And I got a big 24
quart pressure cooker, and so we'd can together. We'd go to
the neighbors up towards the waterworks and get apples. And
when we lived at Laporte, I got a thing to dry corn and apples
and stuff in. I can't remember who we got it from. It was
already made, and we bought it. But I dried lots of corn. I
loved dried corn.

I've made a lot of hominy. I like that. Every once in a
while I buy me a can of hominy. But I don't buy it too often
cause it don't taste like homemade. And I don't use enough of
it to. . . . I guess I could freeze it, but I forget I've got it in the
freezer.

Victor was born February 15th, 1915. And Jack—his
name was John Jackson—he was born October the 12th, 1917.
Henry Albert, "Bert," was born March 31st, 1920. And let's
see. And Robert Charles was born April 24th, 1922, and
Richard Villars Tamlin, March the 15th, 1923. And Francis Lee
Tamlin was born July the 15th, 1931. And Betty Elena was
born November the 24th, 1933. She was born the same year as
the Dionne Quintuplets. I forgot what month they was born,
but. . . . Six boys. And a girl.

My husband kept wanting a girl after Victor was born.
He was just bound the next one was going to be a girl. He was
a-helping a neighbor put up hay, and he was a bachelor. And
Victor was just little, you know, when Jack was born. And he
kept saying, "How's the baby sister?" He had told this neighbor that he was going to have a baby sister. And he'd always
tease him. He'd say, "It's not a baby sister, it's a baby brother."
But he'd tease him all the time. It was so funny.

Course, not all my children are living. I lost three boys.
Jack got hurt playing football. Down here at Laporte. He was
almost 17 when he died. He broke the femur bone, and it filled

up with pus. I took him to the doctor, and he said, "Oh, there's nothing wrong, just bruised." A big 200-and-some-pound guy fell on him. And he was small for his age. So the doctor told me to just take him home, put him to bed for a day or two and he'd be OK. Well, he got worse and worse all the time. So finally it swelled up there where the pus collected, and he just run a knife in there and drained it, and it'd heal up, and then it'd fill up again. So finally I took him to Colorado General. And they said that that should never have been cut into. Because every blood vessel that knife passed through—when you pulled it out—put it in the bloodstream. Said it should have been tapped. Just drawn out that way. But he didn't. So he was almost seventeen when he died. I think he must have been about 15 when it happened.

Robert, he had leakage of the heart. He had bronchitis when he was tiny, and it caused a leakage of the heart. And he was nine years old when he died. When he first got bronchitis, he was just a tiny baby. Less than a year old. And he was sick all the time. Doctor told me to never be surprised if he was out playing and I'd go out and find him gone. So you know what I lived under. And then Lee died. He choked on a carrot. He come in—his dad was outside and they come in, and I was peeling carrots. He wanted a piece of carrot so I gave it to him. I'd always give the kids carrots. But then he went outside then, and his dad got ahead of him, and he went outside and he couldn't find him and he started crying and he sucked it down his windpipe. He was about two and a half—maybe a little over—when he died. So don't give your baby carrots. Raw carrot. It's all right to give them cooked ones. Or if you grind them up, it's OK. And to this day, Victor, he has a fit if he sees anybody give a kid a piece of apple or anything like that. He just can't hardly stand it. He just jaws them.

Bessie's remaining sons, Victor, Richard and Bert, all served in the armed forces. Victor was in the Marines in World War II, and was in the second wave to go ashore at Iwo Jima. He was seriously wounded and was awarded the Bronze Star, but refused to accept it, saying he did nothing more than the rest of his comrades.

And he was in the hospital a long time. He has an awful
lot of trouble with his arm. All the time. And Bert, he was in
over 23 years. Till they were going to send him to Vietnam and
he said he thought it was time to get out. They were in Alaska
when they wanted to send him to Vietnam.

And Richard was in the Korean War. Him and Bert was
in Korea at the same time, and they got to visit each other.

It's a wonder I'm not white-headed. People that haven't
had as much grief and worry as I've had are white-headed. But
they say that it isn't worry that causes white-headedness.

If you don't have much to lose, a depression can have little effect.
But the travails of Nature are something else.

We had to make do with what we had. And I can remember the Dust Bowl, also. I had a cloth strainer that I strained
my milk in during the Dust Bowl, and I washed it out. I
washed it out every time I used it. And I always hung it on the
line to dry. Well, it was late when we got the milking done that
night so I just washed it and hung it out on the line. The next
morning, I wouldn't strain milk through it. It was just full of
dust. Fine dust. And it was gray as any gray thing you've ever
seen. So I said no. I wouldn't have strained milk in that. And
after that, I didn't hang my milk strainer out till after the dust
storms were over with. And then the wind would come up,
and it'd blow again. There was no rain. I can remember that.

And the Depression. We had to buy some meat. 'Cause
he was working in the stores then, and we didn't raise meat or
anything like that. We'd have to buy meat. But we always had a
garden. Ever since we was married, we had a garden.

He worked on the WPA. He was timekeeper on that. So
that helped out a lot. And then we got commodities, you know.
Government commodities. You had to sign up for them and
whatever they had, that was what you got. And that dry milk
that they gave out, you could stir it henceforth and forever
more before you could get it mixed. It isn't like it is now. You

can just put it in and just stir it a little bit and it's dissolved. But then, it (would) feel like coarse cornmeal or something when you'd rub it through your fingers.

I made over clothes for Betty till she got pretty near in high school. Somebody'd give me something, you know, and I'd make it over for her, and it didn't bother her a particle. Some kids won't wear hand-me-downs and made-over things. But she never said one single word. She was glad to get it. And we used feed sacks for everything—dresses and aprons and underclothes, and everything else. And flour sacks. That's when stuff all come in cloth sacks. And feed used to come in white sacks. And I'd use them for quilt linings and tea towels and make clothing out of them.

Women didn't used to, so many of them, go out and work. But nowadays, I think it takes pretty near two, unless a man is getting a good salary. But I think that a woman doing the same thing as a man should get the same amount of money for her work.

Their children miss them. Now Vickie's a-having a terrible time with her little boy. Because she works. She got worried. He'd vomit, and cry and carry on. So she finally took him to the doctor. She wanted to find out if there was any-thing physically wrong with him. Well, there wasn't a thing physically wrong with him. It was just because she leaves to go to work before he leaves for school, and then they come home and she's not there. I think that makes it bad. But really and truly, I think unless a man is high-salaried, that a woman has to work to help make the living. But like I say, I think if they do the same kind of work as a man does, they should have that same pay. And I also think that there are some things that women shouldn't do.

This going on fires. And there's quite a few different things. I don't know what all. I don't think they're as strong. They're not able to handle that machinery that the firemen have to handle. Because you know those old big hoses are so big, and it takes two or three men, sometimes, to handle them.

But they're going into all branches of the service, and every-thing. Whatever a man does, they think they can do. But to go out and do some of these things. . . . And these women are driving these big old trucks. I don't approve of that. Because I don't think they're strong enough. These big semi-trailers.

Bessie's advice on living life properly was simple.

Well, just work. I don't think work killed anybody. I think if you sit down and not do a thing, after you're older, that's worse than trying to keep up a-doing a little bit. As to religion, I'm not fanatic about it, but I read my Bible, and try to do—you know—what is right. Churches are more socially oriented than they used to be. And then they try to work it out that they have all your time. Seems like that they have something planned. . . . When the kids are not going to school, it's something planned from the church. And you know, kids should have a little—I think—should have a little bit of their own entertainment. Course some of them don't entertain themselves right, I admit that, but. . . . No, I think the church is good, only I do think it has been more on the social order than a regular religious order. Now, people won't agree with me on that.

My kids, when they was growing up, they made their own entertainment. They'd go out and play house, play dolls, the boys would play ball, play marbles, or have their cars and make roads around for them, and kids don't do that anymore. Most girls, by the time they're 10 years old, they don't play dolls. And mine. . . . I played dolls till I got married. Course I wasn't very old when I got married. . . .

I used to know everybody in Laporte. But anymore, I don't know a soul, hardly. They're all gone, most of them. I don't know who lives in this house over here (about 100 yards away).

I don't know. Unless the times are changing (so) that we're more self-centered or something, I don't know what. Now, I don't get out and see my neighbors like I should.

Now my granddaughter from Laporte hadn't been up to
see me since Christmas Eve, till Sunday she came. That close.
Well, they have their friends, and they have so much company,
and they just don't get away. But I used to be able to walk to
people's houses, you know. I have walked from here to Fort
Collins. When we first moved up here, I did. I walked from
here to Fort Collins. 'Cause we only had the one car, and
Henry had to have the car to go to work. (And I walked to
Laporte) a lot of times. And then they used to let us ride the
school bus. And I'd ride the school bus down, and then I'd
walk home. But I walked to Laporte a lot of times. And over
there where Beulah Tamlin lives, you know? I used to walk
over there a lot. And my sister-in-law lived up on the hill in a
log house on the west side. And I walked over there.

Well, Robert was sick all the time, with that heart trouble.
And Henry was sick. He had appendicitis. And he didn't have it
taken care of till he'd suffered with it for so long. He thought
it would go away. And then when he got that infection in his
arm in the service, why, that lasted for several years. And then
he had pneumonia a time or two. Wouldn't go to the hospital. I
had to take care of him at home. Then he got sunstroke one
time, and I had to take care of him. He worked on the road.
And there was a big gravel pit up toward Wellington some
place and they was hauling gravel from there, and oh, it was a
terrible hot day. And so he come home sick that night, and I
said, "Well, why didn't you come home sooner?" "Well, I
couldn't. I had to work." Men. They can be so contrary. I don't
know whether you've found it that way or not. They get sick,
they don't want you to do anything, only take care of them. I
was about ready to dump him outside. He was out of his head,
and everything. So I wanted to call the doctor. He said no. So
he was in the bedroom and the telephone was in the kitchen so
I went and shut the bedroom door and the kitchen door and I
called the doctor. He came out. And he said, "Fill a hot water
bottle with cold water and put it on his head and the back of
his neck." It wasn't no time till he was normal again. And I
never heard tell of such a thing before. Well, I'd never had any
experience with sunstroke!

I had a stroke. 1960. October, 1960. And I was in the hospital nine days. But they never gave me any therapy or anything. I was bound I wasn't a-going to give in. I was a-going to keep exercising and everything. I had it on my left side. And I'm left-handed. But since then, off and on, I've had high blood pressure. There was for four years after the stroke, I wasn't able to work outside. But after that, after four years, well, I started in doing just like I'd always done. I just decided that I'd played long enough. But I've had to take high blood pressure medicine ever since then.

There isn't a piece of music in my body. My dad used to try to teach me the notes. He might as well have tried to teach the fencepost.

Any last words for the people who read this?

Can't think of any. Only not sit down and hold their hands when they get old. That's all. Now I'm going to heat some water for some tea for us.

Flora Spragg Shunn Conard

"I laid him in the shelter of a log in the sunshine."

Family was the most important thing for Flora Spragg. Her happy childhood left her after seeking to recreate the sense of family she experienced as a child. Born and raised in Rock County, Nebraska, she grew up surrounded not only by five sisters and a brother, but by relatives and family friends who had followed the same path her father had taken from Independence, Iowa. Once he arrived in Nebraska, he married a girl named Bassett, whose family had given the county seat its name.

When she started school, Flora's teachers were two older sisters. As a teenager, she and her older brother made several trips to haul an older sister's belongings and drive her cattle from the Rosebud Indian Reservation in South Dakota 70 miles east to Gregory, where the sister relocated following her husband's death. As a young married woman, she followed her husband to Canada, and even changed her citizenship to fulfill Canadian homestead requirements. But she grew terribly lonely and brought her children back to the U.S. to be near her parents, who had moved to Bellvue to be near Jesse, one of Flora's older sisters. She finally prevailed on her husband to join her and the family, and they reunited and lived together for the next quarter of a century. He died in 1947, and 10 years later, she married Clifford Conard, retired minister of the defunct Bellvue Pilgrim Holiness Church. They spent their remaining years in Bellvue. Many weekday mornings they would drive into Fort Collins to visit nursing homes, where Flora would play her accordion and sing, and Clifford would give spiritual talks.

I remember looking on the record at school one time and saw that I was there when I was four years old. I don't think I was a regular attendant, really. I'd maybe know more. And our schoolhouse was just a little one-room school. But we had good teachers. Very good teachers. Two of my teachers were my sisters. My oldest sister and my sister Bertha. And Bertha had been to Fremont. Bertha and Agnes had attended Fremont Normal, and Bertha taught our school. She was sure a good teacher. And Mother was a teacher, and her family, all except Jesse and I, were teachers. I substituted sometimes, but that was all.

Some of my last school days—I didn't care too much ever for history, and I didn't care too much for Civics. Or Civil Government. I've been learning it later, in later years. I don't remember just when I was real young, but I liked Zane Gray's books and what. . . . was our book—the Negroes? What was the name of that old book? We had that, I think, read to us in school. *Uncle Tom's Cabin.* I liked that. I think our teacher read that to us, you know, maybe a chapter a day. And that's something else. We had Bible readings always, in school. I don't remember a teacher that we didn't have Bible reading. And I suppose some of them had prayer. I don't remember that all did. Our main play at school as I was older was baseball. We girls, there weren't very many of the older children in school, then. I had a cousin and myself, and two or three boys was all. Oh, we got up to eight or ninth grade, something like that. Our grades weren't kept track of, like they are nowadays. But that's the only place I ever took any ninth grade, was in our little country school.

I've been so thankful our parents taught us to work. And I did all kinds of work. Another thing there about our school, at the close of our school, we always had a picnic. The families of the school. They'd always have a picnic and program. But at home, we had a good life at home. I don't mean it was all work. We had lots of music. I don't think there was ever a gathering—a school gathering, party—and we had lots—in the wintertime we had lots of parties, in the homes, older folks and children together—and I don't think that we ever had a party or a school doings or anything but what we sang. Played the organ or whatever instrument they had, and sang. We were a great community for music.

The family had acquired a pump organ that no one could play.
Flora taught herself.

I remember the first piece of music I ever played by note.
I wasn't old enough that I was at school with the others, and I
could hardly wait till they'd get home so 1 could show I could
play that.

My brother had that, the last I knew, and of course old
things weren't counted valuable those days, and I don't know
what was ever done with it. But oh, I think we first started
playing, playing chords. Just playing chords. And I suppose the
older girls learned it, and I learned it from them. Now, I never
took music lessons from the teacher, except we had one
teacher. One we didn't count as excellent, but he taught us to
read music. Lots of just vocal music. We didn't have any
instrument in the school, but he put in quite a bit of time in
that. And I suppose that was a help, to me. Must have been. I
haven't counted it much, until just here lately, I've been thinking about it. Why, no doubt that has helped me a lot with my
music. I was supposed to take music lessons. Our postmaster's
wife was a music teacher. I took a lesson on music with her. I
could already play, "The Mockingbird." And it was with
variations. I think there was 13 sheets of it. Sheet music. And
that's all that went over with me that day. Maybe I shouldn't
put this in—how silly I was. I had an animal. I think it was a
heifer at that time that I was going to sell. My sister next older
than I, we were putting our money together and getting us a
saddle, because we always rode horseback and we didn't have a
saddle. And I found out that I was to pay for my music
lessons. I never went back for another one. I wanted the
saddle.

Can't remember when I didn't ride. Got to be a pretty
good rider. And handling the horses, too. We girls. As Father
got older, we broke the horses to ride and to drive.

That was a hay country. Newport—I've been told that
there was more hay shipped out of Newport, Nebraska, than

any other place in the whole country. Just build up great stacks of it in the bales, you know, just—oh, just immense, there around Newport. And of course my folks, my brother and father worked together on it all. They wouldn't sell hay meadows around. They wouldn't be such big ones, but we worked usually all summer. But I don't remember us ever having it baled. It was just stacked and fed. We just raised it for feed and the milk cows.

And I was thinking the other day of my first experience running—I think they called it a check-row corn planter. There was something out to the side of it that kept the row. Followed the row each time, kept me straight, and that machine just planted that corn just the right distance apart all the time. My father bought this new machine, and I remember driving it. Riding on it. I wasn't—couldn't have been very big. But I remember we were taught to take responsibility too. Always. Father, nearly every fall, would go to Omaha to the state fair, and I remember my sister Minnie and me coming home from school and hitching up the team to the wagon, going out in the cornfield and picking corn for the hogs. And Mother, of course, getting supper for us. I remember a stranger coming in there one evening. It wasn't like now. We'd be leery, I suppose, of a stranger. Some young man came there, just when we girls came from the field, and he stayed supper with us. I don't remember whether he stayed all night or not, but I remember Mother had him eat supper.

But now that wasn't anything unusual for us, and we milked the cows and took care of all the chores while Papa was gone. And then another time, two different times that I remember—he was on the jury in Bassett for a week or two, and we took care of those chores and attended school. Walked three quarter of a mile. No wonder I'm healthy. And we didn't—it wasn't any hardship. I really think we enjoyed it. Oh, those things back there are as clear in my memory as what was done last week. In the wintertime, our neighborhood had lots of parties. Taffy pulls, popcorn, and like I say, lots of singing. At home, I can see yet how we sat around the table with our kerosene lamps in the evening. Papa'd read the newspaper. If there was news to be read out loud, he'd read it, and Mother would usually sit with her mending.

Mother's eyes were awfully bad. I wonder how she ever got along, taking care of such a family. Some doctor that she had gone to had used medicine too strong in her eyes and burned her one eye till all she could see out of it at all was light. But we always took a special paper, *The Youth's Companion*. It was a story paper. Good clean stories. There was where some of our reading was used. Someone would read that aloud in the evening. It just came once a week, but we always got it there, and that was just part of our good times. I haven't any complaint about anything. We never had much money. But we were always dressed. We never went like we see folks now. So near nakedness some of the time. We had clothes. And Mother sewed. Mother washed. Did our washing. And 'course when we were out of school, we were helping.

We always, always was to church on Sunday at Sunday School, if the weather was fit at all. It was a Methodist church when I was a kid. And then later it was Free Methodist. We lived, I think it was three miles from the church. It was just a little one-room church. I played organ there for church when I was pretty young. That was a neighborhood church, of course. Everybody came. They had a windbreak out at the back for the horses in the winter, and there was always horses, and buggies and wagons. We would have hated to have had to have missed church. And again, I was back there, oh, it's been quite a few years now since I was back there, with my sister and her husband—sister Agnes and her husband—and we drove up to the old church and we went in. We'd been gone from there so many years, I wish I could tell you just the number, and saw Spraggs' name was still on the blackboard. That was my cousin's family. Still lived in there—or had lived there later. We went in where we'd been so many times in such good services and both of us knelt at the altar and prayed there while we were there. Didn't get to see a lot of folks that we would have liked to have seen, but we were driving through. I can see so many places that were so dear to me, those days. My cousin's grandparents had a farm there and lived down over to Ash

Creek. I used to go with her to their place, and they had an orchard down on the creek. Their house–buildings were up on the level but there was quite a little valley down there where the creek was, and that was just a wonderful place. I don't know. I just thought–I could see that yet, just how beautiful everything was, the flowers and the trees. We had them at home, too. We had the trees and lots of flowers at home. I come home in May, and the lilacs and the apple trees, everything was in blossom and the trees were greening and oh, I just thought, my, this is the most beautiful place I ever saw! It was just wonderful after being in the sand hills.

I suppose I was 16, 17. My oldest sister had drawn a claim in the Rosebud Reservation, opening there. She had registered there and she drew a claim. She lived out about three miles, I think, north of Gregory. She was a widow woman with a family. Her name was Atkinson. Her husband was George. He had died while they were living in Nebraska. They were just living about a mile from us, and he had typhoid pneumonia and died. And she had never got all her things over in Dakota. My brother kept her stock. She sent her boy over, thinking he could get a cousin to help him bring the cows back. He came over on horseback. I tried to get some of the neighbor boys, one of them, to go, and couldn't find anybody. So I came home and told Mother I guess I'd have to go. That's how I come to go. We started out in the afternoon and went to up to an uncle of his near the Niobrara River. We had to cross that, and we stayed all night there.

I'm not sure, whether we had 10 or 12, something like that. Not a herd. It'd have been easier to drive if we'd had more, I expect. And we had to cross the Niobrara. Course we had bridges there. Two places, we had to cross that. Then we went on over across the Keya Paha River. That was on farther north. But there, we had to ford the river. And we went on about 10 miles from Gregory that day–the second day–and then we stayed overnight with friends, there and on the way home. She lived north of Gregory. I drove a team with a load of her lumber over that same road, in the wintertime, one time. I know it was pretty icy off the edge of the river, where we had to ford. It was cold too. We had to climb down off the wagon a lot of the time and walk. That's the first time I ever found out I could get around by walking. Atkinson took a load, too, so I wasn't alone on that trip. About 50 miles, we figured it. There was a hotel on the Keya Paha River where we always stopped to eat. That was just about half way, I think.

On the trip to take her sister's cattle to Gregory, she met Dan Shumm. They were married in 1908.

His nickname was "Buzz." He got that from the older children trying to say "Brother," I guess. French. His father had come from France. He was—and his mother was English. Now I'm not sure that his father or his grandfather, but I'm quite sure that his father had come from France. I know that was his nationality. He farmed there for quite a while. Then we moved to Nebraska, on my sister's place in Nebraska, and lived there. We were just a mile from my birthplace. We lived there until we moved to Canada. His folks had gone up there, and every letter we had, they were wanting us to come. Oh, it was so wonderful. And the wind didn't blow up there. And we had so much wind in Dakota and Nebraska. The day we got off of the train up there, we could hardly stay on the sidewalk for the wind. And we had plenty of them. We were out on the homestead. . . . I can remember when we'd have just like we used to have our blizzards, two or three days in Nebraska. We'd have wind storms, and well, it was just like a cloud. . . . They said it was ashes from forest fires out in British Columbia.

I didn't like it too much and yet I guess I didn't really object too much either, though I hadn't intended to stay in Canada all my life. I'd like to go back and see it again. I was so homesick there. The country was all right, and the people. We had good neighbors. Not any close neighbors, but we had just splendid neighbors. Most of them were from the States. And it wasn't that. I had anything I wanted in that country, but I was just so homesick. My parents visited my sister Agnes and her husband, way north in Canada, several years after we went up there. They went way up in the north where they really hunted and fished. And they were with us the summer my parents came up and visited us. I was there not quite eight years, but just about.

I think my reason was because I wanted to come home. The children and I came down in. . . . I think we left the homestead the 23rd of November, in 1920. We came down on a train, and stopped off at Montana and visited Agnes and her husband and then came on down here. Our folks had moved out to Bellvue in the meantime.

And when Mother was left alone, why, I came to stay with her. We were living in the old stone schoolhouse. All those years, it was used as a residence. It was a big, old thing, you couldn't make like a home very much, but it was a home. I lived there until after Mother died. And until after my family was gone.

Dan came right after. He brought our. . . . I know we had got a little dog while we was there, and he brought it with him when he came. Not very long after we came. Just a short time.

He died the 13th of January. Oh, it was ten years before . . . . I was alone for over 10 years. He died very suddenly. He was working in trees up here for someone, getting Christmas trees out, or something. He was a great lover of horses. He always had horses wherever he was, and had some fine ones. He came from work up there and had driven his team up that morning. That was a Monday morning. We had a little old car, and the boy was working up there, too, and they just came back home in the car. I know I was up at my sister's. She used to live up here after she was left alone. I was up there and saw them come by, so I hurried home because it was suppertime. My brother-in-law from Encampment, Wyoming, had come down. I didn't know it till I got here. They came in and were seated one on each side of the stove, visiting. He hadn't even taken his wraps off. He had some chores to do—get in coal, and such. And my youngest daughter and her family lived in part of the house, the front part of the house then, and I stepped in there for something. I was fixing supper and stepped in there for something. I hadn't much more than got in there till my brother-in-law stepped to the door and called me. "Your husband," he said, "just coughed and was unconscious. He never did regain consciousness. He went that sudden. When he first come, he said that he hadn't felt good all day. It was a cold wind. I laid him in the shelter of a log in the sunshine."

Stella Sapp

She was Bellvue's leading member of the Women's Christian Temperance Union, but she preached abstinence with good humor and ready forgiveness. At Grange meetings, she was an inveterate reader of poetry (that almost always contained advice on how to behave properly in life). She was an expert baker of delicious cookies, which she loved to share with neighborhood children. She canned all types of vegetables in old fashioned glass jars.

I was born in Stanton County, Nebraska, 1895. My father, Thomas Benton Willey, was born in Zanesville, Ohio, in 1857. They all called him Uncle Ben. And when he was seven years old, that'd make it about 1864; they went by ox team from Zanesville, Ohio, to Ringold County, Missouri. My grandmother had, altogether, I think, 17 children. She had 12 of her own; one died when he was three months old. Then their oldest boy Asher, when they had their sixth baby, it died, and his wife died. And the next day after the funeral, he disappeared. They never saw anything of him for years. But she took those five children and with her 11, that made 16. And she took one of his grandchildren and raised it, so she raised 17 children. Course the oldest children, some of them were gone. They weren't all home at the same time. But there in Missouri they just had a two room log house with a loft where the boys slept, and there was no connecting doors. You had to go around. If you went in the other room, you had to go outdoors. And they carried water from the spring. They lived there till he died.

But in the meantime, they never heard anything from this Uncle Asher. He had went south someplace. I don't remember where it was, but someplace—whether it was

Florida— someplace in the south–and had married again. He'd never told this wife that he'd been married. But he got real sick and he thought he was going to die and so he told her about this family, and she got in touch with them and these five children. None of them would have anything to do with her except the oldest one, Mary Ellen. They said, "He deserted us when we were little. I don't want anything to do with him now." But Mary Ellen took him in. And then he was finally living in South Dakota. I believe it was Buffalo Gap. So they moved down there with Mary Ellen. In 1910 he died, and on the way to the funeral the team run away and threw her out and killed her. So they waited and had the funeral, and they're both buried in the cemetery in Rapid City, South Dakota.

And they lived there in Nebraska, in Stanton, Nebraska. Then when I was four years old, they moved to Holt County, Nebraska. That was Page, Nebraska, and we was three miles from the–Venus–that was in Knox County. That was our post office. And O'Neill, Nebraska was our county seat. I lived there and went to school. I started school when I was five years old and went to school there through the seventh grade. Then we moved by covered wagon to South Dakota. When we moved to South Dakota, we had a log house. Then they built a sod bunk house. That was where all the boys slept. In Nebraska he usually had one or two hired men, and then there were seven of us children. My mother had one of those first stoves, Home Comfort I believe it's called. She had two bread pans that just fit in that oven. Every other day she made eight loaves of bread, besides some cinnamon rolls, and stuff like that. Every other day, because there was seven of us and we was all home, and then sometimes one, sometimes two hired men. So she had quite a handful there. But of course we all had to work. We all had to do our share, you know. Everybody worked. They didn't play all the time.

Had a big garden, and we'd go fishing off the Niobrara River. I can remember when we all piled into the wagon to go all day, and we'd take dinner and go fishing. They'd seine fish. I would watch those men go up there with that seine and those fish was a-wiggling in there. We had a big wooden tank to water our stock. Right down on our place there was a draw. There was a little pond down there, and little pipes to go down. Well, my brother Raymond and I—he was two and a half years younger than I—we'd watch those fish, and if we could find one that was wiggling, we'd put it in the tank. My dad was very easy going. He wouldn't say a word. That fish was all right. Then he'd come up and the horses wouldn't drink (because of the fish there) and he'd say, "You kids get those fish out of there!" We'd get some screen and we'd go out there and seine fish and take them down and put them in that pond. They said after we left there, they caught some great big fish out of there.

I can tell you my first grade teacher was Maude Waring. When I went to work in Cheyenne during the war, I worked at United Airlines. There was a woman there from North Dakota. She kept talking about this town in North Dakota. One day I said, "Florence, did you happen to know anyone by the name of Maude Waring that lived there in North Dakota?"

"My," she says, "she's my mother." "Well," I said, "she was my first school teacher!" Then she brought her to see me when we was in Fort Collins.

I never went to high school, because we moved up to South Dakota. It was just team and wagon, and Faith and Sermon. We was 40-50 miles from any town. I went through the eighth grade three times. I just loved to go to school. I'd go, and then the last year or two, why, we'd pick out—the teachers was real good—and I could pick out things that were hard for me and we'd go through that. But I never got through high school.

When I was 19, I was married and then had two children there, and then had two more. My husband's ancestors were from Germany. We farmed. Carl Hampel. But oh, he's been gone since—oh I know Clayton was about 12 years old. Eleven, twelve—it would be a long time ago. So I had the children; I had the two younger ones. He just left.

In the early 1920s Stella and her husband came to Bellvue to visit her sister. They liked the area so much they decided to stay. A few years later Carl decided to go back to South Dakota. He returned now and then to visit, but the marriage was over.

The girls were big enough then—they were through high school. They was taking care of themselves. And I worked. For United Airlines about two, three years. Then I worked in a sugar factory, I worked in a canning factory, and I did nursing. Practical nursing. That's the last thing I done.

At United Airlines I worked electrical. Doing all the electric parts to the planes. These tail lights they had—I don't know whether they have them yet or not. But they had green, amber, and red little lights on the wing tips. Made hundreds and hundreds and hundreds of those. Soldered them together. They were the B-17 bomber planes. And then they had some they called the "ducks." Amphibians for Canadian planes. They had some of them come in there that we'd work on. Yeah, that was real fascinating work. If I hadn't had my people all in the army, I'd have liked that. But my son was a prisoner of war in Germany, and this young son got on a land mine. He was in English hospital nine months, and Fitzsimons about a year. And my daughter's husband was killed over there. So I don't like war.

One night at a dance at the Bellvue Grange Hall, Stella met a fella.

I didn't pay much attention to him. He was just another one of the guys. We danced together, and it was quite a little time when he finally asked me for a date. We went, and just did, that's all. We've had a real good 25 years. We really had. Couldn't ask for anything better. We spent six winters in Arizona, we been up to the state of Washington, we've been by St. Louis a couple of times, we been to Idaho two or three times. . . . We just did a lot of things.

You just take each day as it comes. You do the best you can and that's all you can do. You know you can't do these things and you just don't do them. That's why I have that one woman come once a week to help out. You can't do like you used to, and you just as well recognize the fact. Recognize your limitations. It's all you can do. No use to sit around and fret about it. I had one little lady, I don't think she's as old as I am, but: "You know, I didn't know it was going to be this way to get old," she said. Oh, we enjoy it pretty much. Ernie's not very well, but we just do the best we can.

Nellie Swatman Davis

"All my life was the Depression."

Of the people who came to Bellvue, Nellie Davis probably had the greatest claim to having been led there by the Almighty. If she was, it was into a life of hardship, work and one disappointment after another. Born in 1902, she spent her early life in eastern Colorado, where her father was attempting to prove up on a homestead. The life was hard, and they left the homestead for awhile to a farm up on the Platte. One summer when she was still a young girl, a terrible hail storm ruined the family's fine crops. Long afterwards she remembered financially and spiritually demoralized parents making no progress toward recuperation. But during a snowstorm the winter following the hail storm summer, a visitor arrived.

It was in July that the storm hit. We were on the south side of the Platte River. Papa was in. He stayed in. Mother was not well. She had never been well. I never knew my mother to have a well day. He stayed in to help her wash, and had the hired men working on the machinery because they were going to start to bind the oats that afternoon. He went out and looked at them when he went out to hang clothes. He come back in, and he says, "Well, Katherine," he says, "it looks like we'll go back to the homestead with plenty of money. We can come out of this and have plenty of money to finish proving up down on the homestead." And she said, "Oh, don't count your chickens before they're hatched," she says. "It ain't in the granary yet." And Dad says, "Oh, you old wet blanket." I can see him and hear him yet. He went on about his work and that afternoon about 2:30 there was a big dark cloud came up from the northwest. Come towards us. Oh, it was so black and everything. Before the men could get the teams in the barn and all, it started to hail. One bunch of horses run away. One team run away and come down to the barn, and all.

After it had hailed so, the water was clear up to Mama's knees. She went out and all her little chickens was just floating around and oh, she pulled up her apron and just filled her lap with little chickens and brought them to the house. My sister and I had a fire going and warmed up those chickens. She hardly lost one, but she fished them all out of the water. The hail, you know. Then that storm jumped over and went on and then it landed at Roggen, Colorado and it done an awful lot of damage there.

The next day or two, Papa and Mama went out riding, to see what damage was done. There was a mule—Papa told about that mule, standing up just straight in a field. They had been hit with a cyclone and the wind had jumped over us because we was so close to the river, I guess. That mule was standing up there, dead, and his legs was in that mud up to his knees, you know. That's the damage it done. Well, anyway, Papa went on and he finished the crop as best he could. The beets were all down in the ground, the potatoes, and course the grain was all thrashed, and there was nothing to salvage there.

Then, that fall, he started taking a course on the signal-maintaining job on the Union Pacific Railroad. He worked on that. Then we moved back down just as soon as we could. We stayed just till he could get money enough to get out. But in the meantime, it was in January and it was so cold. My mother would go out and set on the porch. He'd get up and try to get her to come in. She was without a blanket or anything, her mind just went so bad.

There was a minister of the Seventh Day Adventist Church by the name of Mr. Babcock. He was peddling apples between Bellvue and Fort Morgan. He stopped at our house. It was snowing so bad, he wanted to keep his horses in the barn. Papa built a fire up in the bunkhouse and he went in here. My mother was sick. She pretty near lost her mind over the shock of losing so much money. We had 375 acres and didn't have enough to even hardly pay our way out.

In January, February, somewhere along there, Mr. Babcock come peddling these apples. Before I went to school that morning, I remember he gave us an apple, and oh, that amounted to so much. He stayed that night. Mother kept a-saying to herself, "Go tell him to come in and have some supper." And she said, "I'm not going to do it." Finally—it kept tormenting her—she said, that what if that was Harry, which was my father's name, out there and he was hungry? So finally she said, "I don't have nothing to feed him, only some bread and milk." She said to Papa—he didn't dare to do things to aggravate her, or anything, he had to be so careful with her—and finally she said, "Go out and tell him that I have nothing but some bread and milk, but if he'd like to have it, to come in and eat."

So Papa went out. Oh, it was snowing so hard, and all, and Mr. Babcock was sitting there by the stove. He was warm because the stove was going in the bunkhouse. He was so glad about bread and milk. He said that's what he ate every night for supper. So he went on talking and pretty soon Mama looked up at him and says, "You are a Seventh Day Adventist, aren't you?" And he said, "Yes, I am." And she says, "Well, my Mother is a Seventh Day Adventist." They started to talk and they talked till way up in the night. Then the next morning he stayed until around 11 o'clock talking to Mama and Papa. Then he went on and he told them when he came back that he would stop again. That was the turning point of mother's life, right there. Her attitude begin to change, with Brother Babcock's help and everything.

So we went back down to the homestead country and in a certain time, we proved up and we moved into Boyero. Finally Papa and Mama—I don't know how come, I was in eighth grade, in the school in town there—they got to thinking they would leave the country then, but they didn't know where they'd go. So Papa got on the train, come up and run Mr. Babcock down. He owned the house that Stella Sapp lives in.

He lived in that house. Anyway, Papa visited with him. They were talking in the morning and after Dad got there, and he mentioned something about a Lou Hosier that lived up there at Bellvue. And Papa says "Hosier! I got cousins by the name of Hosier." So Mr. Babcock and Papa got in the buggy and they went up to see Mr. Hosier, and here it was Dad's own cousin.

So in the spring, in April, Papa got an immigrant car and put our household goods in one end and we had two cows and two little mule colts. An immigrant car is a car Union Pacific puts out. Just a regular boxcar, and they fixed it that one end they put the animals and the other end your furniture. Papa fixed his bed right in the doorway and rode it up here. It took him two days to come. We got on the passenger train and come up, Mama and my sister and I.

Nothing was hard work for me, then. How I plowed, with plows and everything, when I was a kid, and different things. I was strong as any. . . . I did more men's work. Papa always wanted a boy, but I was the only. . . . I had a sister six years older than I was, but she was mentally retarded, and Mama wasn't well. So we shocked the grain.

We had the flu epidemic. Everything was closed. You couldn't go to school or anything. Papa got a contract from Mr. Black here in town for Christmas trees, and him and I would get on horses and ride up Rist Canyon. I thought all that seemed such a long ways. We rode horseback. Mr. Black had made arrangements for the trees, and we'd cut trees all day and I'd snake them down to the road. Throw a rope on a tree and throw it on the saddle horn and bring it down and undo it and go back up and get another tree. Papa cut the trees. We'd cut a load and then we'd come down. Oh, it was just such a cold time, and so slick. Rist Canyon was just like a glare of ice all the way down. It was such a dip down, when we'd come with the wagon. We'd come down the next day, then, and get a hayrack and go back up and get the trees that we'd cut the day before. We'd bring them down and it would make the horses mad. Papa'd use the brakes and everything, but still, coming such a dip down, they'd run up against the horses and make them so mad. But Papa kept his horse shod in cork shoes so that they didn't slip. The horses didn't slip. We'd put them on a boxcar at Bellvue, there—they had a car on there—a railroad car. We loaded the trees that winter for entertainment.

Later, my sister and mother and I got the flu, but Papa didn't. I was in bed two weeks with the flu. I was really sick. My sister was sicker than I was. The first morning that I was up, Papa was so. . . . He had waited on us night and day and had to cook and do everything, and I felt so sorry for Papa that next morning, I got up and made him a pan of biscuits. I remember I was all in, just making that little old pan of biscuit for Papa. But I got them made for him. Anyhow, he had hot biscuit for his breakfast that morning.

I started back to school after the flu epidemic, and I was behind one year because we left Boyero in April before I took my eighth grade finals. They made me, when I was in Laporte, take eighth grade over again. Then the next year, in the ninth grade, I got diphtheria in March. I was quarantined. I never will forget. They laid there and they all thought I couldn't talk. My throat was so bad and all. I lay there and all I could think of was. . . . There was people by the name of Laws, lived in a little house back of the Bellvue store.

Grandpa Laws talked about making sauerkraut. So I told Mama oh, I wanted some sauerkraut. Well, she knew very well it'd kill me, as bad as I was. That's all I could think of. Mr. Laws was working up at George Bear's, and he walked by the house every morning and come back at night. I said, "Mama, ask Grandpa Laws if he would bring me some sauerkraut." She says, "Well, if you promise that you will not swallow it," she says. "I know it will kill you." My folks always figured sauerkraut was something that'd kill you. Papa always said it was nothing but rotten cabbage. So I told her, "all right." So she went out and she told Grandpa. She said to him, "Put it in something—a bucket or something that you don't want back and set it inside here, cause I don't want you folks to spread this in any way to anybody." And so Grandpa went right home and he got an eight-pound lard bucket full of sauerkraut! We never laughed so, over so much sauerkraut. But that night I ate some sauerkraut. I spit out some of it. I suppose I swallowed some of it like kids do, and next morning I could talk. It had cleared my throat. And I began to get better. I said I owed my life to a bucket of sauerkraut.

Then I started back to school after my quarantine was up and everything, and I was trying to make up my grades. You see, I was in ninth grade and I had to get through. Of course this was in April. My vision—I'd be studying and it'd disappear. I'd blink my eyes and it'd come back. So I'd go on to school. I had a teacher that I didn't like. I was so far ahead of all of them in cooking that it was just ridiculous that I even took cooking again. I still have my cookbook—my school book that I had. She asked us if there was something we wanted to cook one time, and I said I'd like to learn how to make cream puffs. So she got the recipe out, and everything, and she didn't have brains enough to know that for the recipes for this higher altitude, you had to add a little bit more flour. Well, it said sift your flour, then measure it, and I just grabbed it up and put it in and then sifted it. Lottie Lambert was my partner and out of the whole class, Lottie and I was the only ones that had good cream puffs. The teacher wondered what on earth—the rest of them was just flat pancakes. I did not dare to tell her. It was because she wouldn't have taken my word for it. But it was just that added bit of flour, for that high altitude, what raised my cream puffs. I never did tell her.

After I had the diphtheria, I was trying to sew, and I couldn't see to thread the needle and I asked Emma Delahoy, who is Emma Delahoy now—her name was Emma Schultz—if she would thread my needle. And Miss Fountain got mad at me and told me that I was just trying to neglect my own work and trying to work somebody else in. I folded up my sewing, and she wanted to know what I was going to do. I says, "I am through." That night, when I went home, I told the folks. I said, "I just can't take it. I just can't." Mama made an appointment with Dr. Bernel and he took me right out of school and put me back to bed with strychnine. I tried staying in bed, but

I felt so sorry for Mama I'd get up and help her. Finally I began to get better, only that one year they put five different sets of glasses on me. Anyhow, then in July, I decided I was going out and go to work. I answered an ad in the paper east of town. A Mrs. Gordon Rudolph. I went to taking care of her children. She had three children. Mama told her I couldn't work too heavy, strenuous work on account of this diphtheria. She said, "That's all right." If I just took care of the kids—played with the kids and did the cooking, she would be satisfied. So I worked for her until that fall, late. Then I went to work for Mrs. Dykeman-Grandma and Grandpa Dykeman—east of town. And I left their house Friday night and was married Saturday morning.

Mama died in October of 1926. And my son was born in November of 1926. He was my baby. Mother would mop a floor in a rocking chair. She couldn't stand on her feet. She was too overly large. She was full of cancer. But the doctors didn't know it. They done everything for her that they could.

My aunt—her husband was janitor of the Washington School over here on Shields Street. They lived in the basement, there, and she said she would take care of me. So I came to town when it was about time for Helen to be born, and it started to rain. It rained continually and it kept a-raining. Helen wasn't born until the eighth of June. Hershel could not get over here without going clear south when they called him. The telephone lines was in, but the bridges was all out clear down—Bellvue bridges and so forth, and this one on North College Avenue was out, and the old road, from the mill to the three silos, was just water two foot deep, pretty near. Maybe not that deep, but anyhow, he had to go clear down, pretty near to Loveland, to get across the river to get back up there to me. Helen was born at around four or five o'clock the eighth of June.

Then when the 10 days was up, Hershel come in to get me. We didn't have a car, and he used the pickup truck of his boss which was a Model T Ford. You know they were built high. We went in water across from the mill to the three silos with the water clear up to the running board of that big old Model T Ford. The corn was yellow in the ditches where the water line was broken. I got water out of the ditch and let it settle in order to take care of the baby. We stayed there till the next year. Alice was born. Just before that, why my husband quit there and we moved up here by his folks. He went to work driving an eight-horse team of mules on a fresno (a farm machine that stirs up the earth) laying out the land for the cement plant. He went to work there. The guy that had the contract and all went to give him short checks and he had to stop that.

We moved up at Grandma's place, there at Bellvue. We had just two rooms there before little Albert was born. My third was a little boy. We lived there, and Mr. Brubaker's daughter was married to Sam Crane. They wanted a team of horses from Mr. Brubaker's brought over. Papa had went over to begin to help him in beets and all. He wanted another man. They called Hershel, and he went down and got a team of horses of Mr. Brubaker's and started across that morning. Oh, it was cold. He walked from there clear across over to the other side of the Boxelder School out there. Oh, it was cold. He got out there, and he put a load of hay on the hayrack. He got it up by suppertime, ate supper and it started to snow. The next morning all the beets and the potatoes and everything were all froze in the ground. He left the horses there. He was riding back with Papa, and Hershel says, "Where on earth will I find work? I've got to have work." That was before my baby, little Albert, was born. Papa said, "Well, let's stop at Charlie McMillan's. Maybe he would have work." He used to run a transfer company here in town. They stopped there and he said, "Land, yes. If you don't mind driving a team. Most everybody comes in here, wants to drive a truck and I don't have enough trucks." He said he'd have to haul coal and dead sheep cars, and Hershel said, "I don't care, just so it's work." He harnessed a team, and he started to work right then.

Well, on the 11th of November, little Albert was born, out there at Bellvue. Dr. Gleason came out. Oh, my goodness, the snow and all, but they managed to get around out there and the baby was born and the nurse got there. On Thanksgiving Day, Hershel rented a house up here on West St. Little three-room house. They moved us in to be closer to his work.

One morning, on the second day of December, I woke up. I'd went to bed that night, and the baby was so cute and all, and they was all around me. I can remember them yet. The little girls was standing there watching me getting ready for bed, and Hershel come and squatted down with them and was talking to the baby, you know, and put him to bed. I was feeding him at ten and two. I slept through the 10 o'clock feed. Two o'clock I woke up. I had such a dread. Oh, there was something haywire. I didn't know what. I had a notion to call Hershel and I thought: No. I talked myself out of it. He worked so hard and everything and he needed his rest. I had a notion to call him, and have him get up with me. I don't know why. I got up and I went in. Our bed was just right around from the front room. I had the baby in a basket with his feet towards the stove, and his head was towards the south, right at the door, there. I went to him and he was just wringing wet with sweat. I couldn't figure out. . . . I thought: oh, my goodness, have I pretty near smothered him? It was cold, and I thought maybe I had him too warm. So I fixed his bottle, and he wouldn't take his bottle. I spoke to Hershel, and he jumped right up. We didn't know anybody. You see we'd just moved to town. We didn't know nothing or anything.

We waited clear up until the time that Hershel was getting down to work. He just had started a new job and he didn't want to jeopardize his job. I said, "Well, I'll be all right," and he said, "Well, just as soon as I get down to work, I'll call Mom and have her send Pearl in to stay with you. Help you." That was his sister. He went on to work. I said to him, "What do you think, should I try and get ahold of Doctor?" And he said, "Do whatever you want to do." Well, I went around there and finally, about six o'clock, I looked out and I saw a light right back of us. I run over and asked them if I could use the phone. I called Dr. Gleason and he wanted to know about it. He says, "Could I have time to eat breakfast?" I says, "As far

as I know." I says, "The baby's the same as he's been since two
o'clock."

I started back, and the lady stuck her head out the
bedroom door. Her husband was the one that let me in to the
phone. The lady wanted to know if I needed help. I said no,
I'd be getting along all right. I went back home, and the little
girls was waking up . We hadn't been in town long enough yet
to have our lights turned on. We still was using lamps just like
we'd come from the country, you know. I dressed one of
them. I went and looked at the baby and he was just laying
there. I dressed one of them. Then I looked back at the baby,
and I thought he was having a convulsion. But he was dying
and I didn't know it. I took him out of there. There was folks
next door. I jumped over the fence, and I opened the door
and I says, "I think my baby's dying, will some of you help
me?"

Well, this woman's husband had just got home from the
factory. He worked at the sugar factory. She sent him for
some other people and a couple of women came then, just as
quick as they could, and they took the baby out of my arms. I
saw somebody out in the yard. I went to the door, and I still
had the baby, before those women come, and I said, "Would
some of you call Dr. Gleason and tell him to come?" So he
came. Then I told a lady and she went back over there to one
of the ladies and called Aunt Nettie, and she came right down,
laid the baby out and buried him the third day.

I didn't know when the Depression hit. The transfer
company had put him down in Boulder, and my dad come
down and said that the Depression was on up here. We hadn't
even recognized it 'cause we were going through it from the
time we went down there to the mill. I didn't recognize the
Depression. All my life was the Depression. Mama wrote
back to Iowa and told them we had come. A man on horseback couldn't touch the tassels, when we were down there
homesteading. Grandma and Grandpa was in Iowa in the corn
country. Where they just knew we was rolling in money. She

never told them that she couldn't reach over far enough *down* to touch the corn tassels. They thought she couldn't reach *up* far enough. Well, then the Depression hit to the point where Mr. McMillan couldn't pay us. He would have Hershel go up and get mine props. He had orders for mine props up at Cherokee Park. He'd get loads of mine props and take them down to the coal mines, and then bring the coal up here. In order to get our wages, we had to sell coal. We got in such a mess.

He'd get up at three or four o'clock in the morning and leave. One time he was loading or hauling bridge braces, all up to Livermore. My dad went with him one day. On the truck, he couldn't haul only two. I believe it was two. They were steel, you know, bridge setups. Papa said to him—it was in January—Papa said to him, "Boy, you watch that stuff." He says, "That stuff is unpredictable. Don't never get on the lower side of it."

Hershel went up the next day by himself. One of the beams stuck. Hershel went around to pick up the bar, and just as he did, it slipped off and caught him right at the top of his foot. It just smashed every bone in his foot, down clear through the bottom of his foot, on his toes and all. His right foot. He took his boot off. He had rubbers over his high top boots. He put his rubber on and came on down. Didn't hurt bad. He come in and I was standing making gravy. I had dinner ready for him. I'd fried some steak, and I was making gravy and he was over at the sink a-washing. We had kind of a goofy house. Sink was over next to the entry door and stove was over in the other corner, like they made them, them days, you know. He was a-washing. He didn't have no lavatory and he says, "Well, I sure had a mess this morning." I turned around and said, "What? What happened?" He said, "Well, one of the beams fell off and hit my foot." I said, "Oh, my goodness! How does it feel?" He said, "Don't hurt. Don't feel." I made him go in by the stove and take his sock off and all, and I said, "Oh, my goodness!" Of course first thing, I got warm water to put his foot in. When the feeling begin to come back in there, oh, he hurt. I got him to the doctor and all, and

of course he was off for a while there then. That was one of
his accidents.

*Another accident occurred when Hershel, looking for higher wages so
he could pay the rent, took a job in a quarry at Owl Canyon, north
of Fort Collins.*

He didn't work a month there, till his foot slipped as he
was breaking rock. A piece of rock flew up and hit him in his
right eye and put his eye out. So he was laid up for quite a
while. When he got able to see to the children and all, I got
work steady at the laundry. I worked at the laundry for 22
cents an hour. My goodness. If anyone would offer them 22
cents an hour today, wouldn't they die? The sunlight hurt his
eye. He didn't lose his eye, but he lost the sight of that eye.
Bill Hill and Art Anderson were in the Stanley Mercantile here
in town. They were going through the Depression situation
and everything, and they'd foreclosed on machinery and things
like that. It was during the Dustbowl days—just right at the
end of it—1932, and they asked him if he would try dry-land
farming. Well, he figured he was working for himself, and
what little bit he could get. They said they would give him a
fifth of the crop of his work. So they furnished him—took
the machinery out of his share. One of them was a John
Deere tractor. I can remember seeing he had to crank and
work and work on that thing to get it going. I sold eggs—I've
got a thing-a-ma-jig in there where I sold eggs for 10 cents a
dozen. We sold wheat for 52 cents a bushel.

At one time, Hershel was farming 2300 acres of dry land
out there. We made and we lost. We was just ready to go into
harvest, and the wheat would have went 65 bushel to the acre,
and a hail come up and took it and wiped it out. We'd have
went into harvest on a Monday, and this happened on Friday.
We went to work, and we salvaged all we could and had to get
all that straw off from there. We got the balers in, and they
got the straw off, because it was too much straw. You couldn't
work it. And they didn't dare to set fire to it 'cause it was
ground that blows. It was out here by Black Hollow Reservoir.
All this land was around out in there. We bought together a

section and a quarter, and the rest of it was all leased land. So anyway that fall, he had a hired man then that was helping him. We'd went through the war and the boys was in the army, and then the rubber and the gas shortage and all this. I fixed up the house. There was a little four-room house out there, and I fixed it up. Hershel got the men in for breakfast, and I drove out and got their dinner and supper. I drove a truck while I was out there, and don't ask me what I didn't do.

But anyway, we weathered it through, and then that hail come up and took that land. We salvaged as much as we could. He would work until the hired man would come to work at seven. He'd go out at three o'clock and run the tractor, and then the hired man would come up. Then the hired man's wife, or if I got out there, why, we drove truck for him. He loaded straw, and we went around over. Then after the son-in-laws would get off work, they'd run out. We'd work out there in the straw and all till we got all that straw off from that land for him.

While he was doing that, he said, "I don't know what on earth's the matter with me. I just break out in a sweat, so," he said. "I just sweat so." He kept a-having trouble, and finally went to the doctor. One side of his heart had failed. The doctor told him to take it easy you know. On a Thanksgiving he went—he wasn't to do anything—but somebody in town here wanted four bales of straw. He had the hired man put them on his pickup. He decided he wanted to kill a chicken. He told the hired man to do it, for their Thanksgiving, but he knew very well the hired man wouldn't do it. So he put the teakettle on, killed that chicken and got so terribly sick. The hired man was hauling straw for a farmer that wanted some. He was loading out there, and he saw Hershel and Hershel was so awfully sick. He come running down to him and got him in the house. They called me and I got in the ambulance, and the doctor said, "Get him to the hospital." He had a blood clot in his heart. We come pretty near losing him, but he lived then.

He just messed around and didn't do anything until one night he had a bad spell, and the doctor didn't bring him to the

hospital. He didn't want to go. We didn't leave him alone.
That was Thursday night. Friday Helen come and stayed with
him. I was working out here at a nursing home. I'd been
working in a nursing home, because after the hailstorm, why
then we had a drought. Didn't get nothing at the farm. Then
the next year we had a crop again and got another hail. So I
had went to work at a nursing home. I first went to cooking at
Rocky Ridge that year, when I could leave him. Yet I never felt
relieved to leave him. I mean I always worried about him,
'cause I was afraid he'd have another one. So anyway, I was at
work. Alice, then, that afternoon come, and stayed with him.
That evening, I just got home and gave him his supper and he
ate it, and he had a spell. We took him to the hospital, and he
died at one o'clock the next day.

Pastor

Clifford Conard's father, Abner, was born in Virginia in 1851. When he was about 18 months old, the family moved west and settled in Bates County, Missouri, where he grew up and married Mary Burnham Bristow in 1875. They in turn began a gradual move west, first over the Kansas line, then farther west, to Rush County, where Clifford was born in 1898, the youngest of nine children.

And then they moved from there to Beeler, Kansas. That's in Ness County. And from there, Father homesteaded in Stanton County, Kansas. That was just across the line in from Colorado. In 1907. And that's where I spent a good many years. I was nine when he filed on that claim. We was out about 30 mile from town and of course our conveyances, wagons and buggies, were pulled by horses. Our main crop that we raised to sell was broom corn. That's what they make brooms out of. I used to say that was our main money crop and then I got to thinking that sounded kind of funny cause a lot of times we wouldn't get over 25 or 50 dollars a ton for it. But now, where they have it, why it sells for around $500.

I know why they moved out to the west end — to file on the homestead. They'd been renting all the time. And Father was wanting land of his own. It was just all grassland. For a good many years, we had what we called a "half-dugout." It was half in the ground and then the other was framework over the top of it. And then we bought an old schoolhouse and moved in there. There was a lot of them that built sod houses, but we didn't. Where we were it was pretty sandy and the sod wasn't very good. Timber? We didn't know what that was. What lumber we got, I had to haul that 30 miles. And I know Father tried for years to get trees started, and all we ever did get was about half a dozen cottonwoods that we planted right around the reservoir or pond, you know, and we got those to grow and they got pretty good size.

When we first moved out there, we built a little shack. Just a frame shack, one room, and after we got the dugout, we moved it up, just to the head of the stairs and that was we boys' bedroom. And I've gotten up mornings a lot of times with snow all over the cover, all over the bed. From a blizzard, where the snow had drifted in.

When I got old enough for a homestead, why I had to buy a fellow's relinquishment. I got 340 acres. That meant he'd filed on it and then give it up over to me and let me file on it. I paid him $1,000 for his relinquishment. And then, of course, I had to hold it three years, and then I proved up on it. At that time, by the time I got to be 21, there wasn't any homestead land around there, so that's the reason I got a chance to buy this. I had 340. Yeah, I had to pay extra for the extra 20 but it was just on the state line. It was a narrow strip, there. Well, by the time I got mine, why, my father, he wasn't farming too heavy, you know, so I got the privilege of working both places. I remember my first crop on that homestead. I had quite an acreage of rye. And I pulled into the field right after dinner, with a header and barges, and had a crew of men there, and in 30 minutes I had that harvested by a hailstorm. Hailed it all out.

I wasn't married until 1927. I batched there on the claim. Yeah, I guess broom corn, course that was all hand work, the harvesting of it, and we had a machine we seeded on, and then bale it and. . . . We usually hauled it to Syracuse, Kansas. That was the closest town of any size that we had. We was in—our county seat was Johnson but there was no railroad there then. There is now, but there wasn't then. It was all dry land farming. You never saw any pump, that is engine pumps, or anything that way. It was all windmills. Stock and house and everything that-a-way. Well, we irrigated the garden, of course, but that was all. Now, that section through there, it all has deep wells and irrigation. Now our corn, if we had any, we used to think if we got 10 bushels to the acre, we was doing pretty good. Few years ago I was down there, and they was building an elevator in the county seat just for corn. And I said, "How much do you figure on, an acre of corn? To get to the acre?" And they said, "two hundred bushel." So water makes quite a difference.

Then one year, and that was the summer I was married in '27, I had I don't remember how many acres, but a field of wheat. Looked wonderful, for that country, and on a Sunday morning it just looked wonderful. It was starting to head out, and by Monday morning, I didn't have any. We had an electric wind come through there and just cooked it. And that wind started in Colorado, went clear down to as far as central Kansas. I know I went down there to harvest in central Kansas and that summer—after I lost mine—and you'd see fields of wheat look like it'd make 20, 30 bushel to the acre. I rent a combine and by the time you'd get that cut or combined, it was just all shriveled up. If it made six or eight, why it did real well. That's what they called it. It was just a hot wind. It just wasn't just a warm wind, it was just hot. It just cooked stuff and you could just—it just shriveled it up.

You just took a chance on it, seemed like. Now, like the broom corn, sometimes we'd contract it before we'd get it harvested. And usually, when we did, we lost money on that. But the wheat, of course we'd just hauled to market and get whatever the market was. I wasn't any exception. I used to tell them—they want broom corn—tell my neighbors, "Now, you watch and if I contract mine early, well, you hold yours, cause the price is coming up. But if I hold, why, sell early, 'cause the price is going down." I remember when my father was still living and we contracted ours early for $110 a ton. We'd been getting oh, 25 to 50. We thought that was pretty big. We had about 10 ton that year and when we delivered that, why, the same kind of broom corn was selling for $350 a ton. And then after he was gone, why, I was farming, and the same broom corn buyer came out and wanted to contract early and I said, "Nope." I said, "You hooked me one time." He wanted to contract for $100 again. And I said, "You hooked me once, but never again!" I got $80 for that. So you can see why I had good ground for advising those neighbors.

Clifford's first wife was a local girl.

Well, her father had homesteaded in there in the neighborhood. They was about I think about five or six miles from our father's place and she was a schoolteacher. Olive Thrush. There was a family of those. And one of her brothers married one of my sisters. And then we had three children. Two girls, which are living now, and our boy was the middle one and he died when he was ten.

He was in the hospital with a ruptured appendix. From what I heard, gathered from talking to the doctors, and so forth since, apparently they was feeding him through the veins, and the nurse shot something into the tube and apparently an air bubble got in there and hit his heart. And he was gone, just like that. Course it wasn't her fault, 'cause she didn't do it a-purpose, but it happens. They say it could happen that way.

We was living in Johnson. Pastoring a church in Johnson at that time. After I was married, I moved over to the northeast corner of that county. I rented a place over there and farmed a couple of years. And then we moved to out by Lamar, Colorado. And it was in '30, we moved out there, and farmed there for, well, not on the same place, but in three different places, I guess, farmed till '35.

While I was at Hartman, we got to going to church down in Hartman. I lived out about four or five miles. And I got saved. They was having a revival meeting there and I got saved in that meeting.

My parents always took us to church, and they were Christian people, there. Father belonged to what they call the Free Methodist. And I really don't know whether Mother belonged to. . . . She didn't belong to the Free Methodist and I don't know whether she belonged to any church or not, but she was a good Christian woman. And then after I was saved, I. . . . Well, anything in my whole life before that, I couldn't hardly get up in front of a crowd, and say a speech that I'd already learned or anything. I didn't have any gift at all. And after I got saved, I just felt like the Lord wanted me to preach.

And I argued with Him quite a while, and finally gave in. And after I'd preached several years, my mother was still living. She was visiting me one time at a church we was pastoring, and she told me that ever since she'd started raising a family, she'd prayed the Lord would give her a preacher boy. I was glad she never told me that before, because I would have thought, "Well, that influenced me." But I didn't know anything about it, and so I guess the Lord finally—maybe He couldn't get the others, so He picked me to answer her prayer.

I guess the pastor called in our home, and some of their laymen there in the church had come out and called on us. And then we had a neighbor. An elderly couple there. They got to taking us down there to start with. And we liked it pretty well and so we were interested and went along there quite a while before I got saved.

It was kind of odd, I guess. Would be for most people. Of course I'm sure that by being raised in a Christian home, I'm sure that had a lot to do with this. I know even before I was saved, I'd feel conflicted over some things I was doing. We were in this meeting one night. I was a coward. They gave an invitation to the seekers to come forward at the altar. They used to come and pray with them, you know. Don't do that so much anymore, but they used to. And that was a Pilgrim Holiness Church. And I told her if she'd go with me, I'd go to the altar. And she said, well, she couldn't. She was taking care of our baby boy. He was just a little tot and she was taking care of him. And I—I don't remember this, but she told me afterwards that I said, "Well, if you won't go with me, I won't go." And she said all the time I was talking I was getting up and going. And anyway, I got up there and they prayed with me and I tried to pray, and confessed my sins, and I felt the Lord save me. And I told the Evangelist at the door that night as we left, I said, "Tomorrow's going to be the best day I ever lived in my life." He said, "Tomorrow may be the hardest day you ever had in your life." And he was right. The Devil fought me from every angle about it, but he didn't get me. Lord protected me.

Then I don't know how long we lived there, but I felt the Lord, as I said awhile ago, called me to preach. And the pastor there, he felt like the Lord had called me and he had me fill in for him plenty of times, before I ever took any schooling or anything that-a-way. I had been a schoolteacher, too, back there when I was younger. Taught four years, I think. Little country schools. And after I was saved, why, I never went to college—church college, but I took a correspondence work.

I took a church over there over in northwest Kansas.

There'd be a stake. Would be what they call a district in the church. And then we had a district superintendent over that. They still have them, but sometimes they're a whole state, sometimes they aren't. I had met the superintendent from Kansas and I knew the superintendent in Colorado. And this superintendent from Kansas told me about this church that they wanted. It was a country church. And I prayed over it and felt like the Lord wanted me to accept the call over there, so we went. It was about 20 miles, maybe better than 20 miles south of Oakley. Between there and Scott City. Oh, it was about a couple hundred yards off of the highway there. It was a big old rock church and a rock parsonage there. Set back there. And I was there two years. I remember we got there in the night and I remember I got up the next morning and went over to the church and looked in the Sunday school record and saw there was 60, 70 in Sunday School and I went outdoors and I could see one house. Looked every direction and one house was all I could see. Well, I found out where they were, afterwards, but I wondered about it, then. It was just almost canyons through there. And there'd be houses down in those. You wouldn't see them till you was right on top of them, almost.

I just pastored. It was dry land. That was in the middle '30's and it was dry land. It was dry land. And the farmers couldn't raise anything and all they had to live on was that relief work the government had. So it was a little bit rough. And I couldn't get on that because I had to be there—where I crossed the state line—had to be there a year before you could

get on. They tried to help us all they could but they didn't have
nothing to help with, very much. I had two children then.
Well, they felt like we was in the will of the Lord. Well, of
course my oldest daughter, she was only seven when we went
there. And the boy was three when we went there, and they
didn't know much about it. Our girl, she walked about a
quarter of a mile to school.

I remember we hadn't had any bread in the house for a
couple of weeks and we had an elderly couple come. They
called on us a while and while they were in the house, why the
little boy, he asked his mother for a piece of bread and butter.
She hushed him up some way, I don't know how, and after they
left the house, why our little girl went out with them to the car.
I didn't know anything about that till afterwards, but they asked
her how come your Mama didn't give the little boy—her little
brother—bread and butter. She said, "Oh, we haven't had any
bread for two weeks." And they drove on off. And after a
while that old truck come a-rattling back in there, and their son
got out and he had a package in one hand, a sack in the other.
The folks sent it up. The package was a loaf of bread and the
other was some flour. So that's the way the Lord took care of
us there. And we'd get out after so long a time, why He'd send
it in someway, you know. Then after we left there, we went
back to my home county seat, Johnson. And I pastored two
churches there, 13 miles apart, for a little over a year. We
thrived real well there. Each church decided to pay us five
dollars a week and we really thrived. I was there at Johnson
seven years before I left. But after the first year, little over a
year, why they got another pastor at the other place. We just
had the one church. Everybody was poor. Couldn't look
down on anybody 'cause everybody was in the same boat.

If the family had it, why they usually gave something, but
if they didn't, why they didn't. Couldn't, you know. And those
things happened. Course we know, it had to be cheap. Everything had to be cheap. Now, for instance, gasoline. We paid 12
cents a gallon. For gasoline. And groceries was the same way,
you know. There was a little store about four mile from that
little country church and we used to go down there when we

had any money to get a little few things, you know. It was a Catholic man that run it. They were nice people. Course he could see what we needed. He told me, he said, "You come down here and buy anything you want to, that you need, here in the store." He said, "You won't have to have the money." And I said, "Well, I sure appreciate that, but I'd like to ask a question, first." He said, "All right, what is it?" And I said, "If I can't pay as I go, how am I going to pay you back?" I said, "I don't have anything promised me." So we didn't buy, only when we could pay for it. Well, we had white folks in the church there and an elderly—well, she was born into slavery—a colored woman. And her son and her son's wife. His wife was a schoolteacher. She was a colored woman, but they were just fine people. They didn't belong to our church but they came there. They were very, very thoughtful people. Helping us out with what they had, you know, and everything that way. We thought a lot of them. I think that was the only person, white or colored, that was born in slavery times. But she was an old, old lady, then, you see.

We were seven years at Johnson. And then we went from there to Nebraska. We was at Madrid. That's right east of Grant. Then we went to Grand Junction. We was only at Madrid a year. We went there in '44. Then we went to Grand Junction in '45. Was there two years and we went to Campo. We was there six years. And then we went back to Kansas to the little town of Winona, west of Oakley. We was there just a year. Reason I left there, my younger daughter was in high school, then, and we didn't believe in this sports work in school, and in Kansas they wouldn't give a diploma unless they partook of sports. Physical education. Didn't have anything against what they was doing, but the attire they'd make them wear, you know. So we was there just a year and we came to Bellvue.

Mr. Conard remained at the Bellvue church until it closed. People from Fort Collins attended, but decided to move it to town. They sold the church, and its small parsonage. Mr. Conard took a church in Benkelman, Nebraska, in 1958.

And was there just a year. There wasn't anybody there.
Just two or three couples came. It was kind of like that house
that I was raised in. It was about half dug in the ground, this
church was. It was up against a hillside, is really what it was. I
talked it over with my superintendent and with the laymen, the
families there. The one family lived southeast of town. They
was just as close to Bird City, Kansas, where there was a
church. And the other one lived east of Benkelman and he
was just as close to another Pilgrim church, so we decided—
and they was in debt—so we decided if we could sell it. . . .
The superintendent and I went down and listed it with this
realtor. We wondered if they'd ever sell it. He had it sold
before night. I don't remember what we got for it. And then I
moved. Went from there to Lodge Pole, Nebraska. That's up
in the panhandle. And we was there two years. And we left. It
was thriving pretty good. And then after we left, why, I don't
know what happened, but anyway it went down and they
finally closed it out and moved the church to Arthur, Nebraska. And the parsonage, I don't know. They sold it, I think.
The last time I was up there and looked at it, they made me
heartsick. They'd tore every building down, and the church
was gone and they had the whole thing leveled off. Ready to
build something on. A house, I suppose. And that was my
last. . . . Well, no, we was home then. That was in '61 . We was
home a year, and then we went to Pueblo and pastored for two
years. And that was my last one.

Mr. Conard's formal training was nil. He had no theological
preparation beyond that which he gave himself or picked up from
other country preachers. He knew little about the organization of his
own church, its origins, or its philosophy. He had a church manual,
and his Bible. He never felt he needed more.

In 1968, they merged with the Wesleyan Methodist
Church and we lost our identity entirely, and they dropped the
Methodist and just call it Wesleyan Church, now. Now, in the
east, they've still got some of the Pilgrim Holiness Churches
going, I understand. I could look that up, I guess, the history
of the church. I believe that there was a group that called
themselves Pilgrims, and maybe they merged with another

group. I'm not sure how that was. But they believed in holiness in their lives, and I kind of think that's the way it happened. And that was along in—well, I think 1922, was when it was organized, but I'm not sure of that. Before I started pastoring, of course, they had a manual, we called them. Some churches called them disciples. A book, you know. The pastor did. And, well, it. . . . As I had said, my father was a Free Methodist. They believed the same thing. I remember what my father's church believed, and I thought it was all right, so I read this, here, and it sounded about the same. There was a couple of items there, that I couldn't agree with. I told the pastor. He asked me what I thought about it and I told him. One of them was that. . . . I believe that a person ought to tithe to pay a 10th of his income, but that manual said that it should be put in the church. And I took the wrong idea, I found out afterwards. I told him I couldn't do that. I said the tithe is mine, and I put it where I want to. Well, he didn't argue with me, he said, "Well, just think about it. Just keep praying about it." Well, I prayed about it all right, and I discovered that the tithe *isn't* mine. Wasn't mine. It was the Lord's. That's what the Bible says. And so where would it go, but to the place where you was getting some help, you know? So I got that figured out . And then there was another one. I can't remember what it was. Just about as indifferent as that. But anyway, that's how it felt like the Lord wanted us to join. Wife felt the same way, so we joined. It was just a small church, in that small town, there.

Got more than I deserved. No, I never did feel like we was having any hardships. Everything as far as we was concerned our part of it, what we received, was good enough. I always appreciated the people I had to work with.

Mr. Conard expressed regret that many modern churches leave the preaching and most other worship activities to the professional staff, almost as if the congregation comes to see and hear the minister perform, less than to do it themselves.

That's right. That's right. That's the way it seems to me. But of course the other churches, the older churches did that

before. Before these started in And the result was bad, and
the result's bound to be bad on this drift, too.

It isn't any better, anyway, our nation. Standards of our
nation. We read this article, reading in several different papers,
that now we have a saloon in the White House where not only
the Congressmen and the like use the liquor, but they sell it.
Well, our nation wouldn't have stood for that a few years ago,
you know that. And that certainly isn't any improvement. And
in so many places, our youngsters in school are permitted to
use dope. And that is illegal, you know that. There's no law
for that. They're trying now. Expect you've heard them talk
about it—they're trying now to lessen the punishment for
those drug users. And, well, that's to me a pretty much of a
drop.

Course we had smokers come to church, but they didn't
smoke in the church. But they came to church, but none of
our church people ever smoked, or used tobacco or beer or
liquor of any kind, you know. I remember in that little country
church I was talking about. Wish I could have found the
picture of that. There was a family there, and one of the
sons—they was all grown, then the parents was old—but this
young fellow smoked. Just before he started to go out of the
church one night, why, he got his cigarette out and his match,
all ready, to light up. Well, they told him—I never did know
this, but I was told that in that church, the pastor before we
was there, allowed them to smoke in church. I don't know. I
never did know whether that was so or not, but anyway I told
this young fellow, I said, "This is God's house and we don't
smoke in here." He was just as nice. . . . He just put his
cigarette and his match in his pocket and he never got mad or
anything. He wasn't a Christian, but he showed a good
attitude, you know.

Ernie

"If he's got the nerve to hold church . . . I'm going to go help him out."

I was an only child, born in Greenville, Barn County, Illinois in 1894. And we lived there a while and then we moved to North Dakota for seven years. And my dad said he froze to death twice while he was up there. He thought it was time to get out. He came in with his hands just froze in that shape, and his feet was froze, his nose, and his cheeks, and his chin, and he got sleepy. He'd been driven to town to get a load of coal, so he got off and walked behind the wagon, and he guessed that's all that saved him. And then, after seven years we moved down to western Kansas. Syracuse, Kansas. 1906. Dad took a homestead there.

He planted his first crop right in the sod. He had what they call a pan planter. You hooked that onto your plow and it'd roll over and the seeds would fall out through a hole and then he'd take it off. He'd plow two rounds and then he'd put it back on and plant another round. And that was his first year there. And it was a pretty fair year. It was wet. Raised a pretty good crop. And then from then on, why, he had hoed ground to plant the stuff in. And he got into some cattle business, and mostly horses.

When he first started out there, we was in a sod house. Well, first we had a 12 by 12 frame house the first summer, and that fall they laid up a sod house, him and his two brothers. Walls was about 32 inches thick and just laid up like you would brick, with regular old mud and grass mixed up for mortar in between them. It didn't take much fuel in the winter. Just had a small stove in there and the middle room was what they'd call

the living room, and we'd leave the bedroom doors open at
night. And the windows was put up kind of on the outside of
the sod. And my mother used all that space there for flowers.
To start with, we just had a dirt floor. Then a little later on we
got a good floor in. The inside walls they turned out pretty fair,
the rough stuff, and then they plastered it. But you have to wait
a few years before you do that. Sod keeps settling, and I expect
Dad left two and a half or three inches over the windows and
doors and filled that full of rags. Every once in a while you
have to pull them out and put them back in. If you don't, they
get so tight after a while you can't get them out. I think it was
about five years before we got it plastered. Long as it was on a
dirt floor, you could sprinkle that, and sweep it, and it got
pretty hard after a while. I think we only lived on that about a
year. If you plaster that before it gets done settling, it'll break
and come off. We lived there for seven years. Then he traded
that place off for one closer to town. We was 21 mile, and he
got 3 mile closer. And I was left alone quite a little out there, all
by myself, if they wanted to go someplace. Sometimes it got
pretty lonesome.

        That first year we was there, we hauled water from a
neighbor that was three mile away. Had plenty of water and
storage room. Done that all summer. We hauled in a wagon
box with two barrels. Then after we got close to town, why, we
had a well on that place. Our closest neighbor there was about
a half a mile. Then they run on out.

        I've had both men and women teachers. And the men
were pretty good. They'd get out and play with us kids just like
they was one of us

        I moved into town and went to work for the Santa Fe,
the 23rd day of December, 1918. I worked in the roundhouse
at that time, for a while. I was a helper and we worked on
engines. Repairing them, wherever they needed it. Each little
job or whatever it was, was on a slip by itself. Some fellow that
I was working with, he'd pick them up and we'd work them out
and then he'd have to mark them off on a board up on the

wall. And the boss would come around and see how you was getting along once in a while. Sometimes he wouldn't be around till you'd been done for a while. Pretty dirty work. Get in under some of those engines. And at that time they was using fuel oil. And that oil would get to leaking around in there. Sometimes you'd get in the wrong place, it was kind of hot. And sometimes we'd have to get down in them pits under the engine, and maybe there'd be an inch or two of that oil down in there to wade around it. But it paid pretty good money.

Then I quit after about 18 months and went back north of Salina, Kansas, and farmed for about two years and a half. And I got into it with the guy I was renting from, and I quit that and moved back out to Syracuse and told my wife that I'd start to farming again after a while. We had a public sale, and everything started going up and I never did have the nerve to start over so I just finished up working for other people. The next time I went back to Syracuse, I worked in a boiler, a stationary boiler that furnished heat for the Harvey House and the roundhouse and the coal chute. Had to have steam up on the coal chute. It was 40 feet in the air.

Later we moved to Springfield, Missouri and lived down there all one winter. I bought a place there. And I got asthma while I was there, and my wife said it was about time for us to move out. So we had another public sale there and come back to Syracuse, and I finished up there till 1950 when I came up here. I went to work for Curry up in the hills up here on a ranch. And I worked up there a while. Then I went over to Walden in September in '51. And I was over there about 18 months. I saw enough snow over there to suit me the rest of my life. So I come back over here to Fort Collins. And I worked for farmers around here. Last four years I worked I drove a truck for the county maintenance outfit. Me and Stella was married in 1953.

I remember the dustbowl in Kansas. I seen the sun shining just as bright as it could. In five minutes, you couldn't

see the porch posts four inches square, about six feet across
the porch you couldn't see that. Have to turn a light on right in
daytime.

There at one time, I was working on a section, and they
was going to send me and another fellow with the road master
to see that the track wasn't drifted over. Cause that bowl dirt
would derail a train. And this other fellow come up with me,
come up and got me. I didn't know they was going until he got
there, and when we was going back down, we walking in
between the rails going down to the depot. And after a bit he
said, "Uh!" I said, "What's the matter?" "I run right square
into that coupler on that car," he said, "I didn't see it." And he
had one of these here little lights, you know, you can't see
anything with them. They're so people know where you are.
And he said, "I run right square into that." I got down to the
depot and then they had to wait there about two hours before
the road master would take off on one of them little three
wheelers. And they trotted up on that, took off, and then got
down to Garden City and he went in and told them everything
was clear. So they started a-running the trains again. There at
one time we had three trains tied up there at Syracuse. Two
passengers and one freight. Wouldn't let them run. They
couldn't see. The last passenger train that come in that night,
he said, "Last signal light I seen was when I come through
Grenada." That was 35 miles. I said, "Well, what was you
running on, Pete?" He said, "I was running on my good
looks." And, he said, well, he come in there and he didn't know
we was going to stop him. He pulled up and he only missed
the water spout about 20 feet. He said, "I didn't know where I
was till I got into Syracuse here and then the storage cars
sitting back over there . . . ." Had five tracks that was just about
full of empty cars.

And he said, "I knew I was in behind them cars. I just
sort of guessed at where I was going to stop." Oh, that was a
fright. There was a few people down there that died. After the
worst of it was over with, me and the folks took a ride there
one day and we seen these one-ways, stuff like that, sitting out

in the field. Maybe you'd see a little bit of the top of them. Rest of it was all covered up. Had one brother-in-law lived out on the farm, and he had a cowshed there, built out of wire— hog wire and thistles and stuff like that in between them. And he had cans stuck over the top, and that dirt drifted up there till it got clear up even with the roof and a cow walked up, and went out one there, fell through. He said the next morning when he got up, she was standing in the manure spreader with her head a-sticking out. He had to get her out of there.

In those years, Ernie rarely went to church.

Just once in a long while. Not very often. Till I come out here and me and Stella got married. Then for about eighteen months, I guess, they had church here in the hall. So I got started going there. And I felt sorry for the preacher, is the main reason I started going. They'd have dances in there, some of the guys from downtown there'd come out and they'd get pretty wild. You could open up that door and go in there the next morning and it smelled like a brewery. I told Stella, "I'm going to go, and if he's got the nerve to hold church there, I'm going to go help him out." And then he got talking to me one day about the Lord, and I finally give in and joined the church. And it's a good thing I did.

All I was interested in before was maybe get me a bottle and take off Saturday night for a dance some place. I never really got drunk enough I couldn't go, but I'd drink and have a good time. But after I got right with the Lord, why, I don't care about doing that.

One time me and a fellow decided we wanted some whiskey down there in Syracuse. I said, "I don't know where to go." "Oh," he said, "I know." He was a single fellow, and I wasn't. I was married. And we went out to this first place. He asked him about a quart. "Ain't got it. Just sold out this morning." And you know, just one house right after that until the fourth house had some. I didn't know they was making liquor out there but they was. Old fruit jar stuff. And it comes down once in a while, I found. Sell a bunch and get back out home. Some of it was pretty bad stuff. What we got was pretty good that day. Then another fellow that we was well acquainted with got to making it down there. And he made good stuff. But if he come to town selling liquor, he didn't drink any. Sometimes he might come into town and get pretty well hooked up, but he wasn't a-selling liquor. He was just drinking what he had.

I never drank too awful much of it. But some of that stuff, I'll tell you, would burn all the way down. Just like fire. Now this fellow I was telling you started there at the last, he made good stuff and you could just drink that about like water. But, oh boy, it'd spread out when it got down there. It'd kick you. I don't know where he ever learned to make it. Me and him grew up about four mile apart. I thought about it when things was pretty hard, but I was just a little bit afraid. I didn't think I wanted to look through the bars.

II.

Townspeople

A couple of hundred yards west of the Poudre River, downtown Bellvue sits at the intersection of County Roads 52 E and 23 N. Today it is bordered on north by the Watson Lake State Trout Hatchery and Rearing Unit and on the southwest by a second unit of the same name. Watson Lake was created in the 1950s when earth was scooped out to construct Horsetooth Dam at the north end of what became Horsetooth Reservoir, a seven-mile long collection point for snow water that runs off the mountains each spring. Water is diverted from the Poudre into Watson Lake and the fish rearing raceways, then turned back into the river.

Much of Old Town Fort Collins is built of red sandstone quarried from the hills south and west of Bellvue. In the final decade of the 19th and first decades of the 20th centuries, the timber and rock quarrying industries provided jobs for the people who lived in and around Bellvue. At one time three churches existed, all within a block or so of one another. Only one exists today, the other buildings having been converted into residences, one upscale (for the area) and one not.

Bellvue's key architectural landmark is what is now the Grange Hall, on the southwest corner of the main intersection. Besides Grange Hall, its other incarnations have been as general store, hotel, and (according to some old-timers) whore house, not necessarily in that order. County Road 52 E is also known as the Rist Canyon Road. Downtown Bellvue's other streets are Second Street, running north/south, and Laporte Street and Grizzly Street, both running east/west.

Two and a half miles east lies the town of Laporte, along old U.S. Highway 287, formerly the Overland Trail, the mail and stage route leading from Denver to Laramie and on west. Another six miles to the southeast is Fort Collins, today a regional shopping and medical center, home to the Colorado's land grant university, Colorado State University, and site of numerous high tech and biotech facilities.

In 1915, when people spoke of "going to town," they might mean Bellvue, Laporte or Fort Collins.

Sometimes while editing these transcripts, I lose my location in time. Passing houses on the way to the Post Office or wandering through Bellvue, I have to stop and think. Am I here now? Or then? Are the names I attach to the houses yesterday's or today's? I walk down our lane, heading south toward the Rist Canyon road. In 1900, the whole right side was one huge thicket of raspberries. Since then, a few houses have taken root; vegetable gardens and horse pastures, and the berries are gone.

I pass the stone house on the left. It's the Jacksons' now (for awhile). It used to be the Tetley house, where Nettie and Hershel Davis rented. The stone walls are so thick it's like a cavern – so quiet a 70-mile gale can't be heard. The house was built by Jacob Flowers. If not the earliest settler, he was the one who left the biggest mark. Besides his house, he built and operated a store, now the Grange Hall, constructed a road clear up to Pingree Park, and made Pleasant Valley a fruit growing center. Heading down Second Street, I cross the creek that flooded in 1923, washing people away. It's tame today, and mild, but in our time we have seen it a raging torrent filled with runoff from a mountain downpour. For a moment I pause in front of the house where Stella and Ernie Sapp used to live, but where Rev. Babcock, the Seventh Day Adventist long resided. I can almost see Stella at work in the shed where she kept her jars of fruit and vegetables that she canned each summer. Is Ernie inside, anchored to his oxygen tanks? Are the people truly gone, or are they still going about their affairs, screened off from us by a curtain behind which I can almost see their shadows moving?

Lora Shipp

I was born in St. Claire County Illinois. That's down in
the southern part of the state, just east of St. Louis. I was
born in a little community called Oak Hill. The old house is
still standing. The date was September 15th, 1894, quite early
in the morning. My parents had a prize mare that had a colt
that same morning and I don't know which they rejoiced over
more. We lived back there until I was about eight. Then we had
a sale. Sold all our possessions, and moved out on our way to
Idaho. But my mother's people lived in Denver, Colorado, and
so we stopped there for a while to visit. None of us ever saw
Idaho. We stayed there from then on. My folks lived at my
grandmother's house for a year. That was down on Cleveland
Place. It's now Civic Center. We lived in a little brick house and
Grandma paid eighteen dollars and fifty cents a month rent for
it. Then, after a year, we came up to Fort Collins. My uncles
had wanted the folks to look around there, and see about land.
It was just after the big flood in the spring of 1904. Land was
cheap, so my father bought a place east and south of Laporte
and we moved there.

We were right on the bank of the river. The land was on
either side. The house was on the north. It's gravel pit now.
The only thing left of the old place is the barn and the double
row of black locust trees that was our lane. When we moved
from Denver, we moved in a hayrack drawn by a team of
horses, all our worldly possessions piled on the wagon. My
brother and I rode our bicycles. Took us three days to make
the trip. And oh, that would make a story in itself. We camped
along the way each night. I lived there, then, until just before
my husband and I were married. My mother died there. And I
went to Laporte School. I went to Fort Collins High School
for a year. By that time, they had consolidated all their school
districts, and the schoolhouse was at Laporte, much to Bellvue
people's displeasure. They never did like that. But anyhow, they

were in that consolidated district and they had to go. Well, I graduated from that high school, and in later years I taught there. Still later my children and some of my grandchildren attended that school. So it has quite a history. A lot of my life was bound up in the Laporte School, and that's where I met my husband.

Lora's earliest and most enduring memories involved school, always an adventure.

We lived a mile from this little brick school. But we had to go through the field, of course, to get there. So my father took my little brother Harold and me, the first morning. We went on our bicycles two miles around the road north, then east, and then at Iverson's corner we turned south. Well, my bicycle was old. It didn't go as fast as my dad's and my little brother's. We had our lunch in a little tin pail with a little wire bail, you know, and the lid to mine kept coming off and I'd have to get off to put it on. And Dad and Harold kept a-going. And so by the time we got to Iverson's corner, when they turned south, I was too far behind them to see. And I went riding on toward Fort Collins. And I rode and I rode and I rode and I thought that was the longest two miles I'd ever ridden. And finally I met a young man coming on a bicycle. So I stopped him and asked him the way to the country school. Well, I was to go so far north and so far west and so far south and I said, "Well, I don't know which is north and west and south. I guess I'll just go along with you." So I turned round and was riding back with him. Well, Dad had gone down to Number 11 School with Harold and there was no Lora behind him, so he left Harold there, outside the school, and rode back to find me and Dad found me and rode back with me. Well, in the meantime, Harold had waited what he thought was a very long time, and he thought maybe he'd better go and try to find Dad. So when Dad got me back to the school, there was no Harold. And it took quite a while to locate him. So we didn't get enrolled in the little school until long about noon.

Then after that, why, we enjoyed most, walking across the fields. We'd hurry to school. We could make that in 20 minutes. But going home there was quite a crowd out, that used to walk across the field. And it was marshy and swampy. There were little hummocks that stuck up, you know. So we jumped from one of those to the other, and we had a game: Follow the Leader. We usually didn't get a good start for home until we heard the sugar factory whistle blow five o'clock. Then we'd go on. Mother usually met us at the back gate with a little lilac switch. The little lilac bush was well-trimmed in those days.

We had no social studies in those days. It was really the three R's. Reading, writing and arithmetic. And we had spell-downs every Friday afternoon after the last recess. Or else we'd have ciphering matches. You know, choose up sides and one at a time on each side would go to the blackboard. We had our choice. "Will you take adding, subtraction, multiplication, or long division?" And then the teacher would give us a problem, and the one that worked it first and got the correct answer, of course, had won for their side. The other one, then, was eliminated. And we learned our combinations, too—adding and multiplying. Well, the teacher would just take 10 or 15 minutes, you know, and "Seven and eight." Well, the one that'd say "fifteen" first, you know, they were through. And we really learned. And I never did have to count on my fingers, then.

But something funny happened after we came out to Colorado. I didn't think it was funny. I wasn't old enough to have dates, but across the river there was a family that had quite a number of boys, and this one boy was worried. His buddy was going to have a birthday party and the foolish mother had insisted that each boy bring a girl. Well, Floyd didn't know any girls that would go with him, and so he was telling his father out in the barn of his predicament. Of course my little brother was stuck there, all ears. Mister Shader said, "Well, you can take the horse and buggy, and go, and why don't you ask Lora to go along with you?" Well, Harold waited to hear no more. Back he flew across the river and into the house. We were just sitting down for supper. He was all out of breath. "Mama! Papa! Floyd's going to ask Lorie to go to a party!" And of course it took my father by surprise. He never thought of such a thing. And he said, "Why, Sister can't go. She's not weaned yet." Harold waited to hear no more. Back through the woods he went. And got there: "Papa said Lorie couldn't go 'cause she ain't weaned yet'" Of course, then Floyd never dared ask me and I didn't have my first date until a good many years later. I could have wrung Harold's neck for that. I would have liked the chance to say no, anyhow. But that's little brothers for you.

I knew I wanted to teach when I was in the third grade. Mother told me that I couldn't, because I didn't have enough patience. But I learned patience, and there were several of us in our senior year in high school—several girls—who wanted to teach. So instead of taking chemistry, we took a course in teaching. And then, when we were through, all we had to do in those days, you know, was pass the teacher's exam, and we could teach. So I passed it, and the first year, I taught up on the Buckhorn. That would be a story in itself. It was a six months term. I learned much more in that six months than any of my six pupils did. Our schoolhouse was a miner's cabin. The old double desks had been brought in. We had one blackboard, and I taught up there the six months.

That was before the road went through the Buckhorn Canyon. It went up over Dead Man's Hill. And this was on the very tip top of the hill. That was very interesting. The man brought in the logs for our heating stove, but we sawed them. We had two cross-cut saws, one on each end, so it took four of us. Oh, we'd saw to beat the band, at noon. Then the rest of the time, we played games. I wasn't very much older than the pupils, and I enjoyed that. From there I went to Waverly and I taught there three years. Oh, that was the nicest place. They were all very poor people. They were highly educated as far as that goes. One woman was the daughter of a judge. She had several children to send to school. But up there, I think, 60 children was the highest number I had in the one room. Some of them wanted high school. They had graduated from the eighth grade the year before, so I taught, beginning at half past eight, and I didn't play games there. I taught through the noon hour, while I ate my lunch, and then after school. I had the eight grades and then the ninth grade. I had a lady, oh, a couple three years ago, ask me about it. She said, "Could you do justice to so many?" I said, "Why, no, of course I couldn't. But I did the best I could."

Discipline in those days was no problem at all. The parents stood behind the teacher. I was invited into every home. And I knew each pupil's background, and the parents and I were warm friends. If the child got in trouble in school, which he rarely did, his parents backed the teacher up. And there was such a warm relationship there. I never was in a community like that. It's changed now, I'm sorry to say. But that was a wonderful experience.

Because we didn't have much of this world's goods. And we provided our own entertainment. We had so-called literary societies that met every two weeks. We had our basket dinners, our pie suppers, and our social life was the school life. And now, some of my closest friends are my old-time pupils. Not long ago before I left my own home to live with the children, I had three boys come in and spend the morning. I call them boys. They were grandparents. But we reminisced about those old times you know, and oh, it was wonderful. Not bragging on us any, but we had to be of a good moral character, as well as have so much education. That was put on our certificates. And if we hadn't been, we would have never held the school.

And then I went to Laporte to teach. Let's see. I believe I went there in 1918. I taught there until just before we were married. I promised when we were married, that I would never go back to teaching again. My husband was very much opposed to a woman holding a job, you know. And so I didn't, until much, much later. There was a group of the German-Russians who had come in to work beets. They wanted to become citizens. So the government had a night school for them, two nights a week, I think. They learned the equivalent of an eighth grade education. And I got into that by accident. A lady that was a teacher there took sick. She was a friend of ours. She had no place to go, except to our house. It just all happened so quickly, that she didn't have time to get a substitute. So she asked me if I would mind taking her class until we could. So Walter went along with me, and I had no idea what I was to teach, but we went to the schoolhouse. And oh, the school was filled with these people, you know, German-Russians. Some of them are friends of mine. And so I told them at the beginning of the class, "Now, your teacher is ill. Just took sick all at once. I came down to fill in for her and I haven't any idea what I'm to teach you. You'll have to tell me." So, of course nobody spoke up for a little bit. Then finally one big red-faced Dutchman in the back of the room—he had on bib overalls—stood up, and he said, "Well, you see it's like this. We have our books. Mrs. Newport, she has us read our books, and then she asks us questions, like, 'Who was the first president?' And we say, 'Christopher Columbus'." And the minute he got the words out, he knew he'd made a mistake and his face got even redder and the whole class just howled. From that minute on, the ice was broken, and we just got along fine.

Her first date with Walter, the boy who would become her husband, took place not long before the U.S. entered World War I.

My father had farmed with Dick Falloon and Dick was just like a brother to him, and he was a very close friend of mine. Our first date was rather funny. We'd met there at Dick's. They took me home with them one time from church, and Walter came there. So we met there. Then I believe he came down with the Falloon family one evening to spend the evening. But other than that we'd not been in each other's company at all. There was a new movie came to town called— let's see. *Shepherd of the Hills.* Oh, it was widely advertised. They had trained these Ozark people for nine months for this, and oh, I wanted to go. I just wanted to go so bad. And nobody asked me. So my father finally said, "Well, I'll take you if you don't get a date." But I knew he didn't want to go. And Walter, on the other hand, was trying desperately to find a date. He ran around with Dick Falloon and Charlie Graves, and they each had their dates to go. The three of them always went together in Charlie's car. Walter asked everybody that he could think of, and they all turned him down. So Dick finally said, "Well, why don't you ask Lora Ebert?" "Oh," he said, "I don't know her well enough. She wouldn't want to go with me." Dick said,

"Well, it wouldn't hurt to ask her." So Walter called me up as a last resort. And of course he was my last chance. So I just said "yes." We went. Oh, we had a very good time. And do you know, neither one of us ever dated anyone else from that time on. And oh, we had such happy times, the three couples of us together. We went rabbit hunting up where the cement plant is now, you know. That was all open country. We went rabbit hunting and killed so many rabbits and divided them up among us. Of course, those days, we'd eat rabbit. Mother finally told me that if I brought any more rabbits home, why I needn't come with 'em. And oh, I think it was about a year or more before we were engaged.

We were married the 18th of August, 1920. At my grandmother's, down in Denver. My father had sold the old rock house place by that time, and found some land that he liked real well at Cedaredge, Colorado. So we went over there and looked around for a place and finally found this place. My father and mother had a little place in town, and he bought a place for my oldest brother and his wife. Harold was married by then, and had a baby girl. The two younger boys were still in high school. And then Walter and I were to select another place, for us. We were to pay the taxes on it, and eventually own it. We stayed there seven years, and every one of us and most everyone else that had gone into that country at that time and bought, lost everything. Even the shirts on our backs.

We paid $15,000 for Harold's place. Ten thousand for ours. Not all of it under cultivation. But the bottom just fell out of everything about that time. Now, we raised potatoes. We had nine acres of potatoes, and all of us worked. Oh, we worked so hard in those. I remember we paid 20 dollars a hundred for the seed, and about the time that we were to harvest the potatoes, they had a strike. Railroad strike. And we stored our potatoes. We sorted them three different times through the winter and ugh that's a nasty job. Then we sold them in the spring for 15 cents a hundred pounds. See, that was before they could ship freight as fast as they do now. We had a peach orchard, and I remember one year when we harvested our peaches and sold them, we got just enough to buy shoes for the family. The same way with the apples. We had hogs and we fattened our hogs on apples and apricots.

We walked up and down the streets of Cedaredge begging people to buy dressed pork for eight cents a pound. Oh, those were tough times. But we had a lot of fun over there. Several young couples our age had come in there. Their folks had helped them to buy, you know. We'd get together of an evening and play Rook. Spend, oh, most of the night playing Rook. Then in winter, we went tobogganing. We'd go down those roads from the mesas, down into the low place. About six of us get on one toboggan, you know, and go scooting down a hill. Years later, my daughter Mary Margaret went over there with me and we stood at the top of one of these roads where we'd tobogganed down in the winter, and she said, "Oh, Mother, you surely don't mean that you went down here!" But we did! And then we had an old horse draw the toboggan up the hill. He could go straight up, you know. Take a short cut. But that was really fun. Then at the end of seven years, my father had to take two of his places back. And we moved back here, then. Sadder and wiser and very much poorer.

Then Walter and I moved up in above Bellvue. We moved up there. We rented that and put in corn and sold the ensilage. And we made a living there. We had four children by that time two boys and the two girls.

The year that we plunged the deepest into raising corn for ensilage, we had a killing frost the 10th of September, so we lost out on that. Then Walter went to work. They were building the cement plant and he went to work there, as a carpenter's helper. But when they started up the work at the cement plant, he had been gassed pretty badly in World War I and we knew he didn't dare work there then. So he went to work as a carpenter's helper and he really was a very good carpenter. And he worked over the country at one job and another and there was a while that he worked in the railroad yards in Cheyenne. Ten hour shift. And drove back and forth. They had a car pool. Then he went back to the work at the schoolhouse. He drove a bus and was a janitor there. And we all helped out. I'd go down each afternoon with one of the neighbors that drove a school bus, and the children, as they got old enough, worked there, too.

Walter's folks, of course, first lived in the valley. We called it Pleasant Valley. He went to the old rock schoolhouse that's there at Graves' place. After he was through with the eighth grade, his next schooling was over in Greeley. He went over there and learned the printer's trade and he went to a business school there. Then he came back to help Dick Falloon farm the Falloon place. From there he went into World War I. He was in service I believe, about 18 months. The war was ended while he was there and he went on into Germany in the army of occupation.

There was one night when all but two of his group—now, I don't know whether you call it a platoon, or what, but I think there were about 250 men out on the hillside. In the night there came the warning of gas and they were to put on their gas masks. Of course they had them strapped to them at all times. But Walter and a buddy of his had their heads covered up with a blanket and they didn't hear that alarm. And they were the only two who did not go to the hospital. The others couldn't get their masks on in time. He had a huskiness in his voice. Oh, I didn't meet him of course, until he came back from the war. He always had that huskiness in his voice. One time there was a man that came to interview him on behalf of a buddy who was trying to get compensation. He asked Walter if he had ever tried to get any compensation and Walter said no, he'd promised himself that if ever he got out of there, he'd not ask for another thing, and he was going to keep that promise. He wasn't going to do it. But this man said he could have gotten compensation because he was badly gassed.

Now he was under direct fire for 98 days, with only five days of that pulled out of the battle lines. And they were up in close contact with them. It did bother his nerves, I think all the rest of his life.

That was the Meuse-Argonne battle. There's one time
that they were going along, and of course they had those
wrapped leggings, you know, and you had to wrap them just so.
This one fellow was walking along, and he had a hold of the
saddle strings of one of the officers. He was complaining of
the treatment they were getting. Oh, he was just more than
beefing and walking through this mud and slush and all, one
leg came unwrapped and he fell down in a mud puddle. When
he got up Walter said he said, "I wish the Germans would
shoot me. I just wish they'd shoot me." And there were funny
things that happened. Of course, they didn't seem funny until
afterwards. But it was a tough, tough time. There they'd gone
over to save the world, and fought a war to end all wars. When
they came back, all the good jobs were taken. The boys that
had gotten deferred, you know, had all the good jobs, and there
was nothing for them. And the government didn't come
through to help us, until long, long afterwards. But by the time
of his death, we had joined the World War I barracks there in
Fort Collins, and oh, they were good to us. They were very
good. I don't know—Walter's mind—he was a keen-minded
man. He was the best Bible student I ever knew. But about 15
years before his death, his mind began to fail and from then
on, it was rough.

*Despite the hard economic times, Walter had definite views about
Lora's working outside the home.*

Women were not to be the breadwinners. They could
work alongside their husbands, and the women were not
inferior. In fact, Walter told me that one reason he married me
was so I'd be his secretary. I'd had more education—more
formal education—than he had, and I worked with him. I liked
to work out in the fields with him. Then, when we came into
the house, why, he did his share there. We were companions.
Everyone that knows us knows that we had one of the happi-
est relationships.

And there were women that were the breadwinners, but
we always felt that their husbands were sort of a Casper

Milquetoast, you know. The man made what he could and it was up to us to live on that. When times were hardest, and the men couldn't get jobs, we gleaned my father's cornfield and took that corn, and we fed our livestock. We lived in Bellvue that winter. We fed our hog and our chickens corn, and then we made hominy and we lived on the hominy.

One of our friends in Laporte had a large raspberry patch. We all turned out to pick raspberries. My husband had a job at that time. He was working with Jap on what they called the WPA. They were working on roads then, but quite a few of them didn't have work, and they came down into the raspberry patch and picked along with us women

We never went hungry. We didn't have so much along the dessert line in those times. But we had our own garden, even when we lived there in Bellvue. We paid six dollars a month rent for our house there. It was a nice house. It's still standing. We had a big garden, and we had a row of apple trees and blackberries. And we had an old sow. We raised our own pork. We had a cow. And we had all the milk and cream and butter we wanted, so we had plenty. Now, clothing was a different thing. Of course, Mother was gone by that time, but she had sisters who sent us their clothing, and I learned to make over. I remember, I especially didn't like to make pants. I was giving the second son a lecture on true riches don't consist in money, especially, and I had quite a few pants laid by that I knew I was going to have to make over for the boys. So he got the point, finally, and he said, "I know. We're rich in pants."

During the Depression, the Shipps rented a house just off U.S. Highway 287, at the time the main road west. Travelers on foot frequently dropped by seeking food and shelter.

The men were not hoboes. They were not beggars. And they would share anything as they came along, you know. Anything that they could do for the families where they stopped. One fellow was a shoe cobbler, and he mended all our shoes while he was there. We had a big barn on this place that we were renting and they were welcome to sleep in the barn as long as they didn't smoke. And they didn't smoke because they didn't have the money to buy the tobacco to smoke if they'd wanted to.

One man was coming back the other way, and he got to the top of the hill. He'd had word that his little boy had fallen from a freight train and been badly hurt, so he was on his way back to see about him. He got to the top of the hill with his little car and ran out of gas. He coasted down into our yard, and he stayed with us several days. He was a carpenter. Walter was building our home down—oh, not very far south of there, in his spare time. He told the man he didn't have any money to pay him, but he did have credit at the little store, and that if he wanted to work a few days, he would get credit for gas and oil to go on. So he stayed with us several days. And just ever so many things like that. We enjoyed the men very much.

That sense of community carried over in other acts of kindness.

When the Depression was at the worst, our son was six years old. We lived in Bellvue at the time. He became very, very ill, and we didn't know what his trouble was. We took him to the doctors in town and finally one specialist told us that there was a growth down in his throat. Dick was far too ill for him to give him an anesthetic, so that he could see what that was. So he recommended that we take him to Denver to the Colorado General Hospital.

We didn't have a car that would run, only once in a while. And Jap had been working for the government, cutting timber, I believe. A knot of wood flew up and blinded him, and they gave him—the government gave him so much compensation. And with that, he bought a pickup. A Ford pickup. Of course we were close enough that they knew of Dick's illness. Besides that, I was to take care of Mrs. Burgess when their baby was coming. But he knew, so he told Walter to take his pickup. We didn't have any money. My sister-in-law had saved up 10 dollars. She gave that to me. Another lady who was nursing there in Bellvue had 10 dollars coming to her. She had quite a family, but she got her money and gave me five dollars of that.

So I had 15 dollars to go on. And we had Jap's pickup. And that was the kind of neighbors we had in those days.

It took about a year. We'd have to go back every month for them to test him and see how he was doing. At one time they thought it was a tubercular growth. It was on the vocal cords. He was to whisper. They said he'd have to whisper for a year. That was pretty hard for a little six-year-old boy with other brothers and sisters around him. Then the next time we went down, they thought it was cancerous. And of course that frightened us terribly. But they finally decided that it was a growth that was fed from the sinuses. They had a doctor, a specialist, come in from Boulder. It cost us 10 dollars. Later on, that specialist performed the same operation on a man we knew, who had money to pay, and it cost him $2,500, I think. But anyhow, from then on, Dick recovered.

Our entire lives centered around the little church down here in Bellvue. Our social life. When people came—strangers—someone always asked them home for dinner. Always. No matter what they had or didn't have to eat. I remember one time some people had moved in—a man and wife and three children. They came up to services, so Walter and I asked them home for dinner. All we had to eat was a jackrabbit pot pie. My father lived with us and he'd got a nice, young, tender, fat jackrabbit out east of town, and I made a pot pie out of it. We had plenty, but that was what we had. They thought it was delicious. And that was the way you did. And then you'd almost always have someone go home with you for dinner and to spend the afternoon. After the meal was over, the men would get out and play horseshoes, and the women would sit and visit, and the children, of course, romp around. And we knew who our next door neighbor was, in those days. Now you don't.

Lora considered religion the foundation of her life.

Oh, it gave me peace of mind more than anything else. We have had some terrible times in our more than 50 years of marriage. But we were Christians, and we knew those afflictions did have a purpose. They were a lesson. And we profited by them. And we lived long enough to see why they came to us. Why they were sent.

Country Girl

Helen Barnes Burgess learned the meaning of hard work from her mother and father, Anna Elmira Brigham and William Matthew Barnes. In the 1890s, William had married Anna Elmira's older sister, Ad, in Marshalltown, Iowa and moved to Colorado, where they took up a homestead in Yuma County. A bit later Anna Elmira and her parents, the Brighams, followed. Ad suffered from tuberculosis, and William took her to Boulder for treatment. The high, dry climate of Colorado's Front Range was a popular retreat for persons ill with tuberculosis, and often they overcame their sickness, but Ad did not. She died, leaving William with two young children.

After arriving in Colorado, Anna Elmira helped her parents with their own homestead and, in 1901 proved up her own.

My mother had the job of herding cattle on the homestead because there weren't any fences or anything. She was just a young girl at home, helping at home. She would help her folks. Her father would have to plow in the fields and plow up what they had planted there, corn. They raised lots of broom corn, for feed. They had to build a place to live, and she built a sod house and they plastered it inside. They went to some distant creek. They hauled sand and stuff to use in the plastering. They had to have a well drilled or dug. I forget how deep the well was dug. And they usually put up a windmill to pump the water for their stock. I think they were supposed to fence the place before it was proved up on, too. She was very well acquainted with the prairie land. There was lots of things to contend with — like the rattlesnakes. She had a bad scare with a rattlesnake there. When she went to take a step over a crick or some knoll, there was this rattlesnake and it was right down between her feet. It hypnotized her so she couldn't even take a step one way or the other. All she could do was just look at it. It just kept wiggling its tongue at her. Her papa saw her standing there, and he ran over there. He'd been hoeing in the garden. She was just standing there like that, and he got her off and killed the rattlesnake.

A year or so after Ad died, William married Anna Elmira.

Aunt Ad and Papa had had two boys, Fred Barnes and Orville. Orville was riding a horse one day, and he fell into a prairie dog hole. The horse stepped into the prairie dog hole and threw him and hurt him inwardly so that he didn't recover from that. Ad was a schoolteacher. She was very insistent on having a good education. That was a thing that nobody could take away from you. And that was the same as money, for your advancement in the world, and more precious than money because it was something people couldn't rob you of. So when Fred became old enough to go to college, why his ambition was to get a college education. So they came to Boulder. Sent him to preparatory school in Boulder. Then my father decided to come to Fort Collins, to send him to college in Fort Collins. So he did very well in college. He was valedictorian of his class, in the class of 1909.

My mother used to play her accordion when she was out herding the cattle. Keep the cattle together, I guess. Keep her amused. It was rather a dull day, I would think, sitting out in the sunshine with her sunbonnet, trying to keep entertained. Well, her crocheting and embroidery work that she did took up quite a bit of her time, too, but she would speak these pieces and sing the songs that she had learned in school when she was in Iowa.

In Fort Collins William located at the corner of Prospect and Shields Streets, today one of the busiest intersections in the city.

We had a 20 acre fruit farm. Just about every kind of fruit on that farm. Papa just thought that was a great place to

own, you know, after living out in Yuma County, on the—you
might say—desert. Course out there he had planted a peach
orchard. But fruit didn't grow very well out there. There was
wild fruit out along the cricks, but when he came here and
found he could get a fruit farm. . . . He called it the Pleasant
View Fruit Farm. He put up a sign over the gate for it, and he
was quite proud of the fruit. He always tried to take good care
of the. . . . Most of it was apples, of course, and he had the
apple cider mill that he got to use the apples. He was sure that
there wouldn't be any worms in them because he sprayed the
apples five times during their growing season.

I can remember my grandmother. She lived in a little
house in our yard. He had built a place for her so she could
have her own little home. And she used to take the horses and
wagon and the big spray tank out into the orchard. Papa had a
spray fixed on a fishing pole so that it would reach up into the
highest trees. We had a big red sheriff orchard. And the
Jonathan apples made the best cider. And the Wealthies, too.
And we had red Junes and Early Harvest apples and Walbridge.
The Walbridge apples were large. Papa used to say, "Big as a
pumpkin." They were good for baking. You'd cut them in half,
and they were good to bake. And we had crab apples. The
Siberian crabs, and some other crab apple that was good to eat.
They had a big cherry orchard. Then we had gooseberries and
currants and plums. We had three different kinds of plums. He
did pack a lot of fruit in boxes. He had a big sorting table. He
sorted out the best of them, and he shipped them to some
friends or someone that he knew before he came here that
wanted the apples. They brought a pretty good price, I think,
boxed that way. But the ones that weren't as good, the second
grade, he made into cider. At first it wasn't electric. Then when
they put in electricity, why he had an electric cider mill. He
made apple cider in quite a large quantity. Then he built vats.
We had three big, or four big vats, I believe it was, in the
basement. Then one big vat outdoors that he put the cider in
to make vinegar. It had to have "mother." (After it had soured,
a cider scum was put in the vinegar vats to help make the
vinegar. The scum was called "mother" because it was used to

"mother" a new batch of vinegar.) I used to think that was so
funny. I thought they should take that mother off, but they
put that mother on there, purpose to make the vinegar. I think
vinegar was selling for 30 cents a gallon then. I used to have
the job of selling the vinegar. It was put in glass jars, and
people would come there, wanting vinegar. It was something
that I could do. That's when I got a little bit larger. One of the
best things I remember was coming home from school, going
out to the cider mill when they were making cider, and get the
fresh cider, right as it came from the apples. That was really
good.

I went to high school in Fort Collins. I came out here to
Laporte to my last year in school, when we moved to Bellvue. I
had to quit school between the grade schools and high school
because I had—well, both of us had—St. Vitus' Dance. It was
something that held us back from doing anything. It was a
queer disease. It seemed the nerves. . . . Your hand wouldn't go
where you wanted it to. Somehow you'd start to take a hold of
something and it would go the opposite direction. It was a
queer thing. And my brother, they decided to doctor him with
a medicine doctor. And they doctored me with chiropractors,
at first. Both of us took chiropractic treatments, but we
couldn't take that very well. It was kind of hard. Dr. Printy was
my doctor. She was a woman doctor. I took treatments for
about six months from her.

It didn't seem to bother me, but it affected Raymond's
heart from then on. He had an enlargement of the heart.

Mama had always wanted me to be a teacher. She thought
that would be a good thing for me to be. So I thought, well, I'll
take the teacher's examination and see whether I could pass it
or not. Then maybe I could go on to be a teacher. So I took
the teacher's examination. About that time, I had been bap-
tized into the Church of Christ, and I had great faith in prayer.
So I prayed that I would pass the examination. So I had to go
to town to take the examination. When the grades came back, I
had passed it by just one point. So I couldn't take very much

credit for it, I thought. But then I did pass, and that was what I had wanted to do. But I hadn't made such good grades that there was anything to brag about. So for two years then, I was able to teach. Then they told me if I'd take a refresher course at the college in Greeley, then I could have my certificate renewed. So I did that. Then I got the school at Masonville. I taught school at Masonville that next year.

Papa had also bought a place at Stove Prairie at the same time that he bought the Bellvue place. He thought it'd be nice to have a place up there in the mountains where we could go and get wood. It had an old house on it, but it wasn't fit to be lived in. We'd go up there, the cows would be in the house. My first sight of the house was a cow standing in the doorway looking out at us when we drove up. I used to not look at it as a home, it was just a place. But later Mama moved up there. We had to sell the 10 acres here in Bellvue and move up to Stove Prairie to live.

We used to imagine there were bears. We'd hear the cows bawl. We'd think it was a bear. But I think it was just the cows. But anyhow, we thought of it as being wild country up there. My brother got busy and put the fences up so the cows couldn't get in, and they remodeled the house and fixed it up. She liked it in the mountains. She really thought it was beautiful up there. She enjoyed the mountains and the spring. We had a lovely spring. I suppose it's still there, because springs don't usually dry. . . . That one didn't ever dry up. It would just run all year. And the ice-cold water—it was just great. We'd have to carry it from the spring to the house, but it was worth it.

She kept getting worse all the time. I taught school up there. Course that was after we had been married for quite a while, and I couldn't leave Jap and the children to go and live with her. And yet some of them thought that I should be taking care of her. Jap spoke about building a house down here in the yard, but we didn't ever get around to that.

She was born in 1869. And she died, I think, in '42.
Anyhow, I had taken the schoolhouse up there at Stove Prairie
and Stratton Park. I taught at Stratton Park for a while, and
then I could get over to see her and stay with her, because it
was just a few miles from Stratton Park School, on up over
Stove Prairie Hill to her house. I stayed with her quite a bit
whenever I could.

That was pretty hard. When I think about it now, it must
have been so lonesome for her. She liked the mountains, but
she would get afraid. The rats or something would bother
around. She'd imagine things and course there were things
that'd get her chickens. She had tried to keep some chickens
and one time a hawk came down to get her chickens. It was
just about to fly off with one of her chickens, you know, and
she went out and fought it. She fought with that hawk and
made it let go and it just scratched her hands all up and they
were just bleeding and bruised. When she had to fight it off,
she said she just vowed she wasn't going to have her biddy hen.
She made such a pet of the chickens. They all knew her and
would come and talk. She'd talk to them.

She was a country girl. Really a country girl. She liked to
be out and doing things out in the ground, making things grow.
She experimented up there at Stove Prairie with different kinds
of fruit that she thought would surely grow here. She planted
different kinds of trees: the cherry trees and the apples and
walnut trees. She just thought sure that that ground is so rich
and good up there, and she had such wonderful luck with her
plants. Her houseplants and geraniums and all would just grow
so good up there.

*Helen met Jasper, or Jap as he was always known, at the Bellvue
Church of Christ.*

I guess the first time he made any impression, maybe,
was over at church. He had come to church, and there were
several young people in the church. And of course his

brother's wife introduced us. That was after I'd been out in
Yuma County and taught and came back here. We were
married in the church. That was '26. I think it was December
26th. And then we went to live with his folks, down here in the
next block. The next summer we went to Fox Park, and he was
mining for gold up there, and worked for Mr. Dowd that year.
Then the next year the folks had a little room on the back of
their house—one-room house that they moved in there. We
lived there for a while. Then the Depression came, and Alice
came, and it was hard times there for a while. The neighbor
lady came over and helped. Mrs. Dewey Schofield. She was a
good nurse. She really took good care of me. The doctor came
when he was called. But anyway, she had taken care of me. We
didn't know about going to the hospital in those days. All our
neighbors, or some of the folks, took care of them in the
homes.

When Ruth was born, Mabel Sidney took care of me. She
lived down here at the end of Second Street where Kahlers
live. She was my nurse, I guess you'd say, then. Doctor came
out at that time. Then Dean was born at Mrs. Read's down
here. At another neighbor's. I went over there to her house. At
that time the government had let us take mattresses to help out
the people that needed them. We saw we were going to need
this new mattress, having this family. She had had a mattress.
But how was that? Well, I don't remember just how the
mattresses got mixed up in this. Anyhow, the doctor came out
there then, and he waited for Dean to come. Then after two or
three years, why Jerry was born. And in that time, they had the
hospital built in town. We had to go to the hospital to have our
babies after that. So Jerry was born in the hospital in town.

Along with the children, the Depression soon arrived.

When Alice was a baby, I made her clothes out of old
clothes. Her best Sunday dress I made out of a brother-in-law's
white shirt, and trimmed it with pink tape and embroidery, and
made a real pretty Sunday dress for her. We got by with that. I
think the shoes maybe were the biggest problem, but Grandma

Burgess knew how to make shoes. Kinda more like moccasins, I guess. And then she always knit the booties for the children, too. When Ruth was little, why Jap began to get work, you know. When President Roosevelt came into office. Ruth was born in 1931. That year, in '31, Jap had got his pension. They were allowed so much money that they didn't receive during the war, that they had coming to them. He had quite a bit coming to him so he bought the Model A Ford. That's the reason I remember what year—1931. Then he bought me a washing machine. Before that we'd had to wash on a board. And he bought Alice a bicycle. That was it. So we all were fitted out here.

Well, I know we got down to where we didn't have any money to buy even a postage stamp. And they didn't cost as much as they do now, either. We got down to where we just had rice in the house, before we made up our minds we were going to go down and ask for help from the county. So we went down. At that time they were issuing food for the poor people. So we got our rations. They had a place downtown where you could go and get what things that you needed. It would be issued out so much for a family of so many, and it seemed good to get something to eat. They had meat. It was side pork; for one thing I can remember that being good to have. And flour. Of course that was quite an important thing. And lard, and potatoes.

Then of course when Roosevelt became president, he had all these work projects. Elmer, Jap's older brother, went into the CCC's and he was a boss in the CCC camp. Course he was older. Then Jap got work in the WPA with working on the road. They put in the roads. That road up there at Stove Prairie across to the Poudre. They worked on that—he and Ivan Read. And of course others. Don't remember who all.

When Roosevelt took over, I felt that we were having a new breath of life, you know. It was just something that we knew we were going to get out of. There were so many things. I can't remember all the different initials. There was NRA. I don't remember what that was, but. . . . He put folks to work, you know. They had work to do, but it did seem like you didn't know what to do, when you couldn't get work, and you didn't have money. You couldn't pay your bills. We had to run up a bill at the Bellvue store till they couldn't carry us any longer. Then when we got where we did have money, when he got to working on the railroad and sawing logs and stuff, so we could work and pay our bills, the storekeeper wanted to know why we couldn't pay ahead, just as well as to pay the back. That was a new idea. It would have worked, I guess. But we didn't think we had to pay for things that we hadn't gotten yet. But you know it was reasonable. We could just as well pay.

We surely owed them a lot for carrying us that way as long as they could. Then, of course, when Jap got the sawmill and got to making a little bit, with sawing logs for people, and they got to building houses, it got so we had money to buy stuff for the house. We built the cement basement here. But we didn't sit down and count the cost. We had to take it as it came. Forty dollars paid for the cement for the basement, and we had that built for quite a while before we got around to get the logs down, 'cause they had to be sawed and hauled down, and that took gas.

All that time, the family lived in one room.

That was hard living in one room. We had the bed in one corner, stove in the other corner, Alice's bed in the other corner, the cupboard in the other corner and the table in the middle of the floor. It wasn't so bad. Everything handy. But then it was good when we could have our own house. And this, of course, seemed big to us then. We lived in here when Jerry was a baby.

Homebody

Elmer Foster was a true homebody. Elmer grew up in the house in which he was born, brought his bride, Freda, to it when he married, with her raised four children in it, and lived there until he died in his nineties. Nestled against a hillside near the Greeley Waterworks at the mouth of the Poudre River, the house sheltered Elmer and Freda through floods, winter storms and summer heat. Among his older neighbors, Elmer had the reputation of being a fighter as a youth. They said he got thrown out of school for fighting in the sixth grade, and never went back.

My father was born in New York state. His folks came to Parker, Colorado, when he was a boy. My mother came from Minnesota across the plains in an ox team when she was eight years old, and they settled in Parker. That is, east of Parker. My dad did some freighting. They freighted to Leadville when the boom was on up there. My grandfather got pneumonia up there and died, at the age of 42. Then my folks and the Pennocks over here—the Frank Pennocks. . . . See, my father's mother's brother married my mother's sister. My aunt was one of the older of the family, and my mother was the youngest. Them and their family started to Oregon. They got up this far, and they had a sawmill down here. They was hauling logs from the foothills down to the sawmill. Got a job. Finally my mother got tired of moving around in one shack after another . . . one *leaky* shack after another, and she traded her team, harness and wagon, for this 40 acres. She got $1,000 inheritance, and she built this house. They built it in 1901, and I was born in 1902.

I wasn't lonesome. Proctor moved up to the Greeley waterworks. The Greeley waterworks started at 1905. They built these two slow filters in 1905. And Jimmy Proctor moved up here from Denver to run that. He had a boy, and Goddards down here had six kids. And there was Alford Maxfield there on the Kremmer place. We had lots of fights. We did quite a lot of hunting. There was quite a lot of rabbits around here then. Not many deer in here then. Got more deer now than we ever had.

Had work here on the farm, then we had our homestead up in the hills. In the summertime we'd go up there. Take the cows up there. My mother had customers for 60 pounds of butter a week. She'd make the butter up there, and they had a good spring. Keep just like in the icebox. Delivered butter on Saturday. Come down here and in the summertime with springwagon. My dad built an ice box to go on the springwagon. We put up ice here. We'd fill the icebox with ice and deliver butter, with team and springwagon. We got regular ice saws, you know. Manpower ice saws. And cut it in blocks. And then get it out on the ice and load it up. And course you couldn't drive down on the ice. You had to have a chute to put it in the wagon, and then another chute to put it in the ice box. In the ice house. I think we cut them about 18 by two feet. Eighteen inches by two feet. Well, there was two winters we didn't get any ice. 'Cause of January thaw. I remember one after we was married that we didn't get any. We'd put that ice up and just pack it solid. Then put sawdust around it and over it. That'd keep it all summer.

For 13 years I worked up here at the Waterworks in the summertime. Then the sugar factory—campaign—Fort Collins sugar factory. Which isn't there anymore. Then in '41, I got a job at the cement plant. I put in 25 years and nine months there.

Elmer's employment by organizations was as a common laborer. For the waterworks, which collected water for the city of Greeley from the Poudre River, he skimmed filter beds and hauled the mud out with a wheelbarrow.

Those were sand filters. The water went down through the sand. There was sand, and then there was pea gravel, and then a bigger gravel. Then at the bottom there was rocks, and then there was those pipes that picked the water up and took it out into the line. That water wasn't always clean, you know, that come down the river, and they had a settling basin up above. Then they run that water down in the filter plant, through the sand. After it got about so much dirt and mud on it, then they'd have to skim it off. See, the water won't go through it when it'd get sealed. And then you had to wheel it out. Had quite an incline to wheel that up.

At the sugar factory, he sacked the sugar that was refined after the beet crop came in.

After that there was nothing till. . . . All you did is saw wood to keep warm in the winter time. Course we had our own meat and our chickens. We raised a few pigs. Always had a calf to butcher. We never went to bed hungry through the Depression. We raised our four kids on through the Depression there. But we never went to bed hungry, and there was a lot of them that did. About all the work we had was what little there was up at the waterworks, and what we could pick up around the farmers, you know, and haying and silo filling and things like that.

Freda made the clothes for little boys out of the backs of their elders' overalls and workpants and so on. "You can do it," she said. "And many a sugar sack and flour sack got used up making undergarments. You had to sew. You had to mend. You had to can. You had to raise a garden."

Floods came down from the mountains with unpredictable regularity. In 1951, a thunderstorm to the southwest sent a rush of water from LeBow Gulch, two miles south of the Poudre, that washed away and drowned three Bellvue residents. In 1923, and earlier, in 1913, the Poudre flooded.

They had a big flood here in June of '23, and it washed out all the roads and the ditches. Filled this ditch up and they had a big bunch of men working on this ditch. My mother was cooking for Ed Grinstead and his drivers. She was all right at nine o'clock, and 11 o'clock, why, she had what I think was a heart attack. And they had to go up Rist Canyon and fix the road up there—this was all washed out down here, down here by Graves'—to be able to get the hearse in.

We went up through the waterworks here and down by the river. There was an old bridge there they called the old Shipp bridge. Anyway, the doctor come up that far. Then I went down and got him and brought him up here.

That same flood hit Redstone Creek, a few miles south of the Poudre. Freda's family was hit hard by that one.

Freda: How people can be so heartless! After it washed the house off the foundation and the big old trees in the yard, Dad was going to build a new barn. He had his lumber together. The barn was—well, you might say north and upstream from the house. And the weight of that lumber against that house and water. . . . When we stepped out of there that night, we stepped off the porch into water. Oh, must have been knee deep or more. And we crossed that red hill where we lived, on Horsetooth Road, and when we crossed—we waded that little stream—that was up pretty near hip deep. Besides, carry a baby through that. My little sister. We spent the night in Gross' barn over there on Horsetooth Road on the east side. But after that flood we had water in the house up to the windows. Carpets were ruined. Everything down low was ruined and the people from Fort Collins, and around, they'd come and they'd look. They'd park out there and look at you. Look at what the flood had done.

And then we got to realizing that things were disappearing. Looters. My mother had an old fashioned musical instrument called a phono harp. It was just a harp shape, only you put it on the table in front of you, and pluck the strings. It disappeared in that time.

The first flood Elmer remembered occurred in 1913.

We went up to Proctors'. I was just a kid and we went up to Proctors, and at the waterworks, and the water floating around out there in their meadow. Logs floating around in it. Halligan Dam broke once and Chambers Lake broke once.

Medical help was difficult to obtain. Elmer learned that at an early age.

My dad traded for some lumber one time. He was going to build a big barn. This guy didn't get him the lumber so finally he took the sawmill over. We was up there skidding out lumber. I got kicked here in the head with a horse. That happened at eight o'clock, and they brought me down in the Model T Ford and it didn't get sewed up till afternoon. And they just sewed it up. They didn't give me anything.

Elmer recalled that a rivalry existed between Bellvue and Laporte. That sometimes things got a little warm.

They both had ball teams. Wellington had a ball team too. Every time they'd have a ball game then they'd have a big fight. They were friends, but they weren't above a good fight.

Elmer recalled fights of his own.

Oh, lots of them. Yeah, Bus Proctor and I used to. . . . Bob Gibson asked Bus Proctor if he ever whipped me. And he said, "No, I never did." He says, "I beat hell out of him several times, but I never whipped him. He was always ready for another one the next day."

Toughie

She was born Laura Alexander on a ranch near La Veta, Colorado, on May 17, 1897, the fifth child of a group of nine. In 1908, diphtheria struck, and in one week she lost two brothers and a sister.

The doctor that came to see us, all he'd ever doctored was sore throats. And he thought it was tonsillitis in the worst form. That's what he said. And then there was a young doctor come. Just out of school. He found out we had diphtheria. And then, when he got to the door, he said it was black diphtheria in the worst form. Course the folks had had this other doctor come until the second youngster was pretty near gone, before the young doctor came. And then he drove. . . .It was the first car that ever hit La Veta. All the brakes was on the outside of the car. And he went to Pueblo from La Veta to get the antitoxin. And he gave us the antitoxin. And they give it to us in the back. In great big tubes. They hurt like everything. I didn't have to have but three of them but some of them had quite a few of them, because they were so bad. All eight of us would have died if it hadn't been for the antitoxin. But I wasn't as bad as some of the children. Course we was quarantined. Nobody'd come see us, and there was one man came and offered to do our washing for us. Which was very good, 'cause there was eight of us in bed. One nurse lacked six months being a nurse. Graduate nurse. Came to take care of us. And this one guy came to do the washing. And that was all we saw in six months. And when the quarantine was lifted, we burned everything we had. Bedding and everything. We had to go from one building to the other, take a bath in carbolic acid, and jump over into the other room and put on clean clothes. And then people wouldn't hardly have anything to do with us. The preacher preached my little sister's funeral. And after that, they wouldn't come near. And they buried the children after dark.

Because they was afraid of disease. First time my dad ever went to town after the funeral, why, the preacher even run from him, they were so afraid of it. And you couldn't blame them being afraid of it, either, I guess.

My baby brother was only 13 months old. He died first. And then my little sister not quite three years older than he was, died. Then my brother, six. And I was to be the next one, but I was too tough to die so the rest of them had to live. My sister six years older than I was asked me, "Laura, ain't you ever gonna die so I could?" And I looked up above the door and my dad had a shotgun up there and I thought, "Well, if I could get that I could blow my head off," but I couldn't get it 'cause the nurse wouldn't let me out of the bed. So the rest of them all had to live.

But they were sick a long time. Their voices were gone, and lots of them had no sense of smell and such like that. Nowadays they're awful lucky to have something to give them—antitoxin—so they don't have that. 'Cause no one realized how awful that was.

You couldn't forget it. No. I don't see how my mother and dad took it. The nurse was all that contracted. She didn't care about the doctor so well, that we had. She didn't like. . . . I mean she was a young nurse, you know, and she didn't think the doctor knew so much so she wasn't crazy about him. So she really didn't use precautions like he told her. When she got home, she got the diphtheria after she'd left us. And then her brother took it and died with it. But that's the only ones that got it. But our books and everything they had in the house was just like a fire. They got rid of all of it. Which I guess was a wonderful thing to do, but there was an awful big loss to us. We had those books, but they had to destroy everything. At that time. We even had to give the dog a bath in that carbolic acid water. And the guy that done our washing, he'd wash on a board with carbolic acid water in the tubs. That's what we had them days. And the carbolic acid was so strong it took the hide off his arms. He was an awfully nice man. Old Civil War veteran. But he said he was going to help the family out, so he came to help us. And that was a godsend.

My mother and dad never caught it either. Just the children. But we all slept two in a bed. Except for my brother. He was the only one left. Was two brothers died, and only one left, and he slept in a bed by himself. In one room. Eight of us. Imagine what a mess that would be for one nurse to take care of? Around the clock? Night and day? She'd swab the throats every hour and feed us every two hours. So she didn't get much sleep. I don't know how she stood it. No wonder her system was down when she went home.

But people don't realize what people had to put up with them days. And, of course, my folks was pretty badly broke up. I don't know how they took it. I don't see how they stood it. They had an awful lot of faith or they couldn't have made it. My mother. . . . All that noise out of the house. The next Christmas was terrible. And then the next Christmas when my baby sister was born, the sun shone again. God's blessing. No. People don't realize what a little old youngster means to a guy, that way.

The first car that came to La Veta was the one that the first doctor had. Took him six hours to go from La Veta to Pueblo. That's 60 miles. He left that evening, after that first antitoxin at six o'clock. And he got back, five o'clock in the morning. 'Course she said if he'd get back soon enough, he could save my—my little brother next to me, but he couldn't do that, either.

With a childhood experience like that, Laura might easily have developed a pessimistic and defeated outlook on life. She did not. She placed a lot of stock in religion, and as she grew older she remained cheerful, optimistic, and physically active. Even when she was in her late eighties, her vigor as she hiked energetically to the Bellvue post office drew her neighbors' admiration. She married Ivan Read, also from LaVeta, and they arrived in Bellvue in 1926. For most of the next 60 years, she lived in the same house next door to the sandstone building that is now the Grange Hall. She even

recalled the 1930s Depression with warmth. There was no employ-
ment, but there was family togetherness.

We did pretty good 'cause we had our garden and stuff
like that when the Depression was hard. There wasn't nothing
to do, much, for anybody. But the kids was old enough to do
some work, and we done a lot of swimming in the river. Them
days, they'd let you swim in the river. So we used to swim, of
course. The Poudre River, here. And we'd go swimming quite a
bit. 'Course my husband didn't have no work either. We could
all go swimming. Swim about half an hour, then come back
and hoe corn in the garden, then go back swimming again.
Best time of our lives. Was a lot of fun doing that. But he'd get
maybe a week's work, something like that. But if it hadn't been
for gardening and things, we couldn't have lived.

It was hard on some people. It didn't bother us too
much. On this ranch, we had a cow and our cream and pigs,
and then people run out and got a deer whenever they wanted
it and had their meat. And we had lots of whipped cream and
everything. Made clothes. Everybody. A woman usually had a
house dress to go somewhere and didn't have too many
clothes. We was all hard hit, that's no joke, but we had a lot of
fun living. Enjoyed life.

I never worried about clothes 'cause everybody was all
alike. Now, maybe they had one pair of shoes but maybe had
to tape up the soles. But then, the other people was like you. It
was hard times for everybody. Then when we was living with
Dad, and the grasshoppers got so bad. . . . That one year, the
drought was so bad, and the grasshoppers were so bad that
they was landing on the posts, and you could take a gallon can
and just about rake them off the poles. And they ate up
everything. Onions and everything, clear down to the ground.
There wasn't a chance for leaving anything. I know we felt so
bad about it 'cause everything we had, there wasn't a thing
hardly. So I went to a neighbor's one day, and this neighbor
and I, we decided we'd go to town. And went in the house
downtown. This woman was keeping college students. And so
she said, "I'll tell you what you do. You go to the show. It's a

good show and you'll feel a lot better when you see it." She says, "It's The Good Earth." So we went to the show, and that was worse than staying home 'cause that Good Earth showed pictures of the cows all dying over there and ponds all going dry. So we were sorry we went to the show. We got a good laugh out of it 'cause she thought it'd be a good show for us to see. But there was always something to see, funny. We weren't near as bad off as a lot of them, I don't think.

Had better times, I think, then than we do now, because, like I say, we had parties and things like that, you know. First year after we came here, they had that Christmas party over here at the church where Whites is now. There's where we had a Christmas party. And everybody got a little sack of candy, and all the neighbors and friends come in to visit, and enjoyed theirselves. My husband's name was Ivan, our son's name was Ivan, and there was three other Ivans there. I was surprised because I didn't think Ivan was such a common name. They called for sacks of candy, you know. And they used to go places. Go to people's homes and have a dance or something. We didn't have to go out.

We bought a Model T Ford, went down east of Denver and drove it. I think it was about the second time we drove it, we went up a hill, and the crankshaft crystallized and broke all to pieces. But we didn't have the company fix it, we just fixed it ourselves. It was funny. Them days you didn't do that, I guess.

Ab came along and he said, "Mrs. Read, why don't you go fishing with us?" Well, I was afraid of the worms and afraid of the fish—stinking things—I didn't like them very good. He said, "Well, I'll take your fish off the line if you'll go fishing." So, I went fishing with them, and he took the fish off the hook and baited the line, and you'd no more than throw out till you'd get a good fish about that size.

And of course I'd throw way out, because I'd wanted to be sure and get them, and he'd get them and unhook it. My husband set between him and me. I imagine it was good fishing. And then he'd go back and get his fish out, 'cause he'd

have it out, and then come back and get mine. And so we done
that all the time we worked up there. But when we came home,
the men wanted to go fishing. So I went. But it wasn't long till
I started pulling out a few suckers and things. He said he
wasn't about to take them off the hook. So then I had to turn
and do it myself. But I kind of liked it by that time. Fishing
and worms didn't bother me.

Sure love it. I love fishing. We remodeled this house after
we retired. Used to go to Horsetooth when they first started.
And there was a lot of fish up there. You could go up there on
the bank, and in an hour, come back, both of us. We enjoyed
it. Get the big ones. Nowadays, they don't know what fishing
is, do they?

We used to catch a lot of them. We used to go up every
day and get our limit. And we just enjoyed it.

It ain't no fun fishing with yourself, and you take a bunch
of women with you, they usually want you to untangle their
line, or want you to pull the fish out for them, and such like,
and you know, that ain't no fun. So I quit. I've been going to
get a license but I haven't. I've been going to get my license
now for three years. I mean I'm going to get my life license,
but I haven't done it. But I enjoyed it. Sure had a lot of fun
fishing. And I got so I could clean them just as good as he
could, and everything. We'd go up to Hohnholz Lake and all
around fishing. And down over Sand Creek Pass. We fished all
the time. Enjoyed it.

*Her husband died suddenly one summer morning. Instead of
frustration at having no time to say goodbye, she felt glad he did not
suffer long.*

He had been sick for a long time and really had had
throat trouble all his life. He'd had quinsy an awful lot of his
life. He never complained. He had heart trouble at the last. He
got up in the morning. He never complained about being sick.
Got up when he was sick unless he was real sick. But this
morning he got up and had breakfast, and he went down and

got the mail, and then we read the letters, went out, and looked at the flowers in bloom, and went and got some gas for the mower, and he said, "Now," he said, "I'll finish the mowing back here in the back while you finish your ironing." I had three dresses to iron. And he said, "Then we'll go fishing." So that's what we figured on doing. And he talked to the storekeeper. Mr. Fuhrer was the storekeeper then. And he talked to Mrs. Boyd's father. He was out here hoeing in the garden. And he went and got some gas down from Mr. Fuhrer and come on back and filled the mower. I had three dresses to iron. The other one on the board. And I thought, well, I'd look and see how he's coming. I could hear the mower going so I knew he was still mowing, but I stepped back in the bathroom and looked out. The mower was going, but there he was. He was gone. His hand just above the mower. Pretty good way to go when you got to go. Didn't have to lay around in one of them homes, or nothing. Nothing like that. He didn't have time to. I heard a woman tell me the other day, one of her folks was about ready to die, they called for the undertaker and the preacher. But I don't think you do that when you're going to die. His hands was all folded up, just like that. Just like they were took off the mower. I was the first one to find him out here. The neighbors was all surprised when I called and told them because they'd all talked to him.

It's a good idea. You bet it is. After you see so many of them just like. . . . Just to lay around, suffer for years before you die. Well, 'course he'd been sick a long while with heart trouble and throat trouble and everything. And when he died, why, God bless him. . . . And I see—I know so many friends that have folks in a home. Been there 10 years. Some of them don't know nothing—haven't known nothing. Some women go over at noon and feed them every noon. Go back and they don't know they been there to feed them or anything. It's sad. Oh, there's lots worse things than death.

Laura felt the religion's value throughout her life, ever since her brother and sister died.

I couldn't get along without it. Without faith, there would be no living. I don't think anybody could get along without religion. They might think they can, but they can't. They all come to it if they got caught in a pinch. It's like the airplane. Kid goes on the airplane. It come down, he done a lot of praying. Maybe he had never before, but he did a lot of praying.

It's been my life, all my life. Since the children passed away. If it wasn't for faith and religion, I couldn't make it. That's all there is to it.

Lily Fry Hout

Lily Hout's great grandchildren were the seventh generation of her family to live on the property she and her husband resided on for nearly 35 years. Half a mile west of U.S. 287, the little house and other buildings sit above the road to Bellvue. Her parents lived in the tiny log cabin behind her house, and her great-grandmother died in the room that was to become her and Lee's living room. Lee made furniture for their house and dug the cellar underneath, and Lily stocked it with jars of vegetables and fruit she canned. And from the kitchen table in that house Lee, having been painfully ill a long time, stood up after breakfast one morning, went into the bedroom and shot himself. That ended their marriage, but not her love for him. When real estate boomed in the neighborhood, her friends asked Lily why she didn't sell out. She could get a good price, they told her. Lily would not hear of it. She had roots in that land, and she had been happy there.

I always liked school. I remember one eventful time in high school, well I was I guess a freshman or sophomore. Anyhow, we'd always had Washington's Birthday off. Well, this one year they decided not to. Well, the kids in the upper grades got their heads together that we'd take it anyway. So we did. And all walked out but two. We stopped at this little store down there—where Lloyds live was a little grocery store. So we all stopped there and got knick-knacks and they credited us with it. Let us have it. Then we all hiked clear up here to the railroad track and down the railroad track to the Loo Stone. In there, somewhere. Had a heyday. Had to walk back, of course. We got in there on time for the buses. But the next morning when we went to school—I lived then, at that time, way up past Ted's Place. Anyhow, we all got settled in assembly. Mr. Jordan got up there, with his hands behind him. I can see him yet. And he told us what we'd done, and he said, "You know you're going to make up all those hours, an hour every night after school, and those that live far, it's just too bad, you'll still have to walk home." And so we did, about three or four days. And he got up there one morning and he said, "Well, you've always been such good sports about it, and good students, so take the bus tonight." We sure had a heyday up there, while we were there. But two of them wouldn't go. But it was fun. I remember we walked clear up here and we got up where we was going, about 10, 11 o'clock, and we had our lunch.

We didn't stay there too long, but we just thought we should have a vacation, so we took it anyway. But it was fun. I remember one time my friend and I that lived here, we flunked algebra. And then our algebra teacher lived right there in Laporte across from the schoolhouse, and he had an apple orchard. We knew we had to get those grades up. So he let us pick apples every night. I don't know how many we picked. Probably not too many. But anyhow, he passed us. Anyhow, we got our grades up. I'll never forget that. His name was Mr. Johnson.

In the fall of 1927, when Lily Fry was 16, she was invited to a party, and there she met young Leland Hout. That was it for both of them. They would marry soon, and have five children.

He lived in Fort Collins. He came from Denver with his folks. They had a business in Fort Collins, and then they had a little house party over here, and he was there and I was invited, so that's when we met. That was our first date. October sixth, 1927. I don't know why I remember that so well, but it just kind of stuck with me. It was so important. We would have been married 51 years. And I was 17 when I was married. Pretty near 18.

His folks and he had an establishment there in town, on Walnut Street. A cleaner's and furrier. Made fur coats. I know he made Mrs. Hout, for one, a beautiful muskrat coat and he was a real good furrier. Mended other people's coats and whatever. And he was a tailor. And so was Lee, for a while, with his father. Later on ,he and I farmed, and then later he was a painter. Decorator. For years and years and years. He and

his father, when they were in Denver, before they come up
here, painted theaters. One of the pretty ones they painted
down there was the Egyptian Theater. The whole side would
be one big picture, you know, inside.

We hardly knew there was a Depression, really, because
we had turkeys and we had chickens and cows and pigs and
whatever, and when we needed money for staples, why, we'd
run in three or four turkeys, or whatever. So we really didn't
suffer any. We didn't go anywhere, that's for sure. There wasn't
money to do anything like that. Just stayed home and raised a
family. We were happy as could be here.

*Lily and Lee raised five children. Mostly they lived right there, in the
little house near Bellvue.*

I remember one year, though, we lived way high up past
Red Feather on a ranch, Lee and I, and it was before Betty was
born. One time Lee came in the house, an early spring day, as
cold as could be. Said he didn't feel well. He was chilling, and
had a fever. I told him he'd better rest awhile. But he went back
out to work out in the field. I think we was baling hay. We had
an old hay baler there, you know. Baling it from the stack. Day
or two, he got real sick. Come in, feverish. I said, "Well, you
may have a wood tick on you." Said, "Oh, no, no way." I said,
"Well, just strip your clothes down and let me look and see."
Sure enough, he had a great big old tick right there in his groin,
and then one down under his knee cap. Well, and he was all
kind of spotted like, and real sick. So I had to go to a telephone. That was two miles away, down to Log Cabin, to where
the phone was. I got in the car and went down there and called
our doctor, and I told him how Lee acted. He said, "Well, get
him down to Fort Collins as quick as you can." He said, "I'll
call his folks and tell them." So I said, "OK." I had to get him
fixed and the kids fixed and ready to take out with him, and I
was way down the road, and here I saw a streak a-coming up
the Red Feather road, and it was Lee's brother coming after
him. So he got Lee in the car and the older boy, and took him

on to town and boy they was there long before I was. But he
had Rocky Mountain tick fever. He was sick a long time with
that.

I wasn't very happy up there. I was always afraid. If I had
to do it again, I wouldn't be, but at that time, I was scared.
Animals and everything. And so while he was sick in bed, I had
my mother and my brother and my father, and we all went up
there and moved out. Moved down. We had stock then. We
had horses and cows, but I got it done. But he was real sick for
a long time. He'd have a kind of a big yellowish spot and
maybe there'd be a purplish one. And then those things would
kind of shift over his body. Got down there, why, that was it.
So he stayed right at Mrs. Hout's place where they lived, there
with the post office, on South College. She doctored him
through and brought him out of it. She had canned a lot of
tomato juice that fall—V-8 stuff, you know? And she just kept
a continuous stream of that going through him, I guess, and
the doctor said that it probably saved him.

Lee built things – furniture, and even organs.

He built two of them. The first was just a two-manual.
Two keyboards. He gave that to our son in Cheyenne. And
then he built this one. It didn't take him too long. Some of the
parts of the thing he went out to the A-l Salvage and bought
those old springs, you know? And then, like the keyboard,
course, was in another old organ of his brother's. But other
than that, he built it. The console, he built out in the garage.
Birch. And then he, of course, finished it to this color. I guess
he always wanted one. His philosophy was, if you want
anything bad enough, make it. And course his parents were
quite musical anyway, and it kind of rubbed off on him a little
bit, I guess. And then he just liked to do that kind of stuff, like
woodwork. His brother had an organ, and so he thought he'd
build him one. In fact, he built two. Everybody wonders: how
did he do it? But he did. Did every bit of it. And a lot of
people watched him do it. Come over and marvel. And then he
played it just as well as it is pretty. And like I said, it was a lot

of our nights' entertainment. I would sit there, and he would play anything I told him, and it was all by ear. To me, it's fantastic.

So many people have looked at it. And I'm proud of it. Proud to say that he built it. It was more or less his hobby. One time, years ago—like I said, if you want anything bad enough, make it—so he wanted a boat years ago. So he and a good friend of ours got together and built them a boat. And we took that lots of places. The kids would ski behind it. We'd go to the lake and fish all day long. So I guess that's what he meant.

His father was a carpenter, also, besides. His father and he had many talents. Like the little old camper out there in the yard. We always wanted a camper and never thought we could ever afford to buy one. So we built one. And it's gone lots of places. We had a lot of fun in that little camper. We were right at home. We always called it our little home away from home. So maybe he was right. That was his philosophy, anyway. If you want anything bad enough. . . . So he did.

Norma Baxter Salisbury

She remembered her father's brand of forgiving mercantilism at his Laporte grocery during the Depression.

Father was born in New York state. Went to school in the little town of Woodhull. But very little is known of his life as a boy. He migrated to Iowa where he was a collector for a machinery company, you know. Drove a horse and buggy around and collected. And that's all we know about that. About 1883, he came to Fort Collins. At one time, he ran a livery stable. I think he had 100 or 125 horses at one time, and ran that livery stable. It was on North College in that first block.

He spoke of his mother. I think he was quite close to his mother. But as I understood it he and his father didn't get along too well. But his mother had a twin sister and he spoke of her. And that's about all he ever said about his family. So we don't know much about them. He, I think he was in Iowa when he married the first time. And he had one son, Ray Baxter. And after he was in the livery stable here for a while, he went up Rist Canyon on a ranch for a few years and his first wife passed away while they were up there, when Ray was about 12 years old, or something like that.

My dad was 30 years older than my mother. And Ray was two years younger than she. She was married when she was 20. So you see it would make it about that time. Mother was born in 1882. So Ray would have been born in 1884. And then in the late 1890's, Dad wasn't on the ranch too long. He stayed up there a while and came back to Collins. Was very interested in politics. And he was elected as county commissioner in 1895, I think, 1895 or 1896. And he served I think one year at that time, or two, possibly. And then in later years, when Walter and I were married—in 1924 just before that— he was elected as commissioner again. And he served four years at that time, and was instrumental in buying the land where the hospital sits at this time. The county knew they were going to have to have something, so he was one of the commissioners at that time. And he was very much interested in the beet industry here and the farming, and quite a civic minded person, interested in those type of things and interested in politics clear on as long as he could.

He was Republican. Oh, quite, quite strong. We laughed one time. My sister was working in the courthouse for the county clerk. And he happened to be a Democrat. When the election came up, she said to Dad, she said, "Would you vote for Mr. Hubbel, coming up?" And he half-way promised her that he would. But when it came time to make that X he couldn't do it. He had to vote Republican. And he told her, he said, "I just couldn't do it." So you see how he was just almost radical, in a way, on his politics. It was mostly just the local area, as far as politics. He didn't go outside of the county.

Mother's family came. . . . Grandfather came from Ohio, originally. And Grandmother came from Iowa. I don't know much about their lives there. But Grandfather first was located at Cheyenne and ran a drug store. But he wanted a ranch and he came out around Cherokee Park, what they called St. Cloud, and bought a ranch. That's where they lived then. There were four children and they were all born there. Then they sold that, right around 1900, and moved down to Fort Collins here in a big stone home out on Vine Drive. It's still on Vine Drive. About 20, 25 acres, I think at that time. And of course they had a driving horse. That's the only way they had of getting around. And they had chickens and a milk cow and raised alfalfa, just enough to get by on. Grandfather finally had to have cataracts removed on his eyes and he didn't see very well the last few years. I used to go and stay with them an awful lot. I was quite a Grandma girl. I can remember during the First World War, he was very much interested, of course, in that, and all we had was the newspapers. And he just could hardly wait till the papers came every day. And then I'd have to sit down and read the papers to him. Read the war notices to him, because it was too hard for him. He could read with a magnifying glass but I can remember that part of it.

Grandfather was a friend of Buffalo Bill. And when he came to town with his circus one time, I was at Grandfather's when he came out, riding his white horse and all the regalia that he had, you know. So that was really quite an exciting thing for me, to be able to see Buffalo Bill. But I don't know whether he was there any more than that, but I remember him coming that time, and I think there were other times, too. If he was in town, why, he got out to see Grandfather. I don't know how the friendship got started, but I do know it existed, anyway.

I was born November 21st, 1902. Right out here where the filling station is on Shields and Vine. That's where my folks lived. Where that serve yourself filling station is, over here. We lived there till I was about three years old. Then Dad bought the store at Laporte, and we moved out there. And that's where I lived until we were married, and went to school all 12 years.

And the post office was there, so Father was postmaster oh, up until about 1930. Early 1930's he finally gave it up. He didn't have too much in the store the last several years. The cement plant built a store in that area where the Laporte store is now. The cement plant built that, and if you worked at the cement plant, you had to do your trading at that store, you see. That just kind of pushed Dad's grocery business out. Which was all right. He was getting old enough that it was kind of hard for him to take care of it anymore. But he kept the post office for quite a while after he didn't have any groceries in there anymore. And finally then, that was moved up into the cement plant building, too. Our home was quite a gathering place for all the young people. It seemed like weekends we didn't know how many we would have. Maybe somebody that lived on a ranch, if there was something going on in the school or that they wanted to attend. So many mornings, Mother would get up and didn't know how many she'd have for breakfast.

We didn't take trips. We were just busy. Dad was busy in
the store, he couldn't leave. Then all we had was a horse and
buggy to get around. Well, we had a team. Dad had two horses.
And we didn't take any trips. Only just to go to Grandmother's
at Thanksgiving or Christmas, or something like that, you
know. One summer Dad rented a cabin a short way up the
Poudre. Fred Stearly had a sort of a little resort up there, and
he had four or five cabins. Mother and the children would go
up there, and on Saturday evening my dad would hitch up this
one black horse that he had. He had raced him some. He'd
drive up and spend Sundays up there with the family, and then
he'd come back down and be in the store by himself the rest
of the week. I guess he had to do his own cooking. I had never
thought much about it at that time, but he would have had to
have something to eat, you know. But I can remember doing
that. But most of the time we were just there at home, just
with the school activities and whatever. It was just all local.

We didn't have a whole lot of traffic then. The most
exciting thing, I guess, was when the stage came through every
day. They carried passengers, too, you know, and one thing I
remember: this old nigger mammy was going to Cherokee Park
to work at the resort there in the summer, and she had this
little baby. I don't know, it couldn't have been a year old. And
the baby was eating a great big red apple. Well, now to us, you
know, we didn't see many Negroes or anything, and we just
thought that was the cutest thing that we had seen for a long
time, was that nigger mammy and that baby.

One party that used to ride the stage a lot was Lady
Moon. She was quite a character. She lived at Log Cabin and
had a ranch up there. She lived here in town. She had a home
here in town, but she had the ranch up toward Red Feather,
off beyond Log Cabin. And she just went back and forth, you
know. But when she did that, she had to go on the stage. But
she was English. Had had beautiful clothes in her time. And
that's what she wore, on the stage. She'd have these beautiful
silk dresses and hats with big plumes on them, you know, and
she rode back and forth. She was quite a character that we all
remembered.

Each rancher had a mail sack with his name on it. And we had a counter, there in part of the store, where we'd spread those sacks out and sorted all of the mail that went into those sacks. And the mailman would deliver it. Then if they had mail to go out, he'd pick up the sacks as he came back, and stop and leave them. He stopped both ways. Cass Zimmerman drove the stage for a long, long time, and then finally the Scott boys took it over. Jess Scott drove it for years, too. I can't remember when they did away with the sacks.

People got quite a lot of letters. And some of them took like the local paper from Fort Collins, here, and the Kansas City Star was one that a lot of people took. And farm journals. Didn't anybody get a whole lot, but most everybody had something in their mail sack, it just seemed like.

After graduating from high school in 1921, I taught school for three years. My first year, I was out west of Tie Siding at—they called it Diamond Peak. I had children from two families and I taught that one summer. Then I went to Red Feather and I stayed with a family by the name of Wagner and they had one little girl. I just stayed in the home, and they had the school out in the bunkhouse. I was there two years. And then I got married.

Seems to me pay was $30 a month, and I paid $15 a month board. Finally, then, they begin to get a little bit more money in the district, and they got up to where some of the teachers would get $90 a month. That seemed like awfully big pay, you know, for a schoolteacher then.

To be a teacher, I just took an examination down here at the courthouse to teach just an elementary school. That qualified me. You had to pass those tests on English and history and arithmetic and the subjects that you would teach in elementary school.

You just took what was open. You could go to the courthouse and the county superintendent, and they would tell you what schools were open. Sometimes there just weren't any children anymore in that particular area. The family would move out and the children would grow up and leave.

Most of them were just ranchers, you know. And they didn't have very much. This first school that I taught at Tie Siding, there were four children. I wondered sometimes how they got by, because he didn't work out. They just had a garden, and they didn't even have any stock. I really don't know where he made his money. I don't know what he did. Didn't do much of anything. She took in washing and ironing and all those kinds of things. I know a few times when I would come home, which I didn't get to, very often—maybe I'd be five or six weeks in between times before I'd get to come home— usually when I did, why, she would have me, instead of paying her my board and room, take that money and buy some of the youngsters a pair of shoes or something that they were needing. I suppose that $15, $20, whatever they got was quite a help to them, you know. But I don't know how they lived. Actually, I wondered. And the Wagners at Red Feather, they were ranchers. They had cattle. They weren't well off, but they had money enough to get by. You know what I mean. They weren't really poor people like this one family was. I thought an awful lot of them. They were so good to me. But they just didn't have anything.

I had no desire to go on to school at all. I enjoyed the teaching and liked that, while I was at it, but I had no desire to go on to college. I never even thought about it. And, of course, then after I got married, why, my interest was all on the ranch and the family. One sister went on to college. My sister next younger than I. Her health hadn't been too good, and Dad felt that she should have a little something extra to fall back on in case she needed it. I think it was kind of hard for the folks to send her.

After teaching a couple of years, Norma was working for her dad in Laporte when she took a blind date with Walter.

That was probably about 1923, because we were married in December of 1924. I don't know just how long we went

together before we were married. Few months. But that's the
way I met him. Really, I shouldn't say I met him there because I
knew who he was before that. His dad and my dad, for that
matter, were friends in Rist Canyon, you see, when Dad was on
that ranch up there. And I knew who Walter was. His sister
lived in the old Doctor Wilkins house. She moved in there with
the youngsters to send them to high school at Laporte, and
Walter would be there. I'd see him around. But you know, he
was just somebody else. I just knew who he was, you know.

I had one more or less serious affair when I was in high
school. But all of a sudden that just blew up, and so that was
the end of that. I had lots of dates with different boys, of
course, going to school and things like that. There wasn't a
whole lot to do, only to go to town and go to the show, or
something like that. That would mean Fort Collins. And at that
time, of course, people begin to have cars, so we could go.
Dad used to let some of the boys take his little old car that we
had. If a bunch of us kids wanted to go to the show, and
nobody had a car, why, Dad would let him take his little old car.
One of the boys would drive it. And we'd go to the show.
Then after the show, why, we'd go and have a dish of ice cream
or something like that. That's all there was to do. Of course in
Laporte, there was the school activities that took up most
everything. And there was football and basketball. But really,
that was all, was just the school activities that took things up.
They had a building that was down south of Laporte, we called
the old Post-house. They had a big dance hall in it. We would
have high school dances down there. At one time I played
piano for them, some, and my mother used to play for the kids
to dance.

And there was a young man that played the violin and a
man to play the cornet. The three of us got together at one
time and practiced a little bit so that we could play for some of
the dances down there. So that was about the extent of the
entertainment. There just wasn't much else to do. End of the
school year we always had our school picnics. I notice the
schools don't do that too much anymore, but they'd either go
up the Poudre or up Rist or someplace. One of the boys that

went to school, Dave Daily, could always get his dad's team and a big old hayrack. That was before the time of cars. We'd go on our school picnics, on the hayrack. They used to have hayrack rides at night, too. They'd do that. That was another thing. I think Walter and I went on one of those. And that's about all there was to do.

The Great Depression appeared not to affect Norma's life materially, though she recalled her father having difficulty collecting accounts at this store, and his generous nature with his debtors.

We didn't feel that there was a Depression as far as we were concerned. We had plenty to eat and plenty to wear. And Dad seemed to do pretty well in the store. I think at that time he probably did lose a few charge accounts because if somebody came in with a hard luck story, they never left without at least a little piece of bacon and a sack of flour or something that they might need. Whether they could pay for it then or not. The majority of them came in time, when they got to where they could. But there were some, 'cause he had quite a charge account, you know, at that time. People didn't have very much money.

But as far as just the family was concerned, we didn't think anything about it. We had a garden and we had a milk cow and we had chickens, and as far as our food was concerned. . . . I guess one thing: if we needed a can of something, why, Mother just went out in the store and picked it off the shelf. We didn't have to put in a supply like people might have, that lived out farther, you know. But I know there was no money, as far as that goes, in the general area. People would trade or they would ask for a little credit. And someday, why, here'd they come in. They'd got a hold of a little money. Maybe it was only $5 but they'd come and pay it on their account. And that part, why, people did real well. I can't say that it really hurt Dad very much.

If a man gave you his word he was going to do something, you could depend on it. That's the way it would be. I think it was their pride. They took pride in saying I'll do so-

and-so and I'll do it. And people nowadays, it seems to me, have a different attitude about those things. They don't seem to care, in a lot of ways, about those things.

My dad gave the people credit. Yes, he did. But it was a different situation then. As we said a minute ago, most of the people then were honest. They wanted to pay their debts when they possibly could. If they needed a little help, why, they felt that they could ask for it and they usually got it. Most of them did. And I think a lot of it was their own pride. If somebody had a charge account with Father, and maybe the man died. Left the family, you know. He'd pull that out of where he kept all of those charge accounts, stick it in an envelope, and write on the outside, "Paid by God." And that was the end of it. If they came in and wanted to pay. . . . But he never would dun them. He'd never say a word to them. A lot of them did. They came in and paid. Paid what they could on it. One family I thought about. The girl and I went to high school together. They had a charge account there. Her dad was working all the time. But he wasn't as honest as he could be. She was working weekends, and in the summer like that. Of course girls, then, they didn't make hardly any money. But she was kind of doing house work and helping a little way that she could. I never will forget. She came in one time and gave Dad $5 and she said, "That's on our grocery account." "But," she said, "don't tell Dad I did it. Because then he'll just think—well, he don't have to try to pay it. Somebody else can pay it." But we knew she didn't have $5. She probably could have used it for herself, much better, but no sir. She thought Mr. Baxter should be paid. If he could. So here she comes with her little $5. Dad didn't want to accept it, you know, because he just felt that she needed it. But she was determined he was going to take it. So he did. He gave her dad credit for $5 on his grocery account.

He did use credit himself. He did. The companies that he bought groceries from and like that. I think it was on a 30 day basis, all of that. And of course through the Depression, the recession, of course. It was a little hard sometimes cause he felt that he had to pay them, you know. And some of these other bills were a little slow coming in. But he'd eventually get it done. But then he was on that 30 day basis and that's the way he wanted to keep it. He had to keep it that way. He didn't have to buy a whole lot at a time, you know, but a case or two of this. I suppose he'd buy quite a lot of flour at one time. And sugar. Sugar, you didn't have to put in. People just bought, mostly, at the store just small amounts. But certain times of the year there were people that wanted 100 pounds and he either had it or could get it for them. But flour, he laid in quite a supply of flour. Slab bacon. He sliced off whatever they wanted, or a chunk. Whatever they wanted, why, he'd cut it off for them.

Katie

Born in Missouri in 1902, Katie Worthan Davis came to Colorado after she married Ted Davis in 1920. They started in eastern Colorado, but eventually found their way to Salida, where Ted ranched a bit and worked as a butcher. They separated when their daughter came to Fort Collins to attend college, and Katie came with her, working as a waitress and bowling alley attendant until she turned 60 and started drawing Social Security. About that time she moved into a house trailer and half an acre in Bellvue, and lived there the rest of her life. She truly had a green thumb, and raised tomatoes, corn, cucumbers and other vegetables, as well as poppies and many other flowers. Many times she nursed sick or hurt animals and birds back to health, never hesitating to move them into her trailer with her. The summer after she and Ted married, they went on one of the last cattle drives from Colorado to Kansas.

We lived down east of Lamar. This uncle, he had a ranch out south of there, and he drove the cattle in to where we lived. Then we took them down east, to Lakin, Kansas, cross-country. I drove the wagon and they rode the horses. I don't know how far we got the first day. Not very far, I don't think. We'd camp at night, you know? Stake out the horses and fight the rattlesnakes and one thing and another. Then when we got east of Lamar, there, oh, quite a ways, we had to cross the Arkansas River. These old—I believe it was two mules they had on the wagon, I'm not sure, and they balked. They didn't want to go across that river. So they had to come back and get them, you know, 'cause they was ahead. They had to come back and get the horses across the river. Then from there we cut across country, kind of, to the northeast, I guess, to get into the west part of Kansas. I don't remember how many days it was. It took several days. Then we got to where they was going—this pasture. We stayed there a couple, or three days, I guess. I know his uncle, when he'd come to a rattlesnake, he'd kill it with his rope that he had to rope the—you know, if he wanted to rope a calf or something. He'd just whip it with that rope and kill it. They'd climb up on the wagon wheels, if you'd stop long enough. That's how thick they were. So when we got down there, at these people—their name was Gay. Don't know their first name. When we left, he had a lot of chickens, so she gave me quite a few eggs. When I got back to where we lived, I borrowed a setting hen and I set them and I raised those little chickens. I don't know just how long it took us. We were gone a week, I expect. Camped out, you know, and it was fun. But it was kind of hard sleeping on the ground, too. All we had was the bedroll, you know, to sleep on. But we was young. Didn't make any difference, I guess. As far as I know, that was the last cattle drive that went out of there. But it was fun. I get to thinking about it now. We did enjoy it. I did.

During the Depression, Katie and Ted were living at Salida. The game wardens there were understanding.

When we lived up there at Salida, the deer would come down and graze out in the pasture with the cows. And eat your hay. But we didn't mind, 'cause there wasn't maybe more than two or three of them, you know. But they'd come down there in the pasture and eat with the cows. Just wasn't a bit afraid. That's the only wild animals we had any trouble with. Once in a while we'd see an elk cutting across the pasture. Sometimes during the season they'd get shot at and they'd run, you know, and get on the wrong side of the Arkansas River. If they happened to get up behind our place during deer season, or shot at, or elk season, then you'd see them going back across the river. They'd go through our place, and head back to their herd.

Ted hunted. We always had deer. He'd always get a deer. It was about all we had for meat. So the game warden told him, he said, "Now we know you farmers feed these deer. Don't run out of meat." He said, "If you want to have meat—need meat—you go and get you a deer." "But," he said, "don't let any strangers in, 'cause," he said, "they're not entitled to them."

Edna

Edna McLennan Denham was born on a ranch near Albany, 45 miles west of Laramie. Second youngest of nine children, Edna grew up on the ranch and in Laramie, where she went to school. Her dad was a freighter who had been born in Scotland.

She and Art had been married more than 50 years when she recalled for an interviewer how they met, and what young married life was like. Rugged but fun, especially living on a mountain ranch.

A depot opened in Laramie. The old depot burned down. So they had to build a new one. And they had a big opening night. I went there, not with Art. With my sister, I guess. Everybody in town went to that depot. And Art was there, too. And he. . . . It was a dirty trick. I knew his girlfriend, or I had known her a lot more years than he had. They had a boy with them, and they wanted somebody to be a girlfriend of this boy. I didn't really want to, but I went. In the end, it turned out, why, here *I* am with him. He took her home first, that night. He had a car, and the other guy didn't, and he had to take us all home. And he left me to take home last, which was out of the way, but he did it that way. Wasn't my idea. And so that is when I met him. And then we were married in 1926. Came down here to Fort Collins and got married.

Then we worked. *He* worked. I don't think I worked too much, then. Well, I did when we went up into the northern part of Wyoming. I worked in a hotel. He went up there to work in some mines that some relatives that some of his folks had. And the mines weren't paying too well. Nice winter that winter. And so I went to work in this hotel. They had a big construction thing. They were building some irrigation ditches in there. And I cooked at the hotel. About then, why, they decided they wasn't making anything on the mines, and so everybody was laid off from the mines. While I was at the hotel there was a fellow strolled in, and he needed a man to work on a ranch. And I thought Art needed the job, so I got a hold of Art. See, this man that Art was replacing had been killed when they were rounding up cattle. The horse he was riding—its feet went out from under him and he hit the man's head on the ground hard enough that it killed him. They were coming back from the funeral, and they had to have a man to take this man's place.

So Art went to work up there. I stayed down, oh, for about a month. Then I went up there and they furnished us a log house. Two rooms. That was a little better. A two-room log house. We lived there I guess about a year. And that was a fun time because like in the spring, when he had to go up and fix fence to get ready for them to take the cattle up a little later, why, I would go up with him. Everything had to go up on pack horse. See, there's horses, horses, all my life. But I still don't want a horse. We packed everything in, on horseback, to take, you know, up there. Ahead of us there had been others, and they had packed in a little stove, and some lumber—I guess for beds. And built some tables out of just rough lumber. And our cabin, I got the biggest kick out of it. It set on a side hill, and you had to look, I guess, for a flat spot. It set on a side hill, so they dug holes up here and holes down here, so when it rained and come down off the hillside, it just went through in little streams, instead of just washing. . . . And I remember the bed was just a board frame outfit. They put just pine boughs, and then we had a bed on top of that. I guess there was a mattress. There must have been a mattress on top of them; it'd have been kind of stickery. And everything had to be kept in cans due to what the mice didn't get into, the chipmunks would. The deer and everything really were plentiful up there, so that I could go out and go to the edge of where the forest was thick, and there'd be these clearings out in the center, and there'd be deer eating, and all kinds of animals around, even bear.

And so we had a lot of fun up in there. We lived, you know, much different than you do now. You had outside facilities, and had your irons on the wood stove, and we'd go

after wood. Usually on Sundays we'd go get our wood. That'd
be a day he didn't work, and he'd take a team and wagon. Their
dog always stayed with us. It didn't stay at home. It stayed with
us. I don't know why, but it did. And it would go with us. And
the bobcats were so thick they'd keep that dog right under the
wagon all the time. He didn't dare get out or they would have
him.

One Sunday afternoon, we was laying down, and I heard
the dog barking and I got up, because the dog didn't bark
unless there was something to bark at. I had thought I'd like a
cat. He said, "Oh, Doyles have got a cat. You don't want one,"
or something to that effect. Anyhow, I didn't have a cat. And
he said they only had that one black cat. And I said, "I thought
you told me Doyles only had a black cat." He said, "Well, that's
all they got." I said, "Well, who does this pretty yellow one
belong to?" Why, Doyles didn't have a yellow one. I said, "Well,
there's one here." About that time, it come at the dog. At the
door was a big rock, probably oh, three feet square, or so. It
was pretty big. And the dog tumbled in, and that cat stopped
right on that rock. He said, "That's not a housecat, that's a lynx
cat!" And it was. It had the tassels on the ears.

Anyhow, why, it run away when Art opened the door and
let the dog in. And so, we'd send the dog after it and the cat
would wait until he'd get outside the gate. Then he'd chase the
dog right back. Art would open the door and the dog would
come in and the cat would stop. He done that about three
times, and Art said—we didn't even have a gun—and Art said,
"Well, I'll take the ax, and I'll go over and lay behind that bush
right at the gate." It had a pretty arbor over the top of it, at the
gate. So he said, "When I get the ax and lay down there, you
send the dog out after the cat. And when the cat chases the
dog back, I'll hit him with the ax." And so that's what we
thought we'd do. I sicked the dog on the cat and away he went.
But the cat jumped him before he ever got back to the gate.
Now, whether he sensed that Art was there, or what. . . . And
Art left the ax and run down there, and it scared the cat away

from the dog. And so we gave up on that. We couldn't do it that way. But that was how thick the cats—the bobcats and lynx cats—were around the ranch around at that time.

We were never sure whether it was that cats were fond of Mrs. Denham or the other way around. But while we were neighbors she always kept a crowd. For the mice, she would say. It was always a close call as to whether there were more mice or more cats around. Several times a year she would send Art over to the river with a bagful of new kittens to drown before they opened their eyes and captured her heart. One summer Sunday morning Art was working on his truck in their driveway. I saw him pause and catch sight of something in the road. Slowly walked out and stooped over, and peered down studiously. After a minute he reached down and took hold of something. He lifted, and up came a dead cat, stiff as a board and flat as a pancake, just like in the Tom and Jerry cartoons. Art held the carcass by the tail, resting its nose on the ground, and turned it slowly. "Well," I observed to Alice, "looks like Mrs. Denham is down to her last eight or ten cats."

If a rancher needed help, sometimes he would ask a neighbor for the loan of a good worker. That happened to Art. For Edna, it was a step up to a bigger house.

I don't know how come he went to work for Kline. Anyhow, why, he went to work for this neighbor. Kline needed some hired help and I guess Lee just let Art go to work for him because he had more men. And so he worked over there, and Kline had a large ranch, too. They would go out and feed the cattle every morning off the sleds. The snow would get so deep. And if we needed beef, Kline would just ride along with the men when they was feeding, shoot one, just put it on the sled and bring it in and dress it out. And then we would take part of it and they'd take part of it and then we'd have meat. A little different than nowadays. I don't remember too much, other than that was where we had our very first radio, was when we worked for Klines. That was between '26 and '29, because it was before Lee was born. So we had lots of company while we were up there for people coming, listening to the radio, because they were kind of rare. There weren't too

many up in that country. It was a Spartan. Darn near as long as
the coffee table there, and about—oh, 14 inches wide. And
then a great big round speaker set on top of it, and I don't
know how many batteries it took. It took some wet batteries
and some dry batteries. But we always kept the batteries up
because we liked it ourselves, and the neighbors all liked to
come and listen. And so we always had plenty of company
then. And at Klines' we had a larger house. I think it was the
old ranch house, and they built them a new house.

I used to do a lot of things for Mrs. Kline. We got more
from them, in a way, because there were so many things she
couldn't do and I would do, like churn the butter and so on,
and so, of course, then we got our butter furnished and
various things, taking care of different things for her. I think
her big problem was she couldn't see very well. And she didn't
talk above a whisper. Something was wrong with her throat, so
that she couldn't talk very well. But they were real nice people.
Some people thought they were crabby, but we got along with
them fine. They usually, you know, would board their own men
if they weren't married. But she wasn't really up to do the
cooking and so I boarded him for her. They must have had a
bunkhouse because he didn't sleep in the house where we
slept—where we lived. So they must have had a bunkhouse. I
don't remember it because I probably never was to it.

Our closest town was Manderson. It was only just a post
office and grocery store and a railroad depot. And that's about
all Manderson consisted of. And then Basin was a little larger.
It was about 10 or 12 miles on from Manderson. And Worland
was the opposite direction from Manderson. I think it was
about 20 miles from Manderson. So if you wanted to do much
shopping, you went to either Worland or Basin or Grable. Art
had, I guess, four head. Four broncs. We went to Manderson.
So it didn't take us long to get down there, but when he put
five ton of salt on that wagon to come back, and it started to
rain, that morning that we left. . . . See, we planned on spend-
ing the night. Well, they figured it'd take a day to get loaded, so
we was going to be gone three nights. And so he got his load
on and was all ready to leave the next morning, and I think he

had some problems with one starting ahead of another, and broke something and he had to get that fixed. When we finally got started, it was probably getting close to noon. The roads was getting slick and the mud would ball up on the wheels, until those horses were pretty well broke by that evening. We had to stay at a house. . . . Some bachelors'—the two Smith boys'—along the way. We stayed there for two or three days, till the rain stopped, because those horses could not pull that load through that mud any farther. I think when we started out the next time, again, those horses were pretty well broke by the time they got home.

So we had quite a time. I cooked for them. They had, you know, food to cook, and I cooked for them and the men played cards and this and that, and the other. We had to all stay in out of the rain. I think they only had a two-room house. I know we got the bedroom. Where they slept, I'm not sure, but they was always up when we got up in the morning.

Some people are like that. But not all people are. We'd pulled into one place about a half a mile back off that we knew had a big house. Art thought he could make arrangements for us to stay there. No. They couldn't have strangers in their home. The funny part of it was he had two daughters, about our age, or maybe a little older, visiting them out there. These girls took their car and was going to town. They had cars, for going to town and so on, then, but they didn't have trucks to do this other work with. And we, for some reason, happened to be going in that same day, and here they were stuck, with a flat tire. Two women. Had no more idea what to do than nothing. Why, I was for letting them sit there. "No," Art said, "We can't do that." I said, "They didn't take us in, and it was storming." But he was better-hearted. And so he stopped and fixed their tire for them. And that's the last I ever saw of any of them. Never give them another thought after that, because. . . . It takes all kind of people to make the world. It'd turn out. Everything'd turn out OK anyway. But these people were well off, and we knew that they had a large house. And here was these two bachelor brothers. Had two *rooms*. So that's the difference in people. . . .

Edna's view of religion was derived from her observation of people she knew who practiced, or didn't practice it.

I've always believed, pretty much. Art seems to do his best work on Sundays. He should have been a Seventh Day Adventist. I don't know. It seems like he always does think up the biggest jobs to start on Sunday. But I've always enjoyed going to church. I haven't too much lately. And, yet, they are getting more people going to churches than ever before. I actually believe they do have more. Most of the churches have more than they used to have. I do know the Catholics have changed an awful lot about their nuns, and what do they call them—priests. And I think now, they're kind of going back again. You hear that they shouldn't be doing this and they shouldn't be doing that. And I went in the Mormon Church, a couple of years ago. Because they had an outlook that I thought seemed more real, and yet promised more, if you lived right. If you lived by it. And they definitely do not believe you can go out and do whatever you want and then have your sins forgiven, and all. Of course, it does say that the Father will forgive you. But, you're not supposed to keep repeating it and expecting Him to keep doing it. They don't believe that way. They believe more in trying to live a more religious life. At least as they see it. Maybe not as other people see it.

But there aren't any polygamists in the church anymore. And there was. But they said there was a reason for it. 'Cause so many of the men were killed. There were all these women had to be taken care of, and these men would take care of their own wives and their brother's wife and so on, that had been killed. So, the way I figure it, that really wasn't my business, now. And however they lived then, I know what they did. Because I knew families . . . . See, Art was in construction work. We were in Ft. Bridger, Wyoming. It wasn't too far out of Evanston. About 45 miles east of Evanston. And in that settlement, around there between Limon and Mountainview, I met ever so many women that were half-sisters, half-brothers and so on. Their fathers had homes, complete homes, for each wife. And these families was each raised in their own homes, and the man could have as many wives as he could support. I guess that was way back years ago, because the women was, a lot of them, about my age or a little older. You couldn't ask to meet nicer people. And I wasn't a Mormon, then, and so they wasn't being nice just because I was a Mormon. I wasn't. So they treated each other very well, and you know, half-sisters and half-sisters and half-brothers—it was very confusing. So you didn't say a word against any of them, because you didn't know—you might be talking about the brother or the sister. And besides, it's not nice to talk about anyone, anyway. But there, it would have been bad to have. We had a lot of fun, and we lived there visiting with the. . . . Of course I visited more, because Art didn't have time. The men, they didn't—you know, they worked. They put in a day's work and was ready for bed at night. But the women, we had the days to put in and maybe we'd all go to this town and that town and have dinner, do our shopping and such, and we had a lot of fun that way.

III.

Mountain Folk

Rist Canyon is one of three canyons leading west from Fort Collins into the mountains. Buckhorn Canyon is the southernmost and also the narrowest, leading up past Crystal Mountain to Pingree Park, where Colorado State University has its College of Natural Resources mountain campus and conference center. Poudre Canyon is the northernmost and most famous, with the scenic Cache La Poudre River that eventually flows into the Platte and thence to the Missouri. Until well into the 20th century, though, Poudre Canyon's steep rocky sides at such places as the Lower Narrows and Upper Narrows prevented easy access all the way up the river, and road construction had to await massive public works projects such as those facilitated by the Great Depression of the 1930s.

In the latter 19th century, trade between northern Colorado's Front Range towns and the North Park area to the west followed a path that went north from Fort Collins up to

Tie Siding, just across the Wyoming border. From there, draymen hauled to Walden and on to Steamboat Springs.

For years, Rist Canyon provided the best entrée from Fort Collins into the mountains, though the canyon itself did not really go anywhere except up into semi-wilderness. That was fine with some folks. There was good hunting, good logging, and not a lot of neighbors to get on the nerves.

Stoic

*He had been born in 1889, and by the time of his interview he was
so far from his parents that he could no longer recall how they came
to Colorado, or why. He knew they had started for Idaho, but when
they reached Larimer County there was Indian trouble in the west,
and they decided to settle around Bellvue. His memory was still
excellent in other respects, especially concerning his early working
years. And though his fingers were stiff from age and labor, he could
be coaxed to play a dance or two on his old fiddle, which he had
taught himself to play 70 years before. His full name was Oliver
Jasper Burgess, but to everyone in Cache La Poudre Grange No.
454, he was Jap. Among the old-timers, his father was remembered
as a prospector. Jap, too, tried his hand. Even in his 90s, he
remained close-mouthed about just where he had looked.*

He got enough, I guess, to get by on. A little gold. Not
much. Find it panning, you know? Get it off and beat it up real
fine, and then pan it, and get the gold out of it that way. A lot
of it, he had to burn. With that placer gold, you don't have to
do that. Course you can always retort that, catch any quicksil-
ver, retort it, and use it that way.

Did you ever do prospecting?

Oh, yeah.

Where did you prospect?

Well, all over. It's real, real worthless, unless there's
uranium, up there in Wyoming. I was up there and looked all
over the mountains and one thing and another up there, and
we done a little digging on a couple of places.

*Do you remember about how old you were when you were doing that
prospecting? A young man?*

I don't know. I always was great for looking at different rocks, you know, and things, anyhow. I think the richest mine they ever found was somebody just picked up a rock, you know, and followed up the placer and down the hill. They followed it up till they come to where it rolled from. It's pretty interesting. I always liked it.

Dad, he farmed, and he done a lot of blacksmith work down here. And then we moved up to Stout stone quarries up at Stout. He was a blacksmith up there, with workers up there. That's quite a sight to see. If you was up there, you can see them big long quarries clear along the mountain. You can see rock dumps all the way along. It was quite a place.

We always had to walk to school, you know. That was down in Spring Canyon. They call it Stout, now. Stout used to be up there right at the end of the railroad And that's where the big quarries is. You see the little quarries from there on down this way, north, but they're right by then what they call Stout, there. That's Spring Canyon. Spring Canyon School is where I went, while we was up there I forget just how many years we was up there. I know after the quarry shut down, we stayed there a long time. And they hauled rock from there out to these reservoirs. Several teams'd haul them. I don't remember just where we moved to from there. I think we moved down to the old Akin place, up on the mouth of Rist Canyon there. He worked on the Greeley Basin there. They were just building that basin. He worked there a long time. I don't know, when they had a job over there anytime, he wanted to work.

We had one man teacher. His name was Henry George. I ought to remember his name. 'Cause we didn't like him. The kids—any of the kids didn't like him. He didn't stay. I don't think he stayed the whole year. Seems to me like they got another teacher in. Let him go. My first year in school I was up at Rist Canyon. And then we moved out down here, and I went to what they call the Number 10 School. That's out there at the four corners. As you go to town, you know, you come to them four corners out there on—I don't know—I forget the name of the blooming streets and roads. I went there a year, anyhow, and then he had a job up there to Stout and we moved up there.

My oldest brother, Carlisle, he's dead now, we went off to work. And that ended my school. I went down and weeded beets for Franz. He was in down along Spring Canyon Road. That's when we still lived at Stout. And we left there. We didn't like that. Had to crawl on your hands and knees all the time, in along the rows, you know, and everything. Thin them. And leave a beet in each place you know. It was quite a job. And when I left there, went down to the college and got a job to thin beets there. I think I only worked there one day. Had enough of that. We done a lot of thrashing. Elmo Willis had a thrashing outfit. I done a lot of thrashing there, and hauling water and stuff that way. That was always a good job. Sometimes take you a little over a month. Sometimes pretty near two months. Get over the whole country. We thrashed a lot of ground that ain't even farmed, nowadays.

I was up in Montana for three years. I found a logging camp, up there. We cut logs. Had to cut with a sawing number, and they wasn't payin' very much. A thousand foot logs, you know. And we stayed there, I and Carlisle, and cut logs for a while. Then I went filing saws, and then he had to saw alone. He didn't like that, so we pulled out. Filing saws was a good job. All of us come to timber, then. They like me to file their saws, they just paid that out of their pockets, you know? Made a whole lot more than both of us made, cutting timber.

We left there and went down to Darby, Montana. That's where we left our outfit when we was traveling through. And we got a job cutting logs for Chet Logan down below Darby, there, on the big south hill side, and we cut there all winter. Stayed there all winter. We kind of made our home there at Nicholsons' there, and they'd fix our lunch and everything, and we'd go and work. Chet, he and two other fellows, Bob Nicholson and Cass Nicholson, they worked up there, too. But Chet, he had his team up there, and he dragged the logs down to the river bank. When we got the hillside all cut off and the water came up in the river, why, we just turned them logs down the river. Had a crewman down there, and we used to pull them out. Had a little donkey engine there. A steam engine that pulled the logs out of the river there, with that. And we'd just pull them up on the chute there. Had a board in there at the end, and when a log came up and hit the end of the board. that was in there kind of cross-ways, you know, like that the end of the log hit that, I'd just turn it over that way, and it'd just roll off down. Had a big grey team there, piling them. And they'd just hook on to them and pile them. And they really had them up there, high as this house. Logs piled up all the way along that railroad track. Just switch where it come off the railroad track. We got that all done. They hauled in logs. Train dumped them down at Hamilton, Montana. I forget just how far that was. About 20 miles below Darby. We worked there a little bit and then we pulled out and went to Butte, Montana.

There wasn't no work, then, so we went to a garage there, and thought we'd get a job at a garage. They said, yes, they'd give us a job there, as mechanics. And they wanted 30 dollars. Pay them 30 dollars for us to go to work. We said we didn't have no 30 dollars. "Well, you go ahead and work." So we went ahead and worked in there. We done all that. Had to do all the fixing and cleaning up and everything. Sometimes we worked way overtime, and all they done, them two fellows that run that garage, all they done was set back there in what they called their office, and smoked cigars and talked and visited with the people coming in, you know. They'd come in with a car or something that had to be fixed, they'd just send them down there to us, and we'd fix it. I think we was there two months, at that garage. And we figured we knew just all about them doggone cars, and we just quit. An old man come in with a Model T—two-seated Model-T—and he been having trouble with it, and he said he had trouble with the oil in it. Wouldn't hold oil. Magneto's always getting . . . . You know how they was. Getting little stuff all over the bands that you pressed on, you know, with your feet. Had a lot of real fine copper stuff that'd get on the magneto and on the point of the plug, you see, where you couldn't. . . . It just quit. So we knew all about

that. We fixed that, all right, when they come in, and he sold us
that car for 25 dollars. We got in there and we hit the hike.

Went back up to Darby. Worked there. I picked apples up
there then for T-Land Orchard Company, they called it. Big
Bench. It trimmed up above us. Just kind of a big flat place up
on the mountains, all the way along. We picked apples up there
for them that had that big orchard in there. We worked in there
for a long time. Then they was wanting men over there at
Anaconda, Montana.

Most of the mines was over at Butte. But they had trees
that was all burned and smelled and everything, and we worked
there. They paid pretty good over there. That is, they paid
more money than we'd been getting around at other places. We
stayed there, well, just about half a year. Carlisle, he had to
leave before. He got scared out. A fellow washing his hands
got into a belt, and slipped and fell. Tore one leg about off.
They had to put another leg on him. That Anaconda's a big
place. Just big brick buildings you work in. He had a big
building there, and I had a big building. Oh, it was down about
from here to the old store down there (about 200 yards), from
where he was, but when that fellow that got into the belt he
just. . . . Our electricity all run over our heads, you know, and
they had roofs hanging down for each motor. When he
jumped in there, he couldn't do nothing then, he just jumped
on that cord, and shut the whole plant down. Course
everybody's running, there, and we didn't know what they shut
down for. Everything's all right down to our plant, and we
were shut down.

Pretty soon, why, the big man got up there and they got
things started again, you know. Well, I really didn't know what
had happened, till I seen Carlisle that night. So he just quit and
come home. Everything got to tasting sweet to him, you know.
So much arsenic in the air. You take the grounds, there, there's
no grass, no trees, or nothing. The ground's just bare, there's so
much arsenic. Got everything killed off. And the old men that's
been there for a year or more, they just break out in big scabs
all over them, you know? So, I stayed there a month, maybe

two months after Carlisle left. Everything got to tasting sweet to me, and oh, I just thought I better quit. So I quit. They didn't want me to quit at all. They offered me more money and offered me a better job, and everything. Nope. I told them I was coming home.

I think that was 1912, when I come home from Montana. And, my golly. They sent letters down there. Some of the big guys, and then the fellow that was running the plant where I was, he just wanted. . . . He almost cried when I left. I had to give it up. Was a good job, and all I had to do was put the oil in, and looking after two big ore mills, and do the oiling. I'd liked to have stayed 'cause I knew I wouldn't get that here. Too much arsenic. I knew I was getting too much. That stuff was a kind of a slum, the building I worked in. They had a lot of big buildings go clear along, and had that all filled with stuff that's been shipped in, and all, and they had men working all along on that.

The men that haul that hose, you know, working that stuff out, and down, they drop it down on these big conveyer belts. They'd run a horse and mule across the road there to them big belts, and then they had two big mills in there. They had to put them big boulders in them mills, and big iron balls, and things that way, to grind this. This mill was there, all the time turning, grinding this all up fine. Then when it got fine enough, why, that was run out and over to another plant. I was never over to that other plant. I don't know just what they done there.

They'd get that, they'd leave. Them that stayed was all broke out, you know, and big sores on them. They get that in their system, you know, and . . . sores. That killed trees and everything, that arsenic. It was hard times, you know. Lots of people come that didn't stay long, and a lot of them come that wanted to stay, but they couldn't. They'd leave, and them that did stay, they just—they looked like old men. There wasn't so many old men, but they looked like old men. They was just broke out and stuff. I think some of them fellows, I believe, stayed there till they died. I know I didn't want any of it. I

learnt a lot about the ore and stuff like that while I was there.
My job wasn't a hard job. It was just to oil them stuff. They
had an elevator on the mill, from the mill up to where they'd
run out and unload into the other building. I was up there on
that elevator most of the time. Don't take no time to oil it, you
know.

*A few years later, World War I started. When the U.S. went in, Jap
was drafted. After his training, he was sent to France.*

I joined the Third Division, over there. I was a replace-
ment, you see. When we got over there, why they'd take a
whole bunch of us, you know, that had been drafted and come
in. They take them and sign them over to another company. I
was in the Third Division, and I stayed with that the whole
time I was over there. They lost my record. On the first night,
we went up on the front from France, there, and the lieutenant
or whoever took us up there, I suppose, had all the papers and
things. I don't know. But anyhow, we just got up there and the
big bombs—big shells and things—was dropping. We come to
a hole, where one of them bombs or something blew out a
hole there, about—oh, 10 feet around and down about four
feet. Whoever was along, they said, "Jump in there. Jump in
that hole." And we jumped in the hole and we stayed there. I
don't know where the others ever went to, from there. And, by
Jack, here comes the captain with a whole bunch of men. He
says, "Get out of there and come on. Get out of that hole and
come on." We got out of the hole and went on. I don't know
where the outfit that was taking us up there, I don't know
where they went. But we went up with him, and his bunch. I
think there was 28 men, was all he had left. They stayed with
us. Just a squad. And so, we went with them, then.

We went back down around into France. I guess that was
France, where we was. We went down in there with him, and
we stayed with him till we got down there. They claimed the
war was over. I didn't have to do any fighting. Oh, I done a lot
of shooting and things like that, afterwards, just in practice,
you know. We went down there, and we stayed over one day
there in France, and then we started out in the big hike into

Germany. We hiked all the way in there. The German army was
ahead of us about a mile. We could see them marching along,
you know, as we'd go over a little raise, or something. We could
see them. We got in there, and went over and hit the Rhine
River. Went down on the Rhine River too close to Koblenz.
Billeted there on the Platte. They called it "Plat." "Plate," or
"Plat," I've heard it called both. We billeted there, in German
buildings. Our squad just kept together all the time. Where we
stayed was all in that one building. There was two schoolteachers stayed there, and an old German one. I guess her husband
was killed, and she was keeping these schoolteachers. We
stayed upstairs, and they was all dirt floors. Nice buildings.
Solid and everything, but they all had dirt floors.

And the stairs run up pretty steep, from outside. One of
the boys that was with us could talk a little German. He'd
studied a little German. He could talk to them teachers and
things, as they'd come or went to teach. We went to roll call
every morning. He didn't know us. That old guy—can't think
of his name—was a rough talker. He'd just swear to beat the
band. One morning, the sergeant come down. We'd been
standing every morning, and we'd answer the call as they called
out the names, you know. Our names wasn't called out, and we
stood there. And finally one morning the lieutenant come
down with the sergeant. They had roll call, and they called up
to us. The lieutenant, he just walked over there and he had a
paper in his hands and he wrote down the names of the eight
of us that was there. And he told me, he says, "Quick as you
eat your breakfast," we had a call before breakfast, you know—
"Quick as you eat your breakfast, you go up and see. . . ." The
main officer. I don't know what they call him, now. I said,
"OK." He said, "One at a time."

So the rest of the squad didn't want to go first; they sent
me. I went up there. I thought: by golly, I'll get a cussing out.
We'd been with them the whole way. Into Germany, from
France, and on the hike. We'd been in there, and done some
drilling and everything, after we got all the way into Germany
and everything, and they didn't know who we was. They
supposed we was army men, in there with the rest of them. He

got up there and shake hands, and he wanted to know why we didn't turn in before. I told him why, and just the way it was. He jumped up and he says, "By God!" he says, "I remember that." He said, "I remember coming by and telling you fellas to get out of that hole."

"Yeah," I said, "we're the eight that was in that hole." I said, "We just come out." And by golly, he said, "I don't know what to do." He said, "I ain't got your papers or nothing. They're lost. I know they're lost," he says. "It's all we can do. . ." He says, "You don't have to drill. You don't have to do nothing. You don't have a thing to do. Nothing on you at all. I'd advise you to drill, and all, and keep up your strength, and keep healthy."

I thanked him for that. So that's the way we worked it. And, about a month after that, he told the sergeant to have me come up. I went up to him, and he wanted to know if I knew who it was that fetched me up on the hill, there, where we fell in that hole. I told him I didn't know him at all. I didn't know any of the men. I said just the eight of us was together, when we fell in there, and we just stayed together. And we stayed together all during the war. All eight of us. I didn't like none of them. And the Germans, while we was there, they were pretty good to us.

We was in Germany a little over a year. About a year and a half. And then the other outfits was leaving, and coming back across, so they told us we could come one time on one of their trips. Big boats. Them big boats'd haul lots of men. Boy, they crowded us on there.

He fixed our records, I guess. Because we had papers. I didn't know what they was. He just gave them to us when we got into New York. I guess it was New York. I got in there, he just give us some papers. "Now," he says, "You can catch your train home." And we stayed there that night, and early the next morning we caught trains out from the depot and my train come to Cheyenne. I was sent to Cheyenne—I had to report there.

There was a fellow there met the train that took me right up to the headquarters, there, and they discharged me there, in Cheyenne. We went down, after we went to the depot, and found out when I'd get down to Collins. They said the train left there next morning, early. So I had to stay there all night. So I just stayed around in the depot, I and two other fellows. We just stayed in the depot. There was trains coming in, once in a while, you know, going through and all, and a restaurant just across the street from us, and we just went in there and eat, and we stayed all night in there. I come to Collins, and I don't know where them other fellows went. I never seen them since, either. Now I got home, and I come out there where my sister lived on Laporte Avenue. They called up home. Dad lived up on the old Akin place, then, up in Poudre Canyon, across this river there, on this side. They come down and got me. I didn't have much. You might say a kind of a pack of stuff that I had.

Oh, gosh, I was glad to get home. But then I looked around quite a while before I got any work. Well, the last work that I done around here is I worked for the county about three years. I worked on the tractor and grader. Some days we'd have to load trucks. We load that by hand, then. We got where that sand and gravel is, see, like it's all kind of caked in. Have a pick, pick that down and then shovel that into them big trucks, them dump trucks. Way up there, about that high, shoveling into them. That was hard work.

With his brother Edgar, Jap tried coal mining in Wyoming. It was dangerous work, there were problems between labor and management, he could not understand the language spoken by his fellow workers, and in time he grew afraid.

When I come out of the mine, why, they wanted me to go up on the top and weigh the coal. They had a company man up there, and I was a union man, and I just knew that it was dangerous in that mine, there, and I wasn't going to stay in there any longer. I come to quit. I and Edgar, my brother, was working there at Hudson, Wyoming. I was going to quit, and he said, "I think we both might as well quit—I don't like this very good. . . ." Oh, it was bigger than that clock, there. Just a great big slab, fell down. We knew that was loose. It had prop under it, out it'd worked itself around, somehow or another, and it'd gone and tipped over enough, you see, that they slipped. The props slipped out, down, and let that come down. And the last of the coal mining I done was right there then.

The company wanted me to go up there and check on them fellows. They'd load their cars way up high, you know, and big chunks and things, and come up the slope. Pretty steep slope. The tracks was a little rough. Why, some of them chunks would roll off, you know, and they knew about what they'd weigh, the men that loaded that car. They'd come, and they'd get awful mad. You couldn't make them understand, some of them. You couldn't make them understand nothing. They didn't like it, but if you couldn't help it, you know. . . . And I and that company man was up there, weighing the cars. All the weights were all about the same, and there wasn't no difference on that. It's an old building they had there. They'd got a place where you go down and put their tags on. Had them little round tags—the weights and things—and take them down there, and put the weight down. What it weighed that day. But I got along all right. I got along with all of them all right. Some of them were jabbering. I didn't know what they were saying, but it didn't matter to me.

I kind of got scared out on the lightning. We was way up in the air there, and there's days that the sun would be shining nice and the lightning come through there, come up the rails. And everywhere where the rails'd join together, you know, it'd just crack and pop, all the way up along and across the scales and everything. I got tired of that and I left. Got down and left that. Quit that.

Oh, they were quarreling and fighting, I think nearly all the time, up there. I never associated with any of them. I got along good every place I went.

Wanted work, and we just wanted to work where we could get a job. My dad moved up to Wheatland one year. I worked up there. Old Judge Carey . . . on a big ranch that he had up there at Wheatland. Just a mile square. I irrigated there, and we hayed and we done everything there. Stayed there a little over a year and got 30 dollars a month, there.

I made quite a little, just playing for dances around the country. But, it went just for clothes, and things, you know, and eats. I was never much of a hand to go to a show, or anything, that way.

Elmer, my brother, he had a homestead up on Bluestone, and I think I was 15, maybe 16 years old, and his wife played violin. And I went up, helped him fence that. He had the whole place—a homestead, you know, and I went up and helped him fence all of that and everything. He had just a little log cabin. At night, I had a little fiddle. She'd tune that fiddle up for me, and I'd sit around there and play. I wasn't playing any tune. I was just sawing away, but sometimes a tune'd kind of strike me and I'd happen to hit the right string and the note and, why, I'd kind of follow that out. And I'd set there and follow that out, and that's the way I got started

I've done lots of playing, in Wyoming, and Montana, and here. I don't know one note from another., I just really didn't know them, but I'd hear a sound, you know, that I'd kind of remember. And if I'd happen to hit a note that sounded just like some of the songs I'd heard or something, why, I'd follow that tune right on through.

There wasn't nothing to save. I went over to Coalmont. That's over in North Park. I done a little work there. Didn't do no mining, but I cleaned up along the track and things, down when I first got there. Then, first time they had a chance for me to do something else, why, they put me on that. Wilbur Moore was the boss, and old L.C. Moore, I think he and the First National Bank owned the mines there. I stayed there. Well, I saved about $500, I think, while I was there at that mine. That mine there. And after a while they put me on firing

the boilers. They had to have water down in the mines at night
to keep the water down for the men the next day to work, and
all. I fired boilers there. Two big boilers. The engine rooms was
right off from the boilers there, just. . . . I could talk to him,
you know, and it wasn't bad. Turn the steam down the mine,
whenever they'd call up from down there. In the daytime, or at
night, if I was there, why, I just turned the steam down to
them to start the big pumps down there in the mine. And
then—when I was through firing boilers, they put me on the
big hoist, there. Stood up about that high. A big hoist. They
had a shaft down, in the mine, 100 feet. And then they run
from that shaft, down, you see, on down the way the coal
pitched. Trucking it way down in there. I worked there for a
while on that.

I got hurt in that mine. I was riding the cars down, you
know, up from where they were mining up to the shaft. And
then the cars were loaded on this cage. They pulled that up to
the top, there, and a fellow run up below there. He'd send that
car down to the track and dump the coal back to the railroad
cars, and come back up. He'd send a car down to where it'd be
loaded again. That was all. That was work. I didn't like that at
all. Had a little fellow by the name of Buck Buchanan. He
done the caging. It was a fright, there, in the wintertime. Cold,
snow blowing. I was on the hoist there. I stayed right with that
till they shut the mine down. That's the Number Two mine I
was on. The Number One mine was about a mile south from
Number Two. They're all shut down, now. They were all on
fire. The inspector come in there on the Number Two mine,
and I guess a little smoke was coming through the seams, or
something in the coal. He come in there, and he told me that
they had to shut down, so they shut down. I come home, then.
I was up there about three years, I think.

When I was saw-milling, there was about 20 years that I
missed out here, in Bellvue. I was in the mountains all the time.
It had never been lumbered, where I was. I had a 50-inch saw
on some of them big trees. And then it wouldn't go through
till I got the first slab off. It'd take the first slab off, and then I
could turn that.

I got the mill before I built the house. And I had it down there in the pasture. And I squared up on my logs there. I had a little black burro. I went up to Deadman and got my logs cut, and I took that little burro up there and he drug them all out for me. I got some up on the old Flowers Road. I had an old Dodge. Old Dodge pickup. Little burro, he ride right in there. And he liked that. He'd just jump right in there, no trouble atall. And he'd drag out one log at a time. And, got them all piled, and then I went to work and made me a trailer out of a Model T axle and wheels, and it went on back of the old Dodge. I fixed a bolster on the back of the Dodge, you know, see, for turning with a load on, and I got them hauled down, I think I got them all in two trips. I think it was 60-some. They're all in the house. This was all white pine logs. That was up in Deadman. They was mostly eight inches thick. I cut them down to six inches. Probably a little more than eight inches, some of them. But just so long as I could take a slab off of each side, why, I didn't care if they wasn't over that wide. Because I figured on setting them flat sides all together. The big timber that I cut was in Dad's Gulch. Up Poudre Canyon. And that was all yellow pine. Up at Long Draw it was all white pine. When I first started to saw, they wouldn't sell me the green timber. I had to get the dry timber. After that, then, I had to pay stumpage. The ranger come in and make a mark on each tree round he wanted me to cut.

When I was sawing, I always had a helper. A fellow from up in Wyoming, there, Buster Curtis. Buster, he went to work with me, up there when I was in Dad's Gulch. I was in there seven years. And he's the stoutest man I ever seen.

I had a 48-inch saw and a 50. That smaller timber, I used the 48 all the time. Smaller timber, why I didn't need the big saw on that. They just come in after it. I couldn't deliver it. I didn't have no way of delivering it to them. And a Fort Morgan outfit down there wanted a bunch of poles. And Elmer, he was helping me then. He had his team up there in Wyoming. I got—I forget how many—100 poles he wanted down. He sent a bunch of boys up there to cut these poles, and I and Elmer drug them in, with his team. They cut them and piled oh, six or eight in a pile, you know. And Elmer'd just go throw his chain around them and drag them in, where they could get them.

That was in the late '30's and '40's. That's when I built this house. And I'd been working for the county before that. I worked three years for them. Then they sent me up Poudre Canyon and around on the road and one thing and another and that WPA. The last of that was from Stove Prairie Landing up to Stove Prairie.

I got my right eye put out, while I was up on a log, trimming it, cutting the limbs off. There was a big limb on there about that big around, and I was chopping that off, and when I felled the tree, it went over across some big rocks and (they) held it up about 10 feet from the ground. That is, the top of it and all. I was way about at the middle of it, and I was chopping in on that, and I had a big, kind of a frozen chip, oh, about that wide, where I chopped down in there, and I just couldn't get that chip out. I was hacking away at it, hacking away and I finally just. . . . I was standing up on the top of the log and I hit it just my best. I just slammed in there. I thought I'd break the handle off the ax or something before I get that out of there. And heck, that come out of there and hit me right square in the eye. I fell off that log and Osie Campeau was doing the skidding for me then, and that was up Skin Gulch. He was just coming up with his team. He seen me fall off that log. He just tied up his team and beat it right on up there, and I was sitting there pulling my head, and he thought we'd better go down. So we went down to the cabin. We met the ranger coming up and went down to the cabin. Helen got dinner for us and all. I decided I didn't need any doctor for that eye. I stayed up there about two weeks, worked right along every day. Come down here and they wanted me to go down and see the doctors about my eye. I went down there. They monkeyed around a little over a month. I had to stay down there working on what I could. They wouldn't do nothing to my eye. My other eye, they's trying to cure—try to keep it from catching something from this eye, I guess, I don't know.

It just pulverized it. My right eye. I still got the eye, but it's—can't see nothing out of it. When the doctors looked at it they said, "You won't see out of *that* eye anymore." It was just all pulverized. But I can see just a little bit of light out of this corner of my eye when something bright goes by or something like that. I can see just a little bit out of the corner there. But I can't tell what it was, or nothing.

Paul Millington

*Harmony, Colorado, was one of those utopian settlements of the
19th century whose reach exceeded its grasp. Horace Greeley is said
to have visited it during a trip to his namesake city 25 miles east of
Fort Collins, but it has long since vanished as a viable community.
Today it is memorialized chiefly by the east-west thoroughfare bearing
its name in south Fort Collins.*

*Paul Millington was born in Harmony in 1898. When he was three
his family gave up on Harmony and moved to Laporte, six miles
northwest of Fort Collins. During the next eight decades he grew to
manhood, learned to work, went to country dances, labored with his
brother (also a lifelong bachelor), took care of his mothers, nieces and
nephews and eventually went into a rest home, all within a radius of
less than a dozen miles from Laporte. His earliest memories were of
the farm his father bought at Laporte.*

There was about 40 acres of that place and he farmed
that and worked for Asbury Riddle. Asbury Riddle owned the
place that's the Hawkeye place now. He fed sheep there, and
my father worked for him after he'd done his own work. Then
we left Laporte and come to Bellvue, the first farm on the
north side of the road west of Bellvue. And at that time that
place was known as the John Rutherford place. My father
bought that from John Rutherford. He farmed that. And most
of it was in alfalfa. He raised some corn, and we had our own
milk cows and raised garden stuff. It had a big water right, and
we had plenty of water for the whole place. At that time, the
timber haulers bought hay from the farmers, and there was
quite a lot of beets raised around Bellvue. The railroad track
come as far as straight east of Bellvue, and people hauled their
sugar beets there with team and wagon and loaded them on
the freight cars, and they was shipped to the Fort Collins sugar
factory. Also, they was digging limestone at Ingleside, and the

freighters hauled limestone down to Bellvue and loaded it on
the freight cars there. As they went further north digging
limestone, why, they run the railroad from Bellvue on up to
Ingleside. And then they loaded the limestone there.

Ernest was the second brother. Ernest Millington. And
he was younger than my other brother and sister. And we lost
him while we lived in Laporte. He was around nine years old.
We had a big rain and a hail storm, and he got out and waded
in the water that was along the road and it had hailed and that
ice water—he took pneumonia and died 'fore we hardly knew
that he was sick.

Not long after Ernest died, the family moved to Bellvue, where Paul,
his sister and other brother went to a school with one teacher who
taught eight grades to 40 students. After two years, they moved
again. Paul continued to attend country schools until he finally quit
at the age of 15, by which time he had completed the third grade.
His neighbors and relatives always considered him, despite his lack of
schooling, extremely intelligent and shrewd.

My father sold that place to Jud Briggs. And then he
went up Rist Canyon to Buckhorn Mountain, and he bought
160 up there from William Lass. And homesteaded 160. Then
we moved up there, and my father had a few cattle. And we
raised potatoes, planted grain and cut it for hay. We raised quite
a lot of garden stuff. He had about 25 head of cattle, and he'd
have some cattle to sell every year. Well, he only lived a couple
of years and got appendicitis, and before we got him to the
hospital, his appendix broke and he passed away. My mother
and brother and sister, we stayed right on the homestead. My
mother proved up on it, and we owned it till just a few years
ago.

The Stove Prairie school district was a big one. They
divided that in four. And they had the school of Stove Prairie
and a school on the Buckhorn and a school on the Redstone
and a school up there on Buckhorn Mountain. I went to that
school, then, for a few years. And the whole neighborhood
used to get together at the schoolhouses for parties.

Christmastime they'd have a Christmas tree there, and the whole neighborhood would get together for their neighborhood parties at the schoolhouses and they'd have dances at the schoolhouse. They would generally change each year and have the Christmas program at Stove Prairie one year and Buckhorn Schoolhouse the next year and Redstone Schoolhouse the next year, and then the school up there on Buckhorn Mountain would have the Christmas program.

And the first few years that we was up on Buckhorn Mountain when we wanted the mail, we come to Bellvue for it. Then Fred Briggs got the mail route started up Rist Canyon and over Stove Prairie Hill and down the Buckhorn to Masonville and back over and down the glade where the Horsetooth Reservoir is now. So we had mail three times a week then. And we thought that was something to have mail three times a week. Most people come down once a week for their mail, and there would be people in different parts of the country that would take the mail for four or five families. Each one would take their turn coming down for the mail and get the mail for four or five families in their part of the neighborhood.

The Millington brothers missed World War I. Paul was needed at home and his brother had been crippled when a neighbor shot him during a dispute over a fence line.

Him and a neighbor got in an argument over the line fence, and the neighbor shot him in the hip and he was crippled from-then on. The county surveyor surveyed it, and the neighbor put the fence up further north than the county surveyor. That leg was two inches and a half shorter from-then on. Got the doctor up there, and he took him in a spring wagon to the hospital. His leg, then, was two inches and a half shorter, but he got so he done quite a bit of work. Raised quite a few cattle.

And in 1913, my mother married Tom Gary, and they lived at Spring Canyon for about three years. Then they bought this 40 acres from Sol Roberts in 1916, and they lived here till the rest of their life. And they farmed here and had some milk cows and some other cattle, and then they bought 160 acres a quarter of a mile west of here from Lucas Martinez. And that give them pasture to run a few more cattle. My brother and I stayed on the place up there in the hills. Then Tom Gary, my stepfather, he fell from a pile of hay seven bales high and broke some ribs in front and back, and we took him to the hospital and he passed away in a few days. And then my brother and I was down here part of the time. My mother lived to be close to 86 years old. She had had the flu and fell here in the house and broke her hip. We took her to the hospital, and she was too weak for them to operate on her, and she passed away in about a month.

Neither Paul nor his brother ever married.

Oh, we had girlfriends at times, but too much work to take care of, and we just never got around to it. Our sister had a big family, and we helped to take care of them. Helped send them to school and helped clothe them. See, I've got five nieces and one nephew, and they all happen by, two or three times a year; one of them lives right here close on the other side of the driveway. Myrtle Edmunds lives here on the other side of the driveway. They all help me with the work here. Now up on Buckhorn Mountain, there was about 16 boys to six girls. Other girls from around the country would come in to the parties and dances. And I liked to go to the dances and dance. They had the old fashioned dances. Waltzes and two-steps and square dances. I was the square dance caller, and I'd play a few tunes on the fiddle. There was quite a lot of neigh-borhood parties and things. And at a lot of these parties, there'd be some couples right from Bellvue up there. Parties then, they went at dark and danced till daylight.

When we was down here in Bellvue, my mother was quite a church worker. They had different things that they done, and my mother played the organ at the Bellvue church for several years when we lived down here. The Presbyterian church in Bellvue was built while we lived in Bellvue. And my mother played the organ there and when they was building that church, the neighbors around helped quite a bit with it. My father took his team and wagon and went up west of Stove Prairie and hauled a load of lumber down that's in that church. And several others hauled a load of lumber down as a donation to the church. And the women around Bellvue had the different parties and dinners and got donations to build that church. That was the Presbyterian Church at that time. I haven't went to church much. They used to have Sunday School at the Stove Prairie schoolhouse. We used to go over there some. And when I was young, I went to Sunday School quite a bit. I think it's a great thing. I believe in religion.

Paul's brother developed diabetes and died from it in 1950.

He doctored for it for quite a while, and he was in Eventide Rest Home for a couple of years. The old folks used to sing hymn songs there, and he was real good at singing hymn songs. But the old folks had a party at the rest home, and they sung hymn songs for quite a while and he just out sung them all. After the party was over, he went to bed and went to sleep, and next morning, why, he'd just passed away in his sleep.

My father was born in Illinois. He worked there in dairies and farming and he went through school there And through college. He was an expert penman. Spelling was hard for him, but the rest of it he was real good at. My mother was born in Iowa, and she went to school in Iowa and college there, and I think that she went to college in Illinois for a while. That's where my father and mother met. My mother's folks lived in Iowa, and then my father and mother both went to Iowa. They got married there, and they lived in Iowa for a while. Farmed. And that was a wet climate, around Hillsdale and Council Bluffs. And there was another town. But my mother had quinsy so bad there that the doctor told her if she didn't get to a drier climate, she wasn't going to live long. So now my brother and sister were born in Iowa. Then they decided that they would come to Colorado. They heard that that was a drier climate. So they came to Harmony, and that's where they started farming in this part of the country.

From the time I could walk good, why, I followed my father around and helped him do everything that a body done. He would tell me how to do things and why he done something this way or that way, and I learned a lot of things from my father. I was right around with him as long as he lived.

My father showed me quite a bit about one thing. He had set posts around the haystacks and he rounded the dirt all up—as much dirt as he had—rounded it up against the posts and tramped it down and it was sloping, and I asked him why he done that and he said that run the water away from the post and made it last longer. The post didn't get wet at the top of the ground and rot off. And like raking hay. He told me raking hay with a dump rake, when the wheel got to the windrow, why you stepped on the dump and dumped your rake and that kept your windrow straight. When I started raking, why my windrows would keep getting crookeder. So he told me when the wheel got to the windrow, dump my rake and that'd keep my windrow straight. And he told me lots of things like that that I remembered all my life.

At the age of 80, Paul expressed no major regrets about his life, or about the fact that only once he had been more than 100 miles from home. And, he continued to work his hay ranch. Asked what he liked best about Bellvue, without hesitation he endorsed its simple life: "The good mountain air, good mountain water, and plenty of fuel. Plenty of wood to keep warm by."

Town's too crowded. And I like it out here at the foot of the hill best. I don't think an old person could find any better place to live. I liked this area all my life and never had no desire to go any other place. When I was five years old, my mother's mother was quite sick, and they wanted her to come to Iowa. And she took me along. That's when I was five years old. I can remember quite a bit about the trip. We went on the train, and when we crossed the Missouri River, my mother got me up and had me look out the window. At that time there'd been a lot of rain and the river was about a mile wide. I stood up in the seat and watched out the train window across the river. When we got to the other side there for quite a ways, the water was half way up around the haystacks and up to the ears on the corn stalks. And we went on to Iowa—on to her folks—and stayed there a couple of weeks. Her mother got better so we came back. Came back to Bellvue.

That's the only long trip I ever took. I went to North Park in 1919 with my team and wagon. By the way of Tie Siding. And worked in the hay in 1919 in North Park. And after haying, I stayed there for a month and fenced haystacks with buck fence and poles. And I left there the second day of October. It started snowing and I said if I'm going over that range this fall, I better be a-going. I left there with my team and wagon and got over on this side the second day, to stay all night, and there was two foot of snow on the range that night.

The main thing is to get something that you can do and do it. There's people for all kinds of work, and if they get something that they can do and do it, that's the main thing. My folks was ranchers, and I never wanted to do anything else.

I worked out a little. I worked for Herb Mitchell—he lived east of Laporte—for one year. And I worked for John Howard over here on the Howard Ranch for three years. Before that I'd worked for myself, and I figured that if I couldn't make it working for myself, why that'd be my hard luck. So I've worked for myself ever since. I think there's people cut out for every job. And if they get a job that they can do and do it, why it's. . . . If a person likes his job he can do better than if he don't.

There's things that I could have maybe done better, but you learn as you go along. As I have said, after you get too old to do much of anything, why you've learned how to do things.

Ranching is something that you can do without much education. If you get right in there and do it. You'll do things, and maybe later you could see where you could have done it a little better, but generally it pans out you got it done.

I am mighty thankful that I done as good as I did. I wouldn't have to work, but I keep working to keep active. Well, now my left knee, I've had it hurt so many times that it went lame. And then my right knee went lame with arthritis. I've done as hard work as a person my size could, and hard work'll wear in on you after a while. But being single, and I've got five nieces. . . . When the estate was settled up, they signed over to me, and I have run it, and sold everything, and divided most of the money with my nieces. My nephew, he got his share when the estate was settled, but that way we could. . . . Them signing over to me, we got the estate settled quick, because I already owned two thirds of it, land that I bought. Then I sold everything, and I sold it on this 29 percent down and 10 years to pay. And I made four different sales. And you see that run it about 30 years and lowered interest. I have divided most of the money between my nieces. And I've kept some, and I get some Social Security. My brother and I, we was slow about signing up this paying your income tax and state tax and one thing and another, and they called us in and we took our lawyer with us—Bill Allen—and we got that all straightened up and paid up. Then we paid on that ever since, and my brother drawed Social Security for a while, and I have drawed Social Security. And this—my niece buying this 37 acres here—it was 40 acres—Merle got an acre and a half and Grace got an acre and a half, and Grace and Marion, and they sold theirs. And I keep enough so's I can live nicely. Keep a-working. Now I run the tractors to mow and rake and bale. Two thousand and fifty four bales of first and second cutting and 25 bales of third cutting and I've got that hay all under good roofs. When I get the hay ready to haul in, why, my niece's husband and boy, they flock in here and haul my hay and put it in. Now if I just got a small crew like three, why, I'll use the pickup to haul hay in. If I got a bigger crew, why, I'll hook the tractor onto a flatrack I've got. Haul 60 bales at a time. And first and second cutting, why, six of them come, and they'd four of them put hay on the flat bed, and two load and we'd haul 60 bales at a time. And we hauled the first and second cutting all in and put it under roof.

Walter Salisbury

Walter Salisbury's parents, Cassius Rice Salisbury and Hattie M. Davis Salisbury, emigrated from Kansas two decades before he was born in 1901. Whether they came in response to Flowers' and Laidlaw's solicitation is not known, but along with Walter's maternal grandmother and other relatives, they landed for a short time in Fort Collins.

They came here from Kansas in a covered wagon in 1880, and settled in Fort Collins on the corner of Meldrum and Mulberry. I can remember my mother telling about when they went to town, the town was about on Jefferson and Linden Streets, and they just cut kitty corner, right straight down. I don't know how long they lived there. About a year or something like that. Then they moved to the Rist Canyon area. My father hauled timber from there for a year or two. And then he started in ranching a little. Bought a small ranch and kept adding to it until he got quite a little ranch started in there. It's about seven miles west of Bellvue, up Rist Canyon. He had about 160 acres to start with. Then bought several little ranches and added to it. And when he sold it, I imagine there was about 800, 900 acres. My grandmother homesteaded part of it, 160. And the rest of it, I think, he bought it all.

I used to be with my two nephews a lot, and of course we climbed the mountains and gold rocks and into everything that a kid could be into. And course we had ponies, and we spent a lot of time on the ponies. Quite a few squatters were around and they killed the deer and once in a while, they'd kill a bear. There was several mountain lions killed in there, and there was lots of sawmills. Lots of teaming going on and lots of lumber hauled out of there, and logs, posts and poles. All sorts of timber work.

I think there's more deer up there now than there was earlier. Several of those little squatter ranches up there, that's about all the meat they had. And there was some grouse. Rabbit, stuff like that. But there was a lot of timbers hauled out of Rist Canyon. I think Rist Canyon got its name from an old fellow that had a sawmill up there. His name was Rist. And I think that's how it got its name. And if I'm not mistaken, this old man Rist, when he had his sawmill, he was sitting filing the saw and the old steam engine, it'll drop over center and he had his leg up agin' the saw to hold it steady while he filed it, and it kicked over and it cut his leg off. But it wasn't long until they said he whittled out a kind of peg-leg for himself, and he strapped it on that leg and went on with his sawmill.

Then in the early days, it must have been about '82 or '83, there was a tollgate in the canyon. About a mile up from the mouth of the canyon. The road went between a couple of big rocks, and there was a tollgate there. My dad said they used to charge 10 cents a trip or three trips for a quarter. And it was there several years, till an old Frenchman by the name of Tim Lemoyne, he went down there with a load of timber and he didn't have the dime to get through and the old fellow that was the gatekeeper there, he wouldn't let him through unless he paid the dime. Well, it made him mad, and he took his ax and chopped the gate down and threw it over in the crick, and that's the last of the tollgate. My dad showed me right where the tollgate was. It's at what we always called "Devil's Gate." It's about a mile above the mouth of the canyon. Course the road don't go up through that way now, it's across the crick from where that gate was.

And then there was a little chunk of ground, 30 acres, that my father sold off to a consumptive from the east. Come out here and built two rooms and a little barn, and his mother stayed with him. I don't know just how many years he was there. He slept out in a tent all summer to be out in the open air. He finally went back east and died. Then my father bought the 30 acres back from him. Then my grandmother homesteaded another 160 to join that 30, and we had that 190

acres for quite a few years. Then the whole ranch finally went
to the First National Bank and they had it for several years, and
then I finally bought it.

She was my mother's mother. She went back and forth a
lot. She'd go back to Kansas and stay maybe a couple of years,
and then she'd want to come back. And she just was back and
forth. But she finally died in Kansas in Glen Elder. She was
just a common little old lady. I don't know what her life was. I
know in the early days they had a grocery story. She was
married three or four times, and I don't know, really, much
about her life. I remember one remark she made one time.
She said, "Well," she said, "I had the satisfaction of wearing
out four men." They had all died. She had a son that lived
there in Glen Elder, in her last days, and he built her a little
house. Right there on his property. And she was quite
satisfied there in her little home. Until she'd get lonesome to
see my mother. Then she'd come out here and stay a while,
and back she'd go.

*For Walter as for most of his contemporaries, the eighth grade
marked the end of his schooling. Life in the mountains only rarely
involved trips to town. Once or twice a year he went to Fort Collins.
His mother made his clothes, and he did not need many: a few pairs
of shorts and some long pants. The mountain folk were even more
self-reliant than the people who lived lower down. And more prone to
settle their own disputes in their own ways. Walter knew "One-Eye"
Thomson, Pearl's dad, and thought he was quite a character. He
knew Paul and Harry Millington, and where Paul did not want to
speak of Harry's dispute that left him crippled, Walter was willing.*

He wasn't ornery. The trouble with Harry, he talked a
little bit too much. He liked to talk. Then there was an old
fellow up there by the name of John Knox. He and Harry got
into a squabble. I guess it was over timber more than anything, but for a while they was carrying a gun for each other.
And it finally wound up that John Knox shot Harry Millington
in the hip. He meant to kill him, I think, but he just got him in
the hip. Course this old John Knox, he went to the pen for two
or three years for that. And that left Harry with a short leg.

Oh, his leg was probably about three or four inches shorter than the other one. He went through the big part of his life with a short leg.

John Knox was an old Scotchman. And I think how he got to coming over here was, they used to ship lots of stallions from the old country. He would take care of these stallions on the ship as they come over here. Then he'd go back and bring another load over. And he was a pretty tough old guy. They'd ship lots of thoroughbred stallions across. Percherons and Belgians. And he used to take care of them on these ships as they come. That's what I understand. Yeah, I knew old John Knox pretty well. He always seemed peaceable enough. But nobody put anything over on him. He stood his ground.

We had a pretty tough time up there in the winter of 1913, when about five and half feet of snow fell. There was a lot of cattle lost up there that winter. It come the first part of December and it laid on till spring. There was a lot of cattle lost up there that winter. People, well, especially the Morgans, they had cattle out of the range, yet. And they couldn't get to them and they couldn't get any trail broke to them. There was some of them starved to death. And finally, on skis they located . . . they'd be maybe five or six or eight or ten in a little bunch somewhere in the timber. They'd go on skis, and pack hay in gunny sacks on their backs to get to them out there, and that's the way they kept a lot of them alive until they could break trails. But the snow was so deep the horses couldn't get through it. There was—oh, I don't know how long. I suppose there was months, maybe longer, that we couldn't get to town. Course most everybody had a good supply of groceries. I know a lot of them ran short of flour, kerosene, coffee, lard and stuff like that. Be we had a pretty good supply. My father used to always in the fall, he'd buy 500 or 600 pounds of flour. He'd maybe buy 50 gallons of kerosene, and we generally had out own hogs to butcher, and lots of the neighbors would come there and borrow kerosene. And some paid it back and some didn't.

Our ranch house where we lived, it was in the trees and it was dark that morning till I got up, I suppose about eight o'clock. It seemed so dark in the house, and I couldn't see out the windows. I climbed up on the old kitchen table to look out the window and boy, was we buried. Golly. I was just a kid. I thought: Well, that'll be great, to get out and wade in that snow. But it was so deep I couldn't wade in it. I couldn't buck through it.

My dad had a little bay mare. Oh, she wasn't so little, either. If you'd go in the barn in the stall to turn her out, she'd always jerk back, you know. She couldn't wait till she got the halter off. Dad took the halter off from her, and she reared back and out the door she went and boy, she hid in that snow and all you see was her nose and her ears a-sticking out. She didn't like that. She turned around very quiet and come back in the barn.

But the horses, they couldn't get through it. They couldn't budge. Course, after it settled, why, then they'd begin to break trails with horses. And I guess the first ones to break the road up the canyon as far as our place was the Jovison boys. Dick and John. They lived there in Bellvue, and the county hired them to break the road through.

The canyon washed out several times. Of course the road, in the early days there, about all the road we had was right up the crick bottom. We used to ford the crick 17 times. There was a few bridges. But in '23 it just took everything. You couldn't get down through part of it, horseback. When the road washed out, it was always a cloudburst. But the melting snow never caused much trouble. It melted too slow.

When I was a kid up there on the ranch—that was long before the road went up the Poudre—I'd go with my dad. We'd take our lunch. We lived about four miles from the Poudre. I was about nine, ten years old. And I'd go along. We'd pack a lunch. We'd get down to the river about nine-thirty and Dad would fish until noon, and then he'd clean the fish. He had a big old wicker basket. He'd always clean the fish and pull a layer of grass, and then he'd lay a layer of fish and then a layer of grass, and that kept them cool, you know. Kept them kind of separated. And he'd fish until maybe one or two o'clock. He'd have that whole basket just plumb full. Some of them, he'd bend the tails back, to get them in the basket. He'd throw them over his shoulder and we'd get on the saddle horses and ride back to the ranch.

We went over Hill's Gulch. That was right north of the ranch. It headed right at our ranch. And it was four miles from there to the river. But all it was, was a trail down there. And then they finally kind of built a road down through there and there was some sawmills. Remember once Mother telling about one fellow come out of there with a load of timber one day, and he had a mountain lion that he'd killed, and she said it seemed like it was the full length of that load of timber. It was a big one.

In 1913 we had six months of winter school. The schoolhouse was just below out ranch and I was the only kid that could get to school. And oh, I hated to go to school by myself. Boy, I didn't like that. But the other kids around there, they just couldn't get to school, that's all.

The mail carrier from Bellvue, he carried the mail. He made several trips on skis. He didn't bring anything but the letters. He didn't bring no papers or anything, just the letters. But it would take him, oh, two or three or four days to make the route clear around. We used to only get mail three times a week. For years we only got it three times a week. He carried that horseback and in the buggy, and sometimes he had a cart that would carry the mail. Old Dewey Schofield, he lived there in Bellvue just a little bit south of the store. I think he carried that mail for 16 years.

The Depression didn't bother us on the ranch because we had out own meat, we had out own butter and eggs and all our own vegetables, potatoes. They used to raise lots of potatoes up there. And there wasn't too much we had to buy. It really didn't bother us too much. Our food stamps, a lot of ours that was for meat and lard and stuff like that, we used to give them away to guys in town here that wouldn't have enough stamps, you know. There was one old gentleman, he always stand on the corner. He knew about what days we'd come to town, and he'd stand on the corner and watch. And we'd give him food stamps. But he had a big cherry orchard out east of Collins, and when it come cherry time, he always seen that we had plenty of cherries. And he used to make quite a little cherry wine, and he'd furnish us wine if we wanted it.

When I was a kid, why, about two-thirds of the town was livery stables. There was livery stables on North College, in that triangle block there, that was all livery stables. Then on Mountain Avenue, there was a lot of livery stables in there. We lived in town on Mulberry Street for a few years after the folks sold the ranch, and I used to like to hang around in the livery stables. I was always quite interested in horses. And they'd do lots of horse-trading. And these fellows that hang around there that was pretty good bronc riders, they'd get up bets that this one and that one couldn't ride a certain horse. They'd get out there in the street and have quite a bucking contest, and then they'd run races up and down Jefferson Street. Aw, that was great sport for us kids.

And when I was a kid, after we went back to the ranch, I had a friend here in town. His father run the Express Courier printing office, and 'course whenever there was a circus come to town, this kid he always let me know and then I'd come to town and stay with him. And we'd take in the circus, and his dad would give us passes to all the shows and stuff like that. Oh, we'd have a big time. We'd get up three or four o'clock in the morning and go down and watch them unload the elephants and all the animals. Oh, we'd have a great time. But I never missed a circus for years. This kid, he'd always send me word that there's be a circus in town a certain day, and I'd go down.

When I was a young fellow, we used to have lots of little neighborhood dances up there. Either in the Stove Prairie school house or the Thomson school house or in somebody's home. And we'd always have to go either horseback or with the buggy, and of course it'd be dark. We had to dance till morning. Till it got daylight. But the women, they'd always take cake and sandwiches, and they'd have coffee at midnight and they'd have just a good sociable time. Then they finally got some of the people coming from town up here, and some of them would bring a few bottles along and it caused trouble, so they just quit having them. Yeah. I've went from the ranch clear down on the Buckhorn. Used to cut through by the old Thompson Ranch and down over the mountain onto the Buckhorn. That Langston Ranch. They used to give dances there. And then going home, why the sun would come up, and I'd go to sleep and get to weaving around on my horse and about to fall off and then that would wake me up.

There's a fellow by the name of Shorty Reed and I was going down through what they called Devil's Hole. It was dark. Gee whiz, it was dark. And we was going down on the Redstone to a dance, and all of a sudden the horses whirled and they started back up the trail and we couldn't figure out what was the matter. And this Shorty Reed, he said, "I believe," he said, "the horses smell a bear." And I said, "I don't know what's the matter with them." And we turned them around and jabbed them with our spurs and started down again. And I said, "Something's wrong. There's something more than a bear." And come to find out, somebody'd put a fence across the new road, and the horses was hitting that fence but it was so dark we couldn't see the gate. When we got to that certain place and they whirled again, two or three times they done that. Shorty said, "I believe," he said, "there's a gate there." Got off and sure enough there was.

Walter married Norma Baxter, also of the Rist Canyon area. Asked how he and Norma met, he said, "I don't know how we did meet." Norma immediately chimed in, "Through Ralph Alsbaugh. He dared you to make a date with me."

Yeah, there was a fellow by the name of Alsbaugh that lived on the old Hawkeye Ranch just north of Laporte. And I used to chum with him a lot. And I guess he says, "I'll find you a blind date and we'll go to the show tonight." And I said, "All right." So he came down to the store and asked Norma if she'd go to the show. I guess that's how we met. On a blind date to the show. 'Course in the early days, her father had a ranch just above us about a mile but that was too soon for me.

Walter and Norma had three sons. Jim, their middle son, was driving down Rist Canyon in November of 1946, on his way to a basketball game in Laporte, when his car spun out of control, overturned, and crashed into the creek, killing him at the age of 17. Seatbelts were 15 years in the future.

The remoteness of mountain life meant no shortage of unusual neighbors.

There was some Mexicans, they lived about a mile below us and they had a still on part of my place. And I didn't know about it for about a year. We used to sell quite a lot of Christmas trees. This still was right on the north slope of the mountain. I was in there looking to see about the quality of the trees and one thing and another, and I run onto this still. It was dug back in the bank, and they had it all covered. He had two 50-gallon barrels, just a-boiling, you know. So we looked all around to see if they would be a jug or two that had been run off. So we told them Mexicans, or I did, that we was going to be there cutting trees and hard to tell who might be in there, and I wished he'd get out. "That's all right," he said, "them 32 gallon barrels are about ready to run off and," he said, "as soon as we run them off we'll get out." So he did. And oh, those Mexicans, they had stills all over that country. They caught this old Mexican once and put him in jail for three or four months, and all the time he was in jail, why, his son was running his still on me. But there was one still up there that had 36 barrels in it. He was making a lot of whiskey.

This old Mexican, he was a great big old fat guy. He broke his leg, and he come up to the ranch and wanted to know if I'd take him town. I told him I would. And brought him down to the doctor and the old man, all the way down, after we got him up to the doctor's office, he'd say, "Jesus

Christ, I wish I had a pint of whiskey. Oh, I wish I had a pint
of whiskey." But they set his leg and put it in a cast, and I
brought him down several times to have it looked after. You
know them Mexicans would do anything in the world for me.
Anything that I asked them to do or wanted, they was right
there to help. I guess I got on the good side of them.

And people, the last few years . . . . Even still when we
was on the ranch, they'd come up there and they thought
everything was free. They'd trespass and they'd hunt and
tramp all through your hay, and they'd just act like it's in the
mountains, it's all free. And then these jeeps, they got to where
they'd drive anyplace and they'd cut your fences and they'd go
pretty near any place with those jeeps. There's too many
people here. Ain't hardly room for them, I don't think. I
know when I was a kid and even after I was married, there was
very few automobiles come up that canyon. Some days there
wouldn't be any. And now, why, there's just one right after
another. I know I sat on the porch after we built that new
house one Sunday, and I counted the automobiles for oh,
about an hour. And they averaged about one every half a
minute. Just pretty near bumper to bumper.

When we lived there in the brick house, I got up—just
finished breakfast one morning and looked out the window,
and there was a bear looking in the window. He stood up on
his hind legs and looked in the window. I moved and kind of
scared him and went around on the back porch. I said to her,
"There's a bear around on the back porch." She said, "What'd
I feed you this morning?" I said, "You go and look." And
there he was, right there on the back porch, looking in the
door. And by golly, that darn bear hung around there for two
or three days, and he'd keep trying to get in the house. And he
pawed the screen doors, and the back door. He tore the screen
off. Well, not off, but he tore it. That night I said, "Well, I'll
take the screen door, cause he'll tear it all off tonight anyway."
And about midnight, why, I heard him banging on the back
porch with his paws, you know. I was afraid he'd break the
door in. So I got up and turned the light on, and he seen the
light and he went up the road then, in the neighbor's house.

Tipped over some trash cans and fooled around there. Then he came back down to our place. He just hung around the back door there all the time. Well, the kids . . . the daughter-in-law come up the road and a couple of the kids, and they thought it was fun to feed him. And they'd put molasses out or honey or some biscuits or something, and that just suited him.

So I called the Game and Fish up and I told them, I said, "I've got a bear up here and if you don't come up, I'm going to kill him. I can't guard the house all the time." So he says, "Well, I'll be right up and bring up a trap." He said, "Don't kill him." I said, "You get up here and get him or I'll kill him." And gosh, he was tame. He'd come right up within two or three feet of you. And I was going to rope him one night there and tie him to the clothesline post. Norma wouldn't let me. She said, "He's liable to get hurt." But I wanted to see him fight that rope. But she wouldn't let me. She was going to burn my lariat rope, or else cut it up and I don't know what all. But I didn't rope him. The Game and Fish guy brought up a trap. One of them barrel things that they use on the little trailer. He set it out right back of the house, and that night he caught him. He baited it with some bacon in there, and he went in the tube. Just like a big tube. And then they had a trapdoor, and he fastened the bacon to this trap door. So they would trip it, and it fell on and had him, you know. But he was a pretty mad bear the next morning. He was on the fight. But they tranquilized him to see what sex he was. If it had been a male, they was going to take him I think to Greeley or somewhere to some little zoo. But if it was a female, they didn't want him. So he said, "Well, I'll take him up around Chambers Lake and turn him loose." "Well," I said, "before you do, let's mark him with some red paint so we can tell if he ever bothers anybody or if anybody kills him." He said, "All right." So we daubed a lot of red paint on his neck and on his head. And he took him up way above Chambers Lake somewhere and turned him loose. And he come back down around the lake and got to bothering the cabins there, so I think they killed him. He got to breaking in cabins there and bothering some of the people. So that was the last of my bear.

One day I was riding over the south part of the place, riding along on top of a ridge. I had the dog with me, and there was two bobcats, about half-, two-thirds grown. I told the dog, I said, "Sic 'em!" And he took out after them bobcats. They separated. He run his in a rock pile and lost him. And I run mine up a tree. So I crawled up the tree and was going to catch him. I'd get up about level with him. It was a big yellow pine tree. When I'd get up about even with him, why he'd come a-slipping and a-spitting at me, and I'd slide back down the tree a ways. I done that several times, and he stayed down on the limb. I had my lariat rope, and I tossed it out and caught him around the neck. Then I threw it down and got down, and he was up the tree just the length of that lariat rope. I jerked him out, and boy was he mad. It kind of knocked the wind out of him when he first hit, but he soon got his wind. The old saddle horse was standing there, and he made a dive for her. I jerked him back, and then he was going to take me. I kicked at him with some dirt and rocks and stuff, and he backed off. I thought: "Well, how in the name of God . . . I can't get my rope off of him." So I happened to think, I had a strap about that long in my saddle pocket. I made a loop in it and I fastened it on a stick about eight feet long. I put the loop right behind him and then I kicked dirt in his face and he'd back up. When I got it so I could jerk it up right behind his shoulders, then, where he'd make a dive at me, why I could hold him back. So I carried him down off the mountain. There was an old cabin there, and there was one of these great big old coal scuttles. I set him down in that and carried him home. I set him on the back porch and I told her, I said, "Come and see what I got in my bucket."

One time she and I was riding down this hill to a gulch. And there was two little cubs playing in the grass. And course when they seen us, why, they went up a tree. Big yellow pine tree. And them was the cutest little boogers. We'd sit there and watch. And they'd look at each other, you know, just like they was talking things over. Then they'd peek out and look us over, and then they'd looked at each other. They was comical. I wanted to kill them and have them mounted, them two little fellows, you know, and I said, "Well, you stay here and keep them up the tree and I'll go back home and get the gun." No, she wouldn't do that. She wouldn't stay there by herself. So we went on and left them alone. I'd like to have had them mounted. Oh, they was *cute little fellows.*

Jill of All Trades

Pearl Thomson Yager, like other women of her day in Bellvue, never saw much difference between traditional definitions of "woman's" work and "man's" work. There was just work. Hers included draying, farming, logging and rodeoing besides raising a family and helping to keep a home.

I was born to the parents of Riley Clyde and Frances E. Thomson, near Elk City, Kansas, in Montgomery County. My father was a team contractor. He used to work in the oil fields in Oklahoma, and back in those days they hauled everything with a team and wagon, like they do now with trucks. My father would start in the spring of the year when harvest started—wheat harvest—down in Kansas. He would start hauling grain to the elevators, and whenever they got through in that area, why, he took his covered wagons and he would go west until he come to an area where their wheat was just starting to ripen. We had two wagons, and they had grain boxes on them. And then we had the jets and bows that we set on top of the grain box, and this is what we traveled in.

Usually he tried to find someplace where they was just starting to harvest, and some man that had a lot of wheat land. He would get a job of hauling wheat for them. And he'd set our jets and bows off on the ground and pitch a tent, and that's where we lived until he finished that job. When he got through there, he would load the jets and bows back on, and we'd head west until we came to another area where the wheat was just starting to ripen. We'd start back there in Kansas in June, and generally we would get out as far as Great Bend or Burdette or Larned—out in that area—by fall. Then he quite often would get a job at breaking sod. It was plowing up the pasture land, converting it into wheat and farm land.

The last year was 1916. We crossed Kansas five times in covered wagon, and then we lost my Grandmother Jolly. My grandmother and grandpa lived at what they called Card Creek, which was a few miles out of Elk City. We'd always be back there for Christmas. The whole family. The Jolly family always congregated there for Christmas. Dad always intended to be there by Christmas time. Then the rest of the winter, he would work for the city of Independence, or in the oil fields, hauling rigs for oilfields, until spring came. He was an old cowboy, and rather an adventurer, and he liked to travel. He never lived in one house a year in his life after he was married till he moved into the ranch.

We crossed Kansas, like I said, five times, in a covered wagon, but after Grandmother passed away, we never went back. The family has never been together. And that would have been the winter of 1915 was the last year we went back. Then Dad heard of homestead land in Montana. He always wanted to homestead. So in the fall of '16, why we was going to go to Montana and homestead. We got down here at LaSalle, and the snow was so deep he decided to get work there for the winter, and we'd go on the next spring. Well, he worked for farmers around there, stock feeders and things like that, till spring, and the next spring he could see the mountains. He'd heard of Estes Park. So him and a groceryman by the name of Tracy, that lived at LaSalle, started out. We had a team of mules. They hooked them onto the covered wagon and started out for Estes Park.

Well, they got over here to Fort Collins, and they got off on the wrong road. They went up Rist Canyon instead of the Thompson Canyon. And they wandered in. Got to the top of Stove Prairie Hill and there was a road going off to the left. They followed that and they got in there, and there was a widow woman that lived there. Her husband died on the ranch, in the wintertime in a big snow, in November. I don't know what year. The snow was so bad and the ground froze so hard, that they had to burn a brush pile on the ground for, I under-stood, 48 hours, to thaw the ground enough that they could dig his grave. One of the neighbor women, Molly Morgan, preached his funeral. So Dad wandered in there, and he found this place, and he liked it so well that him and this groceryman bought it together.

Once the Thomsons got their place in the mountains, they gave up all intention of going to Montana. They were home. And the mountain folk who were their neighbors were an eccentric lot.

It was 340 acres. But he did increase it to 1,000 acres before he sold it. After Dad bought it, there was possibly about 50 acres of farmland on it. And after he bought it, he pulled out trees and cut timber, and he increased it to about 100 acres of farmland, on this 340. And the rest of it was timber and pastureland. There was an old house there that was standing. It was just an old native lumber house—two story house—and the folks didn't think it was very good, but they thought they'd get by in it a few years, until they could build a new one. The people that Dad bought from had been there 18 years, and he thought they were the worst old moss-backs he'd ever heard of, to live in one house 18 years. He'd never lived in one house five years in his life, before that. Well, he bought that place and he was there 35 years. And we never did get a new house built, and he wasn't ready to leave at the end of 35 years, he enjoyed it so much. But his health failed, and mother had had a heart attack and she had to come to a lower altitude, and dad had broke his hip. But before that, they had sold the ranch. But it was amazing, how much he enjoyed it after he got up there.

At the time we went in there, our main crop was potatoes. I mean our market crop. Otherwise it was just hay. Well, there was a neighbor on Stove Prairie, John Vannorsdel, who had a thrashing machine—small thrashing machine—and he would come in and thrash the grain. Daddy had raised barley and wheat and oats, but mostly hay and potatoes. We had a great big potato cellar. I think it was the summer of '18, as I remember, they had a bunch of soldiers stationed down here at CSU. They called it A and M then. They came in there and hauled potatoes out by the—I think they had a truck—I can't remember for sure. But potatoes was our main sale at that time. But there was a sawmill, and he did saw some lumber. He sawed bridge planks that they used to build a lot of the bridges around Larimer County. And a lot of it went down to Masonville as well as to Fort Collins, to the road bosses down there. We used to cut stringers—bridge stringers—and peel them. We used the Douglas fir timber, and we would cut them and peel them and haul them down here and sell them to the county for bridges. Nowadays they use cement, mostly, but in those days they used wood. But we could only make about 15 to 20 miles a day with the covered wagons. And Daddy usually tried to make it a point, when night come, to find a schoolhouse or churchyard, or something like that, because he felt it was public property. And when we was traveling, why, that was usually where we'd try to stay overnight because there'd be water there. And, in those days, they had outside toilets. And so that was a good place for us to spend the night.

After Daddy bought this ranch, we were living out near LaSalle, out in what they called Peckham. It took us three days to move from there to the ranch with covered wagons. We had a team of four mules on one wagon and they were real fast walkers, and we had a team of big old black horses on the other wagon, and we had some cows and we had a few pigs and some chickens. I had a little adopted brother. Mother and Dad adopted a little boy in Great Bend, Kansas, when we were traveling on the road in covered wagons. I was an only child. And they didn't want to raise me alone. So they adopted. This lady. . . . There were 13 of them, living in one house. Her father was the only one that was working. So she came to my father and mother and asked them if they wanted to adopt him. He was only two or two and a half years. They were traveling on the road, in covered wagon. We were just there temporarily, working in the plowing. Something like that. But anyway, when we got ready to go to the ranch, there was my mother and my dad and my brother and I, and we had two covered wagons and these horses and cows and things to move. So Dad put mother in the lead with the horses, 'cause they walked slower than the mules. Then he tied up the top

buggy behind her wagon, and tied the driving mare and the
saddle horse behind that, and my Shetland ponies. My brother
and I each had a Shetland pony. He tied them on there and he
put Mother in the lead, and then I drove a team of mules two
days and a half on the other covered wagon. And he rode the
horse and drove the cows, behind.

I was nine. I was nine in January, and we moved in there
the 13th day of July in 1917. I can't remember where we
camped, but I know that Dad thought he could drive the cattle
through the little towns and things like that better than the rest
of us. But my mules were real fast walkers. And like most
mules, they were ornery. I was very small for my age at that
time, and those mules kept trying to run into my wagon tongue
in the back of that buggy. I'd stop them and let Mama get
down the road, I thought quite a ways, before I'd let them
catch up. Course she probably wasn't more than a city block or
two. But to me, a kid, I thought it was quite a ways. And then
I'd let them go. Catch up with her.

When we got over here to Laporte, Dad took the lead
wagon and Mom took my wagon, and I got on my Shetland
pony, and I drove the cows from there to the mouth of Rist
Canyon. We got to the mouth of Rist Canyon—our worldly
possessions in these two covered wagons. One team couldn't
pull the wagon up Rist Canyon. It was too heavy and too steep
and everything. So we pulled one wagon over right at the
mouth of Rist Canyon and unhitched from it and let it set
there all night with our worldly belongings in. And we hooked
the four head of horses, the mules in the lead, on the other
covered wagon, and Dad hooked the driving mare on the
buggy, and he put my little brother and I in the buggy, and my
mother took the saddle horse and drove the cows Dad took
the lead with the four-up, and Bud and I following him, and
then Mama behind with the cows.

Well, I was getting pretty tired by that time, and going up
the canyon, the road was very narrow. We crossed Rist Canyon
20-some times in that four miles distance. You just meandered
back and forth across the stream. And there was only about

one or two places in that canyon at that time that you could even pass with wagons. And there wasn't automobiles. There was a few, but very few. But you never met anybody. You'd go four miles and probably never meet a soul in there at all. But anyway, I went to sleep and pretty near run off the edge of the road one time, a-driving. So we went on into the ranch. People by the name of Lass were moving out as we moved in. I was awfully tired, and it wasn't necessary for Bud and I to go back down with them to get the other wagon so they left me up there. And they went back the next day. They had some pigs out there. So I had to carry water for them. And I was so weak and worn out from driving those horses all that time and like I said, I was pretty small at that time, so I laid down on the path, coming to the house with the water. Mrs. Lass, she got worried about me—she come out to see what had happened to me.

But that's the way we moved in there. My father went, before he closed the deal on the place, him and this groceryman went. Had a man take them up there in a car. They went up in a Model T Ford. There was a hill that we call Little Morgan. It was named after these people that homesteaded up there. Model T's, you know, didn't have much power. Anyway, Dad said that they took poles, and there was three or four of them, and as that Ford would pull, they would pry with these poles to help get it up over this little hill. It wasn't a very long hill, but it was rather steep. But that's the way they went in there—the first automobile that ever went into the ranch.

And then later on, he hired a man with a Studebaker to take us up there to see the ranch before he closed the deal. It was in May, and where the relay tower is now, there was still a snowbank there, about the middle of May. They melted snow to make coffee. We had our first meal in the mountains. In those days, they didn't know enough about driving a car and using compression to go downhill. This man rode his brakes a-going down. We went down Stove Prairie Hill and down the Buckhorn, and they were on fire by the time we got down to the Buckhorn where we could get water. We had to put water on his brakes to put out the fire. That was how much they knew about handling cars in those days.

But Daddy had a sawmill, and we used to raise rutabaga. We even raised pumpkins up there. During the First World War, my mother churned butter. She hauled it down here with the driving mare and buggy, and sold it to the grocery stores. The Laurel Street grocery and Scrivner's, on West Mountain, and some of those grocery stores She sold her butter. She got 60 cents a pound for it in those days. Hauled it down with a horse and buggy. We had a lake back on the place, and they'd put up ice in the wintertime. We had an old log ice house. We had sawdust in there, and they would dig out the center of it, and cut these blocks of ice and put them in there and cover them with sawdust. We had ice cream. It wasn't very clean ice to use in drinking, but yet it would keep things cool. But we didn't have any electricity and no telephones of course. We had a dugout vegetable cellar. And we had a great big potato cellar.

I entered the fourth grade up there and went through the eighth. Our school was called Welch Park. When we went in there, our district was 16 miles square. And there was four schools in that district. There was one on the Redstone, and our school was called Welch Park. It was right on our property. It was an old log schoolhouse. It was hewed out of logs and was built right on the ranch. The teacher always boarded and roomed with us because it was practically in our yard. It was just below the barn. She stayed with us part of the time. My brother and I were the only ones in the school, so we practically had a governess. The first year we went in there, I think there was eight of us. The Lasses had told the school board there wouldn't be any children. But I think that year there was eight of us. And we always had problems getting to school up there.

Paul Millington lived just across the fence from us. Paul and Harry Millington. I don't know where they went to school. I think Paul, as I remember, was about 19 when I went in there. I think Paul was about 10 years older than I was, as I remember. Him and the schoolteacher and I used to go back skating on our lake. He was the one that taught me to ice skate when I was a little girl. Paul was always a real good neighbor and a real good friend. And I always thought a lot of Paul. Matter of fact, for our fiftieth wedding anniversary a few years ago, he called and congratulated us, when he saw it in the paper. But, yeah Paul lived up there. They lived just across the fence from us and they had hogs and things like that.

There was times that I was never to town for over a year, when I was a little youngster. When Dad and Mother would bring a load to town, they had to haul the team and wagon, of course, and they'd come one day and stay all night and come back the next, with their team and wagon. And so usually only one, either Mother or Dad, came at a time. If there was some reason both of them had to come, why, the teacher was there with us youngsters, 'cause they boarded and roomed with us. It was always a nice, congenial arrangement, as far as that was concerned. Then the Gabriel girls—the Gabriel children—they lived about three quarters of a mile from the schoolhouse. Mrs. Gabriel was a sister to Paul and Harry Millington. They had a ranch. I think they homesteaded east of there, and those youngsters had to walk that three-quarters of a mile to school. They told us that many times they were so hard up that they had nothing to eat but potatoes, and maybe not even salt for them. Back in those days, times were pretty hard. And Daddy used to go down, and Oliver didn't even have a team. And Dad used to skid logs for him and haul lumber out for him to help him get groceries and things. One or two of their children were born up there without even a doctor. Mother went and stayed with their mother.

So times were very hard back in those days. We had an old neighbor up there, John Knox, and he lived over there all alone. I don't know whether he was a bachelor or widower or what. We never knew much about his life. He'd come over there and if he didn't come over every week or two, why, Dad and Mother would have me get on my Shetland and go over and check on him. Well, like I said, I was just a little kid. He lived mostly on pancakes and plain boiled potatoes. He'd boil up a pot of potatoes and set them on the back of his old wood stove and let them set there until he ate them up. And as a youngster, I always had a horror of going over there sometime and finding him dead and half ate up with pack rats. That was always the horror and feeling that I had of finding him.

One time he came over to Dad and Mother's. Mama always baked homemade bread, of course, and she always made cinnamon rolls. She just took them out of the oven and John was there, and so she asked him if he didn't want some cinnamon rolls. "Oh, yeah." He set there and ate four or five of those big hot cinnamon rolls. And he was not used to it, and I guess he had indigestion. Anyway, the next time he came over he told Mama, "Ah, your old food, it's no damn good. It sickened me." He came over there one time, and he was putting up a roof over his sawmill, and he had dropped a log on his shoulder and he came over to see Mama and Dad about it. He had broke his collar bone and it was all black and blue and here he lived over there all alone and wasn't doing a thing about it.

Well, the man that we bought our ranch from—homesteaded after my husband and I was married—his name was Fred Kemper. He was an old bachelor, and he had an aunt somewhere that sent him oh, I don't know, $10 or $15 a month in the mail. That was what he bought his groceries with. Well, anyway, him and old John Knox used to cut timber together, and they had this old cross-cut saw, that "you want him and I want him" —pull it back and forth. Well, out there one day in the timber, they was working and some way, John got his finger caught in that saw. So he told Fred, he said, "Take your knife and trim that up." And Fred took out his pocket knife and started to trim that up. John said, "Ha, b'Jason, your damned old knife is too dull." And he laid it on his stump and took his <u>ax</u> and trimmed it and bandaged it up. And he never went to a doctor. He told us that, and Fred Kemper, both, told us that.

Another time he was over there all alone, and he was cutting logs and a tree fell on him, and somebody came along that found him. I think it was Oliver Gabriel. But somebody, anyway, who he didn't like, came along, and they wanted to take the log off. "Oh, no, and b'Jason," he said, "I don't like you, you get the hell out of here." And he went and got somebody else and sent him back. Well, John was sick one time, and Oliver Gabriel came over to Dad and Mom's and he wanted something to give him.

So Dad, he always thought what was good for a horse was good for a human. And they used Epson Salts as a laxative in those days. So Dad sent some liniment over to use on John, and when Oliver got over there, he forgot how they told him to do it. So Dad had sent enough of Dad's salts for two laxatives, and I think liniment to use for once or something. Anyway, Oliver reversed them, and he gave old John all the salts in one dose and he stretched the other—the liniment—out, and you talk about interesting times, we had many of them up there.

I don't know how much Paul told you about Harry and John Knox's problem, but I've always got quite a kick out of it. But Harry told this hisself. Harry used to tell us John Knox was out there building a building. Harry was ornery. He was one of those smart aleck kids. He told how he'd set up tin cans along the fence and get back and target practice them tin cans, hoping he'd miss them and hit old John.

Now Harry told us that hisself. Anyway, he told us how one time old John was roofing this house, and he went up in the timber with the intention of shooting old John off of the roof of this house. And when he got over there, his stepdad was over there helping him. And he couldn't get close enough to be sure he'd hit John instead of his stepdad without John seeing him, so he had to give that one up. But there was bullets in old John Knox's, all around the door casing, where he had been shot at. I saw those bullets in the door casing.

Harry was always picking on John. And Harry told us that when he was 16 years old he decided he was man enough. John had learned to carry his rifle to protect himself, because Harry was always picking on him or shooting at him. He saw John down there working, so he decided he was man enough to take that rifle away from John. And he went down and proceeded to take the rifle—he was 16, the way he told it—he went down to take that rifle away from John. Well, they got in a fight over the rifle and it accidentally went off, and Harry was shot in the hip. And he said he didn't know whether he pulled the trigger or whether John did. But John served the term in the penitentiary.

But Harry Millington was one of the most aggravating men in the world. My dad farmed their place at one time, and it was the first time they had deer season across the Poudre. They had four days. Him and a neighbor, Charlie Hollemon, wanted to go over there, deer hunting. And Dad had some wheat back there on Harry's, and he'd cut it. It was down and shocked, and deer season came up before he got it moved in. And, he was going to move it over to the home place and have John Vannorsdel come up and thrash it. Well, he went and talked to Harry. He said, "Harry, will this be all right for four or five days so I can. . . ." "Yeah, that's fine."

Well, the next day after Dad left, Harry went back and loaded up this grain on his hayrack and started to his house with it. Well, Mother saw him. She went out and told him, she said, "You bring that over and put it in my corral. We're going to thrash it, soon as Clyde gets home." He wasn't going to do it. Mama got him by the shirt collar and she pulled him off that grain, and he unloaded in our corral. They put our cattle back there on the pasture, and he went and drove them clear out on the range. I mean, this was his disposition. And he'd go out on the range and drive our cattle off the range and put his on it. The folks would go to town after a load of feed, and they'd come home and Harry's cattle would be in our barn eating hay that Mom and Dad was paying hard-earned money for and hauling for 30 or 50 miles to get up there to feed our stock. Oh, Harry did everything in the world to irritate everybody. Now, as far as we was concerned, John Knox never bothered us in any way. We never had a word.

Although she spent her last days in town, Pearl retained her independent spirit, and her resentment of city ways and city folk.

The way I feel about these things is this: A lot of people feel when they get out of town, everything is free gratis. I mean that's been our experience with a lot of city people any more. And I think that children aren't disciplined in the home as a whole, as much as they used to be, and they have things too free and too easy and they haven't had the sacrifice like a lot of older people, and had the hardships to go through that a lot of the older people have, and I don't think they're appreciative of things. Of course, they've got it the easy way. I know with my own—we have three daughters—we always wanted them to have things better and easier than we had. After they closed our school, and they consolidated and made this all into Poudre-Rl, why, our daughters rode a-horseback from our ranch to Stove Prairie school, five miles each way, a day for two winters. A few years back, there was a church camp. What used to be John Knox's property is now the Methodist Church Camp. A man that was up there and had some daughters that went to Stove Prairie School, he was telling me that they had appropriated—oh, I think it was—l don't know, $40,000 or $50,000—an outlandish amount of money, to change the Stove Prairie Schoolhouse and improve it. And I said, "Well, land, when my girls went over there, they had one room. And one teacher taught it."

A friend of ours lives on the Buckhorn, and she taught that school and had 30-some students there. And she was the only teacher. And I said, "Well, what do they need all that money for, for a little mountain school?" "Oh, my goodness!" he said. "They don't have any gymnasium or any auditorium down there." And I said, "Well, when my daughters was riding 10 miles a day back and forth to that school, they didn't need an auditorium. They got their physical exercise a-riding and walking and they didn't need an auditorium." Nowadays they haul them in a car and everything. This teacher that taught that school, at one time they wanted to know what she wanted in the way of playground equipment. Shoot. We got a baseball bat, and we got our sleds in the wintertime and we'd go out on the hill and we'd make our own recreation and our own enjoyment. Where nowadays they've got to have everything so modern and everything so easy.

There was a time, back in Prohibition days, when there was quite a few moonshiners around up in that country. This John Knox that I mentioned. There's still part of his old still house. Part of the old still house is still standing back there, west of his ranch. He was a Spanish man, and I've heard about him. Dad used to have a horse we called Spotlight. And he knew where all the stills was in the country. And I said it would never have done for a Prohibition officer to ever come up there and ride that horse because he'd have took him to all the neighborhood stills up in that country. One time there was some Spanish guys that had a big still. I never knew where it was—it was back up west of the ranch somewhere—and I was down on my hands and knees out in the fields all by myself, thinning carrots or lettuce or something, and this guy had a lot of scars on his face. Clarence had told me that he had a sawed off .30-.30 that he carried in his pantsleg. And he always had his hand in his pants pocket. He told Clarence one time, he said he could just throw his leg up like that and shoot. I was crawling on up this garden row, and I looked up and here was this guy standing at the end of the garden. And I'm telling you there was a cold chill went down my back when I was out there all by myself. He never said a word. He was a lookout man, and he stood up there. . . . There was timber come right up to the garden at that time. He stood there and watched me a while, and left. He never said one word. I never did have any problems. He didn't bother anybody, but you look back at some of those times and it's. . . . Like I say, things is changed considerably.

My father was a breeder of horses. At one time we had 125 head of horses. And, of course, we didn't have them all broke. Ed and Doug Watson lived south of Masonville, and they had a place down there where they put on rodeos. At their ranch. They had corrals and things. And my father furnished the horses for them. At one time they put on rodeos every two weeks. Like I said, my father was an old cowboy, and his word was law and order. And I grew up under his feet. I was always where he was. I was his boy even though I had a foster brother. My brother was real tender-hearted, and every time something didn't go right he'd break down and start crying. So Dad—we started at the ranch, a-riding calves. And the neighbor boys would come in, and on Sunday, why, they'd bring in a bunch of horses and get out there and ride them. Alfred Benson and Elmer, and some other boys that lived around there. And they'd come up there on Sunday and just have a lot of fun, a-riding. I didn't ride at that time, but I got a little older and Watson used to put on rodeos and I'd go down there. My father wouldn't let me ride bucking horses, intentionally, with a saddle. I had to ride bareback with a surcingle. So they would go down there every two weeks, and I'd ride bucking calves and bucking horses.

We put on a rodeo in Estes Park one time, and I was in the saddle 15 days straight. We was rounding up horses. Our range was 18 miles from the ranch to Masonville. Our horses run over what they called Payton Hill. So I'd been out there helping round up horses 'cause they was going to have this rodeo at Masonville. So I went down there and they had this rodeo. They didn't have too good a corral, and some of the stock got away with surcingles on them and saddles and one thing and another. Mom and Dad had to go back up to the ranch to see about the stock. So I stayed down there, and I helped the Watson boys ride and round the stock back in, and got surcingles on them. Well, the next day we was going to Estes Park to put on a rodeo up there on Labor Day. Mom and Dad and the Watson boys and some of the other boys and myself rode these horses to Estes Park.

We left Masonville at five, and we had them corralled at 10 o'clock at the Blue Ribbon Livery which is at the east end of Estes Park. They just had a small corral there, and chutes fixed. Not too good facilities. And they didn't have any arena. So on Labor Day they went over there, and we didn't have any cattle up there, just the horses. And they had a parade and we rode in the parade. It started up at the old Stanley Hotel. Went down through Estes Park and back around, and it would be a little past where the lake or reservoir is there at Estes Park, now, and over at the west end of that was where they had the chutes. We went back out there on Labor Day. They parked the cars around in a semi-circle. Dad wanted me to ride. So they put the surcingle on the horse. Dad never let me ride in the saddle because he was afraid I'd get a foot caught in a stirrup and get drug and hurt. So I had to ride bareback. Well, I went.

Got on a horse in the chute and came out. And the horse didn't buck good enough to suit my dad and she started running. She run out between these cars. In those days they had old touring cars. Tops up. When we went through between two cars, I thought, well, what was the use of riding out behind the audience? So I reached down and caught a hold of one of those bows on top of the car and slid off. Well, the pickup man come through behind me and like to run over me with his pickup horse. Dad wasn't satisfied I hadn't put on a good enough ride. So he got a horse out in the arena and blindfolded her and eared her down and put the surcingle on her and put me on her. So I had to ride another horse. But during that time, I rode eight head of horses and I think it was four bucking steers during that 15 days I was in. The next day I was sick all day. So we had to stay over in Estes Park. I held up the whole crowd. It was just a little bit too much on me. So then the next day we rode them back down to Masonville and the next day we took them back to the ranch. Back in those days it was all a-horseback and it was a long, hard trip. The Simmonses that used to own the Key Cutter Hardware Co. were from New York. They wanted me to go back to Madison Square Garden that fall and ride. They said they would sponsor me and all that. But like I said, I was just a kid, and Dad and Mother couldn't get away from the ranch so I didn't get to go. But for two years I was the youngest lady bareback rider. I was only 14 when I started riding at the rodeos. I never got out on the big rodeo circuit as far as that was concerned, I mean like Cheyenne and places like that, because we had the ranch to take care of and I couldn't. But I've been piled off of them. I've bit the dirt many a time.

The only broken bones I've ever had, I was going out to the timber to trim some wood and there was a knot sticking out of a tree and I reached up and hit it with my ax. It was in the wintertime and it was real cold and it flew back and broke my nose. The other time, I was down here in high school and I had a ladder fall out from under me and broke a rib. But outside of that, I rode lots of horses and broke lots of horses.

There was one winter Mother and I hauled wood down here to Collins. Dad had the sawmill, and we trimmed out the tree tops and sold them for wood. In those days we got $8 a cord for wood, in the log, to haul down. Nowadays they're selling it, they tell me in Denver, for $95. But here in Collins, they're selling it from $40 to $65. But in those days, we got $8 a cord. Mother and I'd take a team and wagon apiece. We'd come down one day and stay overnight and go back the next. But eight dollars a cord is the way that we did. My husband and I, after we was married, we bought our ranch right in the Depression days. Everybody else was on PWA and on the soup line and things like that, and we bought our ranch. Him and I cut posts and poles and mine-props and sawmills and we worked 12 and 13 hours a day and we made as little as $30 a month, and had two little girls and ourselves to feed. Our neighbors setting across the fence was making fun of us. They was making $40 a month, and he was working two or two and a half days a week, for CWA or PWA or something like that. He was making fun of us, but that's when we bought our ranch and we paid for it.

And we always made our payments on the ranch. And we've had our ranch 43 years. Forty-four years this coming May, I guess, that we've had our ranch. But we've sawmilled. During the Depression days we had men that walked from here clear to the ranch. They heard we had a sawmill. To get jobs. We had quite a few high school kids. But I worked in the timber with the men. My husband never had patience to teach these high school kids how to drop trees and trim them and work with them. So I was the one that went to timber with the men. And especially kids. And taught them how to work. I drove the truck. I've hauled bridge plank to town and I've operated the sawmill.

IV.

Cowboys (and Girls)

Growing up on a farm or ranch in the early 1900s virtually assured a lifelong close relationship with livestock, especially horses. For many young men, horses served as childhood playmates, companions on isolated homesteads, transportation to and from school and, usually around the age of 15, entry to the adult work environment. Young women, too, especially ones who were athletic or were an only child or had only brothers, became expert riders.

"Best Blade Operator in Wyoming"

Toward the end of his life, Art Denham looked back on his stepfather, Harlow, with something approaching objectivity. "He was a good cowboy. He knew things." But one of the things he knew was how to whip Art. "He could just take that line, and hit me just right at the end of it. Just bring the blood." Art took that kind of treatment from Harlow until its cruelty and unfairness got to be too much. At the age of 14 he left, but even then, he kept in touch.

In 1908, when he was two and a half, Art had malaria so bad that the doctor said he would probably die if he didn't leave McComb, Mississippi for a cooler climate. His mother, recently separated from the father Art would never remember, took the infant to Denver, where he stayed with his grandmother for several years, accompanying her when she moved to Byers, 50 miles to the east. Eventually his mother and Harlow came out from Mississippi and settled at Byers too. Harlow soon found work at Walden, in North Park, and took his wife and Art's younger brother, leaving Art with his grandmother. In 1916 the family came back to Byers.

Then he went to work at the Parrot Ranch out there at Byers. They took me, and we lived there, in this little old cabin, and he worked on this ranch. I stayed there till I was 11 years old. Then he run across some people that wanted to buy, and wanted my step dad and another fellow to go in partners and move up to Wyoming, on these ranches. They bought three ranches. So they got everything all gathered up around Byers in a covered wagon. Thirteen head of horses, and my mother, me and brother and step dad. So we left Byers. Headed for west of Laramie about 12 miles. We come through Fort Collins, stopped at the old Stover store that used to be down there.

Stayed there overnight, I believe. Yeah. It snowed about two inches. This was in the fall of the year. I remember him buying us some gloves.

So we left there, got to the Forks Hotel, and my step dad got ptomaine poisoning. So this other fellow, he was following along in an old Model T Ford, he took him on to Laramie to the hospital. My mother went with him. That left us, I and my brother, to bring this outfit through. So we left the Forks Hotel. I can't think of the name of this ranch we stopped at. It ain't too far up the road, off on the east side about two miles. We could see this house. So we said we'd better pull over in there and see if we can ask that rancher to stay all night there. So we did. He kept us. Fed us, fed our horses. Didn't charge us a thing.

We left there the next morning. Got to Virginia Dale, and come a storm and we was snowed in there for 10 days. We tried to go one day, but the horses just couldn't pull the wagon. It was too deep. So we went back and stayed another day or two and it kind of cleared up a little, so we took out. And we went from there, clear on to the ranch. That was a good 25 miles. We cut right straight across from Tie Siding, straight northwest to the ranch. We got to the ranch that night about 4:30. Cold. Boy. And we didn't have any good hay to feed the horses. Some old fox-tail alfalfa. So we fed them horses that hay, and this other fellow—partner—Cocker was his name, he come out and took us to town. Then we come back out the next morning to feed the horses, and them horses had that foxtail all in their mouth and we had to dig all them 13 head of horses' mouths all out of that foxtail. So then we stayed on that ranch. Well, we shipped in a bunch of cattle from Texas— around 400 head of cattle—and we had a hard winter that winter. We lost darn near all of them. They hung on for oh, about three years, on them ranches. Then, I was about 14, someplace in there.

Well, I and my dad didn't get along very good. Step dad. And they were supposed to pay me 50 dollars a month. Well, I never did see any of the money. And I worked like the devil,

tying bales on that baler. It was an old one-horse baler that
went around like that, you know, out there, cold every morning, and I worked there all winter, baling hay. Then on Saturdays, I'd load up a ton or two on the hay rack, take it clear to
Laramie, and sell it. They had a gypsum mill there. So, we just
argued and argued and fought, so that. . . . And he. . . . If we'd
do some little thing wrong. . . . I hate to tell all this, but . . . He
wouldn't whip us like an ordinary person would. He'd take a
line down off of the harness, and stand me over there by the
door somewhere, about that far away. . . . About 10 or 15 feet.
He was a good cowboy. He knew things, and he could just take
that line, and hit me just right at the end of it. Just bring the
blood. So he done that several times and I got sick of it, and I
took off. So I never did go back home anymore. Never did. So
ever since I was 14, I've been out on my own.

So in the meantime, I'd bought a little Indian pony from
him for 25 dollars. I'd worked there on the ranch with him,
bailing hay and stuff. We couldn't get along, so I got on this
pony one day and—I rode this horse across the big hollow.
Great big valley in there. Great big one. Lots of acres. Went
over there and stopped at a ranch and asked him for a job. He
said, "Sure. Did you ever drive a team?" I said, "Yeah." And I
had. So he put me to raking hay.

In the fall of the year, you know, they have cattle round-
ups. They used to. Well, they don't anymore. Everybody turned
out in this big hollow I was telling you about. They had poison
weed out there. I even rode out there watching the cattle for
poison weed. You'd find one, why, he'd be down, probably, and
you'd take a pocket knife out, and chew up some tobacco, or
some vinegar and soda, and give her a drink of that, see. Or if
you had some chewing tobacco, you just wad up a lot of that.
Just cut it right across the tail, underneath, into an artery there,
and that'd bleed good. Stuff all that full of tobacco. But soda
and vinegar, they were good. That'd make them vomit.

That'd slow it down, that tobacco. I remember cutting
this hand, here. Oh, I darn near cut that thumb off. So my
brother-in-law—he always chewed—so he had a great big wad

of chewing tobacco. I fell off, in a crick. There was a bottle down there, and I fell on that beer bottle. Just cut that thumb near right off. But he had a chew. We just put that right on there. Oh, it was an awful cut. I went home after we got through fixing it. Never did sew it up right. I just got along fine. I was pretty small. I didn't know all the details of it, about that bleeding and things. But I done it. If I'd get cut too much, you know, why, you'd bleed to beat the band. You put some of that tobacco on there, and slow it down. I don't know what done it. I guess it just kind of seared it or burned it or something.

They had the roundups all there. They'd all camp. They'd all bring their wagons, and there was a cook shack in a wagon and everything, and they'd camp there. It was all open range back out in that north country. When they'd think they all got them gathered, from way out, for miles, they'd all throw them in our field there. Then they'd take one day or two, whatever it took them, to sort them all out. Put them in another pasture or something, you know, for the different fellows that owned them. Had one black fellow on there. I'd never seen one, you know, after leaving Mississippi. I never remember seeing any Negroes, you know, a black person. Had one of them on the roundup, and he was a pretty good cowboy.

Then after the haying was over, he kept me for a little while, fixing the hay corrals, you know, re-fencing them. Got them all done. Why, then he says, "Well, Art, you can stay all winter with us, if you want to. But," he says, "I can't pay you. But you can stay here and help with the chores." I said "OK." But this fellow I got acquainted with had a mail route in Laramie. He was always out doing something else. He had a little ranch on the little Laramie. He wanted me to come and work for him. He didn't pay me much. Said he couldn't, but he'd board me and pay me a little. So I went with him. His name was Fred Greaser. He'd drive this mail once in a while, and then he'd want me to take it. I was only a little kid, you know. Had that big old. . . . Well, it was a big Reo and it had about five or six or seven seats lined up in the back, you know, and just a tarp, and a roof over the sides, fastened down. It

was a long ways up there to take that mail. About 45 miles. Up
in bad country. Roads with snow. The old town was Morgan.
Had a post office up there. You could see it off of that
Highway 8, back up in there. So I done that for him two years.
Just about two years.

So then I went back to Byers and finished out the 9th
grade. I had an uncle by the name of Jim Morgan. He had five
kids. Three girls and two boys. They was all older than I was.
We left there. I bought me an old Model T Ford. No fenders
or nothing on it. I didn't have the right kind of license on it.
But I took a chance anyhow. Drove that old Model T, and he
had a Model T, and one of the oldest boys, he decided to go,
too. So we all had three old Model T Fords, and we were
headed for Worland, Wyoming. It took us a long time to get
there. In the meantime, I'd known Edna. We got there at
evening at Laramie, and they had a campground out there in a
kind of a park for people to camp in. I camped there that
night. I went over to the house to see Edna, and she wasn't
home. So I went on back to camp and got up early the next
morning. She come over there before I was up. She'd heard I
was in town. So we went and took a little ride in the car. She
had somebody's car, an old Oldsmobile.

So them guys kept a-waiting for me to come back.
Thought we'd better get a-going. I told Edna, I said, "Them
guys want to go on and leave me. I might have trouble with
that old Ford." So we finally took off. I never caught them
boogers till I got to the river. Caught them at the Rock River, is
where I caught them. I just really went fast with that old Ford.
Old dirt roads, you know, and no pavement. So we went on.
We came to some place way up there north of Rawlins, and the
gas was 50 cents a gallon, and we were getting short of money.
So they had to leave this other fellow's—the other boy, Lee
Morgan—leave his Ford there cause of the gas bill. We cut
across there, some way. I don't know how we got across there,
but we did. So we went on up there, to Worland. The next day
I got a job with the oh, whatchamacallit. I can't think of it now.
Could have been the Holly Sugar Company. They all got jobs
on the ranch, too. All worked again that summer. So I made a

little money. I wanted to come back to Laramie and see Edna. So I did. And I had them old plates on, see? The sheriff asked me, he said, "Them plates don't belong on there." I said, "No, they don't." "Well," he says, "we're going to have to fine you $100." I says, "I haven't got $10." "Well," he said, "you'll have to lay in jail 10 days." I said, "OK." So they took me up there. I called this man Woodman. I'd worked for him. So I worked with him in the summer putting up hay. And then, seems like these people-these Morgans went back to Byers.

Harlow and Art's mother had left Wyoming about this time and gone out to Hollywood, where Harlow had hired on as a stunt driver for the movie Ben Hur, in which he drove chariots. When he heard his mother and Harlow were coming back to Wyoming to visit, Art decided it was time he and Edna got married.

So I asked Edna, "Well, why don't we run down to Fort Collins and get married?" She said, "OK. Let's go." So we didn't have no car then, I didn't, so I went and borrowed her brother's—I think he had an Oldsmobile, too. Didn't have a top or nothing on it. Drove that thing clear down here to Fort Collins and went up to the courthouse and got the marriage license, and we got married. So we went back, and Edna's sister had a house. A little old three-room house. Just a shack. So we went and rented that from her. Went up and what little money we did have, bought a few pieces of furniture, and moved in this place. In about three or four days, here they came from California. So he was glad we got married and all that. Tried to tell me, though, "You was too young. You didn't know what you was doing." But "Oh," I said, "I think so."

The Morgans come through and stopped. They was going back up there to Manderson this time, to work in the coal mine. Well, they was going to lay off the people at the shops, and the boss told me I was going to be one of them, so I just had a chance to go up with them, so I just went. I didn't have a car or nothing. So we went up there, and I went right to work in a coal mine. We stayed right with them there for about three months in their house. They had a great big one. Shack, kind of. We stayed with my uncle. My aunt wasn't there. She'd passed away. Edna was taking care of Pete. He was just a little boy. He came late. So we was all working up in the coal mine and the weather was so nice we couldn't sell the coal. And we got down in them mines and shoveled coal. And he couldn't pay us 'cause he couldn't sell the coal. And there we were. And he furnished us coal, all right. We got all the coal we wanted, but we was running awful short of eats.

So I went up to the store to see if we couldn't get some on credit. He didn't want to, but he did let us have some spuds and flour and some slab bacon. When that run out, I went back to get some more. "Gosh," he says, "I just can't. I might let you have some spuds"—they were the cheapest thing there was around there—and some oatmeal. Didn't have no cream for them. So we lived on spuds and just old oatmeal and put warm water on it. That's how we eat for quite a while. So, Edna got a job at a hotel there. She was getting $30 a month. I was a-helping around there, getting the coal in, and the wood, and stuff, keeping the fires and sweeping and scrubbing around there for my board.

So we stayed there for a while, and then I owed this bill over to the store, I don't know, it was about $75 I owed him. Never did get our money out of that coal 'cause it was just summer all winter. Never did. The coal all slack. They had to haul it out of there. A guy took mail from Manderson up to Heartville, Wyoming. It was about 45 miles up there. Something like that. And there was a guy named Tony. He was a fellow up there. Had a man working for him. He got killed, riding a horse on slippery meadows. Fell and killed him. He said he'll be down here tomorrow. He says, "I'll tell him about you." So he came. So I went back up with him and worked up there for $75 a month on that ranch. We had a little cabin, a little log cabin in back there a ways. I stayed there with him I guess three years.

Broke six head of horses up there for him to ride, and they was wild ones. He had about 150 head of horses. And he had studs running right with them, see, up on this range. So every spring we'd go up there and round up all these horses and bring them down and put them in the corral and work the colts over. Some that had some kind of a disease, or anything, we'd just take his 30-06, go out there and run them out there, and shoot them. And if one looked like he'd make a good saddle horse, we'd keep him in and break him to ride. One day we was going up there after them, and I was a-riding a kind of bronc, and I'd just got through shoeing this horse that he was riding, and he was leading it, see, I was following right along behind. I don't know what happened, but this horse kicked. He kicked me right there. I'm telling you, if that wasn't the sorest. . . . That shoe hit me right there. Man. Oh, that did hurt. He wanted to go back, and I said, "No, let's go on." But that thing sure did swell up and was sore, oh man, oh man.

There were about 150 head of horses up there, and then he had about 1200 head of cattle. So, in the spring of the year, we'd take all them cattle up in the summertime and put them up there, too, on the range. Somebody had to stay up there with them. We packed everything up there, salt and groceries and everything. Couldn't get up there with an automobile or wagon or nothing. We had six, eight head of horses to pack salt on, and groceries, fence, barbed wire—spools of barbed wire.

Had a two-room log cabin. It was built kind of in a side hill, that way. And it rained quite a bit up there at times. Didn't have a floor in it, and darn water would build up around back there, and then we'd have to dig trenches for the water to go clear on out through. And the mice was so thick in there. I'm telling you. I was laying there one night, and one bit me right on the finger. Edna, after we got the cattle all set and everything, why then she'd come up with me, and we'd go fix fence and go fishing and ride around. There was all kinds of game, bears, and everything. One day he come up. Edna was down there at the cabin, then at home. He came up and we was walking around, and the dang bears had been killing the calves. So, when he come down this time, he went to a Forest Service and Game and Fish, and told them the bears was killing his calves. "Well," he says, "go back up and kill every one you see. Kill them."

So he come back up, and we went up that evening to start killing them, and we saw one and he shot it, right in the shoulder. It was a long ways away. Broke his shoulder. So we got on the horse again, and followed around in there. It was a heck of a mountain, going way up high. So we was trailing this bear up there, and I was right ahead of him. It was getting dark. His name was Lee—I says, "Lee, we'd better let him go." "No", he says, "let's go get him." It was getting so dark, and he was right behind me. I said, "If that bear starts coming down here," I said, "Now, you get him." And pretty soon here come that bear right out. I looked up and he was a coming, and he was right on his hind feet. He wasn't very far from me, and I told him, I said, "Lee, get him!" And I ducked, and boy, he did, right in the heart with that 30-06.

Then we went up the next day to skin it—he wanted the hide. And something had torn it all up. On the back end part, see? We skinned it anyhow, and took that thing down to camp. He wanted to go home, so we got one horse blindfolded to get that bear hide on him, and I'm telling you if he didn't come down out there with eight head of horses. He took eight with him to bring some salt back. And the horses were just scared to death of that bear hide. A big black one. So then the next day I went around to the same place, and I was riding a good saddle horse. He was a good one. I always rode him when we rounded up horses—'cause he'd outrun them. So I saw a bear. I got down off of that horse and was going to shoot him and that darn horse jerked away from me and went for camp just as hard as he could go. And there I was, afoot. It was only about a mile and a half from camp, though.

It was bear country there. Lots of them. Oh, there were a lot of them. I guess I must have come down the next day or two. Helped him come up with the salt probably. We had a milk cow there. Edna wasn't a very good milker then. But she'd get enough out for herself and Mrs. . . . . I forget her name now. They kind of lived together while we were up there. In the meantime, when I owed this $75 grocery bill, see, I told this guy, "Now, when I get to working, I'll send that money down to you." He heard I went right up there and went to work.

And heck, he couldn't wait to get up there and see—Doyle was his name— see him, and ask him for the money, you know, that was owed him. "Well," he says, "Art hasn't got that much coming. So, he says, "I can't pay you. So he come and saw me and I said, "No, I haven't got it. I haven't got that much coming yet. Wait another month and I'll probably have it." So he come up in another month and I had his money for him. It was hard times.

So then I worked for that guy a couple of years, I guess. His wife was a lot younger than him, see? She was a woman that wanted to get out and go places, and he never did take her anywhere. And he had a new Model T touring car. I come down off the mountain and went over to the house to tell him what was going on up there. "Well," he says, "I'm going to go up." And he says, "The women want to go to Tensleep, Wyoming for the rodeo." And, he says, "You take them." I said, "OK, I will." And he give me some money to spend on them. So he went on up there that afternoon. So we all got ready, and the next day we takes out for Wyoming. That's just about 30 miles, something like that, right straight south of Hydeville. Went to the rodeo. Watched the rodeo. There wasn't many cars in those days up in there, anyhow.

A guy got hurt—got bucked off, or something—on a horse, and there was no one to take him to the doctor in Worland, so they come and asked me if I would, and I did. Took him to the doctor. Broke his ankle, I believe. So I went back on up, and then got the women and went on back home to the ranch. Didn't go up for a day or two, like I should have, you know. He was good to let me stay down, but I didn't go back right up, see? And here he come down, just frothing at the mouth. Oh, he was mad, 'cause I didn't get up there. So he fired me. So I said, "OK." So then another fellow, just oh, about two miles from there, another big rancher, he was looking for somebody. I knew he was. So I went over and talked to him. Said, "You bet, I'll come over and go to work." I stayed there two winters feeding cattle. He didn't put up the hay himself. He had some contractor come in and put his hay up. In the meantime, I'd go down and work for some other

people on the hay. Then I'd come back up there and feed for
him in the winter. I and another fellow.

Then Lee Doyle, the guy that fired me, just couldn't find
anybody else. So he come over and talked to the fellow I was
working for, to see if he couldn't get me back. "Why," he says,
"Yes. You can have him if you want him. You had him before."
Lee come and asked me. I said, "Yeah, I'll go back to work for
you." And I did. 'Cause it was all summer, too, you know.
Wasn't such hard work. Just riding, that's all I done. Then we
left there and went back down to the hotel and started to run
it. I made a little money, and I bought me a 1926 Star Roadster.
So we run the hotel for a while.

They run lots of sheep way back up in the foothills of
the mountains. They'd drive everything down to the railroad.
We had that hotel full. Didn't have rooms. I think about 16 or
18 rooms, that's all we had. Them days, everything was cheap,
you know, so we was running the hotel, getting along there
pretty good, and Edna wanted to go to Basin, up about 10 or
12 miles from there to get something. I don't know what. It
looked like rain. The top was down on this roadster. I raised
the top up and slipped it down over a bolt and put the lock
washer on the nut and I was tightening that nut, looking right
at it, and a piece of that lock washer broke and went right in
that eye. That's the reason I got that bum eye. Blind in it.
That's why. So I went down to Worland to a doctor. He just
took his knives, you know—his scalpel, or whatever they
were—and just cut it out. So it was a mess, and it just wouldn't
get better. I kept going to him, and it just wasn't getting any
better. So everybody said, "You better go to a specialist." So
we had to go clear to Billings, Montana to a specialist. That
was the closest. So I was up there about—well, we left some
people taking care of the hotel, see? And we had to stay up
there. She had to doctor it, and she couldn't stay there and run
the hotel. Had to lead me around. Had it tied up. So we were
there about two months, I guess. In the meantime, the hotel
was going in the red. They wasn't making a thing. I don't know
where it was going, 'cause we had a good business when I left.
We stayed up there about two months and then come back

down. Didn't have no money to buy groceries there, they didn't have nothing. So we had to give that all up.

August 28, 1929, we had a son born. We named him Lee Ervin Denham. We went on working there until fall, I think. Late in the fall. Edna's sister and brother came out from California. The Depression was about to hit then, so I was laid off, and we drove back to California with them. They had a car, and we had a car. We drove back to California and stayed with them until '32 or something like that. Anyhow about 6 months. Then we came back and went to Estes Park. That's when the Depression was really rough. So we got up there, and my mother and step dad was living there and they wanted us to come up so they could see the baby. So we went there and stayed there, and I got a job on the relief working on the roads. Estes Park them days, there was about 500 people was all there was there. Didn't have no oiled streets or nothing, they was just bare.

Well, you couldn't get a job. You had to go to work for the county on the relief, see? We got, I think, seven dollars a week, or something like that, to buy groceries and stuff with. And we trapped a little on the side. Caught coyotes and bobcats.

One job Art took was with the Works Projects Administration, which was building trails in Rocky Mountain National Park. He packed supplies into the WPA camps.

Our headquarters was up at Bear Lake. They hauled it up there in trucks, and things for us, and we packed the horses. We had 11 head of horses to pack. And I think it was about 11 miles back into them lakes. Building trails. It started with a trail from Bear Lake, and just wound it all around down to the lake, see? Then they'd cut the timber around the lakes and clear it— all that dead stuff. Had a lot of experiences with some of them horses. They'd buck the eggs off. A crate of eggs would be on there, and they'd buck it off. Eggs everywhere. Shovels and picks. Just packed in everything over there. Had to, see? And they had a cook shack over there, and a lot of men in there.

After I got off the relief, why, the county hired me. I was driving a truck. He give me a try at it. And so I done fine with it. Had brand new trucks. Ford trucks. So he gave me a job and work. Then after I drove the truck a while, why then he put me on the blade. "Maintainer," they call them, I guess. It's a blade—an old homemade one. So I run that for oh, two or three years.

And we had an old '60 gas tractor. And I run the tractor and the other guy, he wanted to run the blade, so he run the blade. But this other blade we had, we used that big outfit, mostly to clean the gutters, you know? Pull it up on the road. And we'd use the other one—it was a homemade—made out of McCormick Deering 10-40, they called it. Homemade outfit. But I got to run that thing pretty darn good. So I stayed over there until they changed the administration, or whatever you call it. Changed county commissioners and everything, so we was all laid off, every one of us.

I knew enough, then, about how to run one, and what a road should look like, and everything. So I takes off out of there and goes to Cheyenne and hire out with a big outfit. And I went to Laramie and got a job there running that blade there. Nice big diesel. Stayed with him every summer for about two summers. I think I got 70 cents an hour.

In '43, I guess, I got a job with the Union Pacific as watchman on the railroad. And a watchman out at the tie plant. That's during the war, now.

The railroad was worried about sabotage, but the real problem was weary trainmen.

There was a train went through there about every five minutes. You know where the tie plant is? I was out there, too. I'd have to go over there, and them engineers, they had a red light down there in the yards for them to stop about a mile out of town, see? And when it turned green, why, they were supposed to go. But I kept a-waiting for him, and I'd wait for him a while, and they wouldn't wake up, so I'd have to go over there and shake them out of there, get them going. Them trains would be lined up clear back to Tie Siding where they had that wreck there, you know. And they was sleeping, the engineers and firemen. They were just sound asleep.

His job as watchman led to employment as a deputy in Laramie.

When they had some real bad guys, why, they'd come and get me, too. When that guy killed that woman up in Telephone Canyon, it's been years ago, he killed her and raped her and everything, up there. And he was a mean—, he was a mean one. He'd just as soon kill you as look at you. And they finally got him to jail, and he set fire to all his mattresses and everything, so they called me to come in there and get those mattresses out. I told them, "Now you guys stand at the door, now. If he goes to bother me, why, I says, 'Let him have it!'" He was a big, husky guy. I cleaned all the mattresses out. Guys that were hoboes, and things, they didn't want them there on the railroads. So we'd have to run them off, over onto the highway. That was quite a job, sometimes. It was mostly night work and all, and I got tired of it. I had a few head of cattle we was gathering up. Planning on coming down here and buying a place in Berthoud. So that's the reason I quit. They sure didn't want me to quit. Oh, they begged me to stay. So we moved down—bought this place down in Berthoud, 160 acres.

The farm at Berthoud was a good one, but farming was hard. A few years later Art and Edna sold out there, and bought a small ranch up Rist Canyon, west of Bellvue.

We had 100 head of cattle. Put up enough hay for them. Had lots of springs on the place. World of water. And then we had 1200 acres leased from the government. Cost us so much a head for cattle, you know, to run them out there. It was only about 18 cents when we first bought the place. To pasture them out there on the government, 18 cents a head. Until it got up to 34, and then they kept cutting the head of cattle down. So we just couldn't hardly run any cattle at all on it. It was 30-some head on 1200 acres. So we had so many cattle,

and we was pasturing them out around our neighbors, and
places. We always milked a few cows. About six head of cows.
Fed those calves till they got big enough to wean, you know,
for the buckets, and then we'd just take them over in the big
meadow across the hill. We were just doing wonderful on that
ranch.

So we stayed there how long? Couple of years, wasn't it?
Three years. About three. A guy come along and wanted to buy
that ranch. I didn't want to sell—we didn't want to sell it. We
was off to a neighbor's one night, and he come up and left a
note on the door. He wanted to buy the ranch and wanted to
buy it right away. So we went home and found the note and
went down and talked to him, and yeah, he wanted it right now.
So I priced it pretty high. Paid $14,500 for it and priced it to
him for $27,000. And he paid it, too. Then we made a bad
move. Made money on every place we've ever bought and sold.
This is where we went wrong. We cut out an ad in the paper,
from Arkansas, for a 500 acres ranch down there. Well, Upley
and his wife, and Edna, we just took a trip down there to look
at it. He was kind of interested in a place down there, too. We
went down there and looked at this place. Got in there at night
and didn't know where he lived or nothing, so we went to the
hotel, to get a room. They didn't have any water in the rooms.
He was out of water. But we went to bed, anyhow. The well
had went dry. So we called him up, soon as it got daylight.
Come right over there and took us over and give us breakfast.
A nice fellow. Then after we got through eating, and everything, I said "Well, let's go in the jeep and go look at the
ranch." And we went. Looked fine to me. A little old shack of
a cabin on it. Part of a well. It wasn't very good. But we
bought it. We give $6,000 for it. Paid him cash for it. It was a
terrible place to live. Them darn copperheads, everywhere
you'd look, you'd see one looking at you. Boy, they were thick.
Oh, man.

*One year of that was enough. They sold out and returned to Colo-
rado, first to Loveland, then near Cedaredge, then to 12 acres just
off North Shields in Fort Collins.*

Then we had a fire in 1967 and burned our house down
and everything we had in the house. It was about two o'clock
in the morning. We was all in bed. We had a dog, one of those
black dogs. Labrador. Just a pup. Nice young one. He was a
good dog. And it got so hot in there, he woke us up. Tried to
get us out of there. But we didn't pay no attention to him, I
guess. Then Edna, she woke up and said, "I smell smoke." She
was getting ready to go to Denver the next morning. She woke
up and smelt that smoke and I says, "Yes. The house is on fire.
Let's get out of here." We got out of there and ducked to get
under that smoke. We couldn't see any daylight through the
window. The front porch was all windows and we couldn't see
daylight nowhere. Too much smoke in there. We got outside
and the back end of the house was shooting in the air, oh,
15–20 feet in the air. The blaze. We thought the dog went out
with us, but that darn dog didn't come out. He went back into
there and got under the bed, and he just suffocated under
there. The spring mattress—good springs—they just melted
right together. Edna, she had to have a little oxygen. Tried to
call the fire department and the darn girl down there, "Just a
minute, just a minute," and heck the fire was burning. It was
getting so hot she just throwed down the phone. I got in the
pickup and went up to the neighbor's a little ways. Told him to
call the fire department. They got there, finally. It was all gone.
Everything was gone. It was an awful fire. Boy. Just burned
everything we had. She was running around in her night-gown.
I did sneak in and got some overalls, on my hands and knees.

They say yet, they don't know how we got out of there.
Gosh, it was awful. It rained a little bit that evening. Well, I
guess it was raining when she went to bed. She was taking a
bath. Got to bed a little later, and about two o'clock, why, she
was a-going. They claimed a short. The two wires got together.

*As a laboring man, Art took the most pride in his skill with a
"blade" – the road grader or maintainer that he operated on county
roads in southern Wyoming and Northern Colorado.*

If I was looking for a road job I could always get one. Always. 'Cause everybody knew me or had heard of me, running heavy equipment. If it wasn't for my eyes, I could still do it. But I can't look down the road, oh, 700 feet and see a blue-top—you know, a stake—and tell where to set my blade and hit the top of that, that far apart. I used to could do that.

Since I had that eye hurt, why, I never have read too much. I strained my eyes a lot working, you know. On working machinery. People didn't see how I could do it. Run that machinery and put the road up to grade right on the specs, you know. With just one eye. But it just comes to me just naturally. No effort to do it. Take a cap and set that blade just so much, like that on the ground or a little closer and just go.

And just like that blade—running that blade, you know, you're setting there and you can tell where there's a little hole, pretty soon. It moved just a little. Well then you put the blade down it'll raise it up. Well, I guess they claim I was the best blade operator in the state of Wyoming. Everybody wanted me. Didn't like the cats too well. They're dirty things. Them old tracks, boy, they let dirt right up in your eyes.

Charlie Howard

*Most modern day dwellers in Colorado's Fort Collins-Loveland area
are familiar with the Big Thompson Flood of 1976. If they weren't
alive and in the storm, they know people who were. Many reminders
exist in the form of plaques commemorating those 145 who were
washed away and zoning commissions who view with great skepti-
cism proposals to put housing developments in floodplains. The 100-
year flood, it was called. Or the 300-year.*

*But the real old-timers, people with nearly a century of personal
experience with Colorado's weather, realized that storms of similar
tremendous magnitude are much more frequent. Perhaps the main
difference lies in number of human lives lost.*

*For Charlie Howard, born near Walden in North Park and raised on
a ranch in what is now Lory State Park south of Bellvue, the biggest
storms occurred in 1913, 1938 and 1951, with some other bad ones
along the way. For him, the terrible winter storm of 1913 was
unforgettable. And for him, as for all ranch people, the true measure
was how it affected the livestock.*

The first day of December was Monday that year. And it
come about a two-day storm, got about two feet of snow. And
then it kind of cleared up one day, and we went and got the
cattle in some, and I believe, I don't remember whether
Wednesday or Thursday or Friday morning—Friday. I went out
and we had one of these here old-time spring wagons. Some
people call them hacks. Missourians called them hacks. And
we come out—I come out. I got up and was going to go out to
the barn and milk and feed the stock, and the snow had drifted
over the barn. You see the barn was over here, and then there
was a yard here between and then the house up here.

Well, you see the wind was from the north. So the snow
just from the level of the seats—you could just see the back of
the seat sticking up out of the snow. So there was a pole fence
around there, so I went around. I tried the doors on the south

side and I couldn't get them open. It'd drifted plumb tight. So I
went around on the north side of the barn, there was a hay
corral there, and the snow had blowed off of that, part of it,
so I could go in on the north side of the barn. But the snow
averaged about three feet and a half, on the level if it hadn't
drifted. But everything drifted, and you see, up there, there'd
be a flat place. Well, that is open, you know, and then the snow
would go in these gullies. Well, the snow of one gulley would
blow into, from that gulley on, so we had about—some places,
them drifts was 30 feet deep. Boy, it was deep. Well, it happened, we hadn't turned the cattle in there, yet.

We wasn't looking for that bad a snow. But they was up
west of the fence on the foothills of the mountain, there, and
we thought, oh Dad, he thought the cattle was all killed. But
Saturday morning it come up clear, and we looked around and
saw the cattle commence to drift up. And the ground was
pretty bare so they could get feed. If they hadn't have been in
the place where they was, they could have got snowed in and
they could have got buried, too, but they got up there somewhere where it had blowed the snow off, so they wasn't so bad
off. And then we went along. They was up on these ridges, you
know, to get out of the snow, because the north slopes was
bare. Well, not bare, but mainly. And then we just opened the
fence and started to let them down into on the flats there, and
there hadn't been anything on the grass, right there, since
spring, so they had plenty of feed, soon as they got down to
that.

Now, now you take out here even up here, anywhere
where you get away from the hills. You take a bunch of cattle
and there ain't no shelter whatsoever. They're just going to
turn away from the storm and just drift with the snow. Hard to
tell where they'd go, and they can't see and they'll fall over
things and then they stop and get tired and the snow kind of
blows over, like they was in shelter and the snow would just
cover them all up. I know the worst snow we had for that was
in New Year's of '49, I believe it was. Had a big storm and
blowed the cattle down along Cheyenne this way. Down in that
country. Well, we didn't lose hardly any. Because it struck them

in the fall of the year when the cattle was strong. They was in good shape from the summer, you know. And they was in good shape so they could take quite a little. You take them in the spring when they're weak, and boy that's when it gets them.

It was just a toss-up, now, whether the flood in September of '38, or the one in '51 was the worst. We had some horses drown in that '38 flood.

Now wait a minute, now. I'm getting ahead of myself. The worst flood on the Poudre that I know of, that is a regular real flood, there was a big flood up on the north fork of the Poudre and it took all the bridges out. That was in 1904. Just a big flood that come from that branch of the river up that runs north from Livermore. What they call the north fork. There come a big cloudburst up there.

And then these other two floods, the one in '51. Why, it didn't hit so much on the Poudre, but you take up on the Buckhorn and the Redstone and oh, I've seen Rist Canyon go out several times, with cloudbursts.

That one in '51 drowned a few folks up there that lived up there over by Paul Millington. Well, it was around the Brewster place, where them corrals are, when you go up around there, to Paul's. Their name was Post. It was Mrs. John Jovison. He died here, before, and she married a fellow named Post and they both drowned.

And then there was a fellow that had a place right over south of Bellvue on this little crick that comes through there and he—it washed him and his house and everything away.

Charlie was born on September 19, 1890.

My father was a Swede by birth. He come over to this country when he was about 16. Come west about '82. When he landed in America, he landed at Quebec. He had cousins there. And then he come west, and he worked for the Union Pacific Railroad as a bridge carpenter for a few years. And then

they was just opening up North Park about that time, and he
went up there and he carried mail from Pinkham to Tower on
snowshoes one winter. And then he commenced to fix up his
homestead and get stock and stuff and start a ranch. And my
mother, she was born in Golden. I think that was where she
was born. I know the folks lived there.

His name was John A. Howard. He lived with some
people there that taught him. They was good people, and they
told him how to talk the English language, to understand. And
he practiced talking English so he didn't have a brogue. He just
talked like anybody. Like you and I do.

*Charlie's mother's folks were originally from Kentucky. Her father
was a prospector, and he would locate mines and then sell them out.
He worked up around Cripple Creek and Breckenridge and up
through that country.*

She had a sister living in North Park, and she went up
there to teach school a couple of winters, and that's the way
they met. Walden's the biggest town there, but the place we
had, where we lived, was on the Michigan. In on the east side
of the park. It's just down the river from Gould. About 10 or
12 miles out there north of Gould, I guess you'd call it, the
way the river runs. Down towards Walden, anyway, down on
the highway there. He was ranching. Well, in those days, you
could take up 160 acres for a homestead, and then by develop-
ing the land and putting water on it, you could take what they
call a desert claim. And then you'd get another 160.

You'd get 320 right there. And then the main thing for
that was, the main industry up there, was cattle, and then they
had to have irrigation to raise hay, because that's rough country
and you had to feed. That's the way that works. And then there
was open range there, then. So for the summer, they'd just turn
them loose and the cattle all mix up. And then in the fall,
they'd have round-ups and each one would take his cattle in.

It was just ordinary ranch life. I remember we had the
post office there at our house, the post office, and I remember

quite a few of the people used to come for their mail, there. And I don't know. I know we had cold winters, too, up there.

Walden was just a ranch town, a port. And course they had saloons there, them days, and they had a stage station, and so on.

It was awful high up there. It was too high for my mother, and they wanted to get down to a more milder climate so us kids could go to school. That was the main reason. So they traded places. Got that place up there under Arthur Rock.

That was before the real farming commenced to come in. Then we got so we broke out a lot of ground, there, and we planted alfalfa and we raised dry land hay and we pretty near always got one good hay crop. We didn't go to Laramie, but we come through a place they called Woods' Landing, and Tie Siding, and through that way, yes. That was the old freight route that they used years ago, at that time, there was a fellow by the name of Post. Had a freight outfit there in Walden. And he had a couple of big freight wagons, and he'd go to Laramie and buy the stuff—they'd get it wholesale, you know, and then he'd get down there and pick it up by the stores. And then he'd haul it up to Walden. Whatever they needed, you know.

It was a road. I don't know whether it was graded too much, but still it was a fairly good road. Where it needed it leveling up and stuff, why, they graded it, but ordinarily it was just wagon tracks.

When Charlie's folks moved him to the Bellvue area, they settled in what is now Lory State Park. The town of Stout was still there (now it's at the bottom of Horsetooth Reservoir). The quarry business was going good, then, and the sandstone was in demand by Fort Collins, Denver and towns throughout Colorado.

Well, you see, they had a railroad up the glade. And they'd load the rock on the cars—flat cars—and ship it different places where they wanted it. You cross the track there, at Laporte. And then you go up around there and then there was—that cutoff there right around the hill, and went up through that Brewster place. And got up on the west side, where the lake (Horsetooth Reservoir) is. We were right at the foot of that first hog-back there, and run right up along that road—hill there; the quarry was in there.

The fellow we traded with, he'd taken up a place where we was. I went to—they had a little schoolhouse, they called it District 40. Right inside of Soldier Canyon there, about a quarter mile. And it's ail covered over with water, now. They consolidated that school in 1912. They'd have a schoolhouse about every six, seven miles. One room, one teacher. She taught every kid they happened to have. Sometimes they'd run about anywhere from seven to eight to just or one or two, sometimes.

We used to walk to school about a mile—little over a mile from our house down to the school. And then we—they'd hired a teacher there, and most of the time she'd board at our house cause there wasn't anybody else to board them. There was one winter, the second winter we was there, there was just me and my brother to go to school, so they had school down at the schoolhouse, but that was what you termed a hard winter. So we had school most of the time in our front room. Because there was no sense in getting out in that weather to go a half mile to school and back. Or a mile to school, and back. Teacher boarded there and we just had—it made it pretty good because it was an awful cold winter and we didn't have to get out. And we were small. Her name was Titty Campbell.

Outside of school, we just monkeyed around, and when we got big enough, we'd go—we had a pony or two, and we'd ride around with Dad looking after the cattle, and stuff. Had to do quite a bit of riding. Keep the cattle. 'Cause they'd scatter so much, we'd keep them gathered together. There were several different bunches of cattle, and they all run together. Then they'd—each one would go out and put out a salt, so they'd have to—each ranch would put out about an average what he thinks his cattle would need, and they'd all do that, so they kept in salt pretty good.

We had quite a few rattlesnakes. Quite a few rattles, as you say, and coyotes, one thing and another. We had quite a time keeping chickens up there at the ranch. Coyotes would sneak in and get them. Yeah, we—I never paid much attention. Well, I was afraid of rattlesnakes, but I never worried about them. I'd generally see them before they'd see me, and it was worse on them than it was on me. If I had a club, I'd kill him with that. But most generally we'd just throw rocks at him. Hit him in the head with a rock.

That Watson Lake in Bellvue is reasonable recent. You see, they started in '47 to build the Horsetooth Dam. And they put the water in, started the water, the 20th of April, 1951. So you see, that's fairly recent. And then they started the bridge in '52.

Prospecting never held much interest for Charlie.

I've seen so many dry holes up there that I didn't figure it was worth while to do that. There's a lot of prospect holes up there. And then that copper mine that's up there, well, that was along about the turn of the century, 1900 and stuff like that, you'd have thought that was really a mine. It was pretty well at the north end of the place. It was up in the hills there, was north of Arthur Rock. It was right straight west of the pay station up that big gulch there, about a mile and a half. And at that time, when that was running, they run that all with steam. They had a big engine out there and steam boiler, and they did chip some rock out of there, and they struck a pocket or two. Just a pocket. And it didn't test very high then. But they did chip and build a new road around the hill there.

And that mine that I found, it was a pocket and it had jewels in it, crystals. But I let some people go up there from Denver, den mothers, and then we sold it and I didn't get back.

Charlie's mine had wulfenite in it, a crystal containing molybdenum, used in making steel alloys. His mine was never developed commercially, though.

*One of the things Charlie missed most about the way Bellvue
changed over the years was the end of the Friday night dances.*

We'd get invitations to go to dances. Course they used to
have a schoolhouse up on the Redstone, just across the road,
just across the mountain from where we lived. I'd go there, and
it'd be daylight when I come home. I belonged to the Grange,
and we used to have dances there at the Grange. If it was too
bad to get the car to go out, I'd walk down to Bellvue, and
Vern's. Drunk a few beers and monkeyed around and visited
with somebody a while. I wasn't going to stay up there long
enough with myself to go nuts.

*Professional medical help was scarce in those days. Of course, there
was no such thing as health insurance.*

There used to be one doctor in Laporte, I believe.
Doctor Wilkins. Yeah, I remember him, we went to him some.
We just— we didn't have a doctor very much, and then there
was a whole bunch in town, but I know them days, when a
baby was born, they'd just charge you a dollar a mile to go and
take care of them, make two trips. A dollar a mile for each trip,
you know, and it was about, well it was according to how far
from town you was, but 15, 20 dollars was the whole cost for
that. Took care of them and took good care of them.

*Charlie was married twice. The first marriage was fairly brief, but
the second, when he was 65, lasted nearly thirty years, until he died.
During our interview, Miriam, his second wife, related how they had
met during a trip she made from her home in Lincoln, Nebraska.*

I came out on vacations and went fishing. And I had
some friends that knew Charlie, and—well, these people that
he was telling about that lived close. And they took me up
there and introduced me to Charlie. And I'd been up there for
three different summers and didn't even know he existed.
Nobody introduced me or us, or. . . . I think they were afraid
we would get married. But—oh, we just wish we'd met sooner.
The nicest man in the world.

Bulldogging Steers, Bucking Horses and Rodeos

Loyce Creed's father emigrated from Kentucky to Texas, where he met and married Myrtle Pearsall, who became Loyce's mother. For his mother, going forward in life meant going west. Loyce inherited that same love of relocation, and before he finally settled down in Bellvue, it led him throughout the United States, Mexico, Canada, Great Britain and Australia. A belt buckle he was mighty proud of reads: "Presented to Shorty Creed, by Madison Square Garden Rodeo for record time bulldogging, October 20, 1939." The time, four and three-fifths seconds, held up for 17 years at that New York rodeo. By his own admission, that was the fastest steer he ever threw. And he stayed on lots of bucking horses. When he was 75, he still looked like the athlete he had been at 25, compact, narrow at the hips but broad in the shoulders, with a six-foot frame that nowadays would spell running back to any football coach. But in the 1920s, he threw in his lot with traveling shows descended from Buffalo Bill's and the other wild west productions that capitalized on the mythic qualities of the American frontier experience and for good measure added all the exotic animals they could acquire.

We rode bucking horses and steers and bulldogged and stuff on the Miller Brothers' 101 Wild West Show. Course they had elephants and they had buffalo and they had everything, the Miller Brothers' big outfit. We traveled all over from Canada to Old Mexico to England and Australia. We traveled all over. Everywhere there was a rodeo, we went.

Loyce was born in 1903 at Kingfisher, Oklahoma, northwest of Oklahoma City. His parents moved there from Grapevine, Texas, in Tarrant County. After awhile, the family moved on west into Beaver County, in the Oklahoma panhandle, just about on the Texas line, and began to take up quarter sections of land.

We was there in Oklahoma for 14 years, I guess, on that place. They homesteaded. It was all open land. There was no fence, no windmills, no water, no nothing. It was all prairie land. There was lots of buffalo horns. There was antelope in there. There was wild game, but it moved on, shortly, because it begin to settle up. We were 48 miles southeast of Liberal, Kansas. It was all dry land in them days, you know. Horses and teams, and no tractors at all. No automobiles. All dirt roads.

My mother said that she always wanted to go west. And she never wanted to look back, you know. She never wanted to go back. Everywhere she ever went, she never did want to go back. Some people go some place and stay awhile, but they turn around and go back. But she never did. She never wanted to go back. So any move that they ever made, they made for the better, or tried to find a better place, I suppose. She said, "I never want to look back," she said, "I want to go forward." They raised wheat, and broom corn, and row crops—maize and kafir corn. It was all dry land, but if they could raise a half a decent crop, why, they could get by. My Dad took up a . quarter, and my grandfather on my mother's side took up a quarter, side by side. There was a quarter on the east side, and there was a quarter on the west side. So they put the two together, finally, because my grandfather passed on—that was on my mother's side. So Papa took his piece of land over and paid for his keep, or took care of him, or paid the taxes or something. It wouldn't be very much, you know, in them days. So we had them two pieces of grassland, and then we had some south of there.

It was all open country, you know. You could just run cattle out in open country with no fences. The only fences there was, is ones that had homesteaded, and they had to fence their piece of ground. So we had plenty of country to roam over. It was four miles from our place to school. We had to go four miles to school after I got old enough. I'll never forget that, because you could take your choice. You could walk, run, trot, or ride a horse, or hook a horse up to a buggy and go to school. And it would be cold in the wintertime, you know, and the blizzards—they call them blizzards down in that country.

When they left there, they kept the land. They moved to Liberal, Kansas, and they had a big apartment house, and times were bad. That was in '20, '22 or somewhere there. And that's where they stayed for several years until they moved to Colorado. They moved to Rye, Colorado for a few years with us. My father was pretty well knocked out with his hands and arthritis.

I'll tell you, we had some rough times, and we had to make our own entertainment. We had our own entertainment on riding all kinds of wild horses. If we could catch him, we'd sure try to ride him. And we'd be out in the wild country, and if we could get a bunch of them hemmed up somewhere into a corral, why we'd have the day. We could have a whole day of riding bucking horses all day long. Some was good, and some didn't buck very much.

Most of 'em were wild horses. We didn't have any wild horses, exactly, on our place, because there were so many of us, we kept them pretty well tamed, you know, 'cause we used a lot of horses. Everywhere we went we was on a horse or driving a horse to a buggy or a wagon. We didn't have no other way of going. We didn't have no motorcycles or bicycles them days. We went horseback, and then we would make our entertainment, too. Anything. We had a lot of fun. We played baseball. The kids and neighbors would get together and we'd run. They'd have big picnics. And we had big covered dish dinners. They'd just spread the table cloths on the ground and eat it that way, you know.

For Shorty, those get-togethers led directly into bucking horses, bulldogging, and on into rodeo work.

Every Fourth of July in our picnics and stuff, we had some fellows that was grownerup than us kids. They lived about 10, 15 miles west of us. They were good cowboys and they dressed good, you know. I was kind of a small shaver, but I would see them with them nice boots on and that hat, you know, and then they'd be riding bucking horses, for a hat collection or just for fun. Just for entertainment, at a Fourth of

July celebration. So I thought: Oh-oh. That's for me. That is for me. So we just kept on, riding bulls, cows, or mules or horses, anything we could ride that would buck. Then when I was 18, 20 years old, 21, why I just kept on, and I was a-breaking a lot of horses at that time. After I got old enough to break horses, why, I broke and trained a lot of horses for the ranches and different places. So then I just kept a-going and, you know, if you'd go get a job, well, it was pretty cheap wages. You could make so much more riding bucking horses, that way. I'm sure that's the way I got started.

You'd break him and ride him for three or four weeks or a good month till he was pretty well safe. Broke so most anybody could ride or could get on so that he wouldn't buck, you know, and hurt somebody. And as long as you could ride him and show him to the fellow that you were riding him for, and he'd say, "Oh, he's all right. I'll take him back. He's all right." And if he wasn't, why, you'd ride him a little longer. Keep him a little longer. If you could get $10 a head for them, for each horse, why, you thought you was a-making money. Now they get $100, and $250 for that.

To break a horse, you get a hackamore on his head, and if he's rough, you put a rope on his feet. You hold him and keep him from striking you, or pawing you or kicking you. You get your saddle on him. He's a-fighting you all the time. Finally, he's so wild or so jittered that he thinks you're trying to hurt him, you know? You be easy with him as you can. Then you finally get on him and get all that gear strapped on him and then get the ropes off of him, and you get in that saddle and just let him have it. Then when you get that done like that a few times, why, he turns out to be a pretty good horse. If he's a rough horse and he don't want to be broke very easy, you have to give him more. And some of them, they're easier to train. Some of them, you can ride them two or three weeks or so, and they just want to be nice. There's different disposition in horses. Some of them's rough, and some of them's nice.

Should be rode every day. We didn't have anything else to do and it was no trouble for us to ride a horse every day.

Maybe more. More horses we had, the more riding we did. You know? You could take two or three, four head of horses at one time, but you could ride all of them. Easily.

There wasn't no sandy places. It was all hard sod where we lived. If we had a sandy place, it would be about 15 miles west of us. What they called the Palo Duro Crick. It was about four feet wide. You could jump across it. But us kids thought that was the biggest creek you ever. . . . we thought it was a river, 'cause it was all dry land there. We had windmills, you know, for livestock, pump water for our house, and stuff like that. Then the Beaver River was north of us, between us and Liberal, Kansas. It was wide and sandy. It would be about 24 or 26 miles up to that river. And that was where the wild plums was. My mother would take us kids in a wagon, and we'd drive that. We'd start way early, daylight or before daylight, and we'd drive up there and pick wild plums all day long. We'd get almost a wagon box full of plums. And we'd get them chiggers on us, off of the plum bushes. Well, my mother would can those plums. She would make plum jam or plum jelly, and work all those plums up.

If she didn't have enough sugar to fix all the plums, she'd can them but leave the sugar out. Then, as we used up these other ones, sweet, after awhile, why, if they had money or something, they could get money to get sugar. Then she fixed the others, which was already canned. We had fruit like that. We had a peach orchard. We had apricots. Every year we didn't have them, but most every year we could have some fruit. She dried some of those apricots, and she dried fruit out of the orchard. 'Course if they would have had irrigation water, we could have had wonderful fruit there. But it was all dry land, and they'd take care of it just like a garden. They'd disk it with the teams and horses, you know. Sometimes it just shriveled up. Just dried up. Too hot and dry. Not enough moisture. There was another place east of us where we could go get wild grapes. My oldest brother would take my brother just older than me and myself. The three of us, we'd go and we'd be gone three days, and we could come back with a whole wagonload of grapes. My mother would work them up. Grape jelly and jams and stuff like that. The wagon load would be on the stem, you know. We'd put about a foot of straw in the bottom of the wagon and pile those grapes in there, 'cause we'd have to trot back about 30, 35 miles from that wagon and team.

We'd get poison ivy and poison oak all over us. Wild grapes grew on trees and they'd grow up, you know. Well, we'd just skin them trees and pull them vines down and pick grapes. Then when we get home, we had poisoned ivy or poisoned oak all over us, and Mama would have to straighten us out on that. I had experiences that I'd never forget, of lots of things. I wish I could explain it, really like it was.

We had a lot of stuff to eat, I'll say that. We had everything to eat, and we had plenty of meat. We had plenty of pork, we had plenty of beef. There was a large family of us, and there'd be large families around. If all them families come in at our place, any day, they could all eat because there was plenty.

My mother sewed a whole lot. She made lots of clothes. and she would trade. Those peddlers would come by with some cheap clothes, you know. I suppose they was cheap. They didn't cost very much. She would trade meat, pork. We had cured meat, and them people would just go crazy for that stuff. She would trade for clothes and yard stuff. I think they had stuff rolled up in a yard. You could buy it. Well, I think she traded for that, because she sewed a whole lot. She sewed lots of clothes and dresses. I had two older sisters and us, and then my youngest sister was a baby sister. After all of us boys was growed up, why, she came along, and naturally I guess she was spoiled because all of us had grown up. There was 10 of us in the family. She raised 10 of us. We lost some of them that was younger. There's good days and bad days in those times. But us kids didn't know nothing about it. Long as we was eating, and we was plenty warm, and had a good place to sleep and a wild horse to ride, that's all *we* cared about.

We were just north of that big XIT ranch. And the Hitch
brothers was west of us, south of Guymon, Oklahoma. I
worked for them. I drove teams. Mules, with a wagon. Hauled
cottonseed cake from Guymon, Oklahoma, to the Coldwater
Crick where the Hitch ranch was. That was Henry Hitch. I
worked for them for quite a while. One day—he used to call
me Casey—he said, "Casey, you're going home." I said,
"Why?" He said, "Well," he said, "your folks haven't heard
from you." And I said, "Yeah, I wrote them a card." He said,
"Well, I got a card from them." And he said, "They wanted to
know how you was." Said, "You're going home." So I think he
fired me. Not exactly fired me, he just thought I ought to go
home. And I think their work was caught up some, too. They
run lots of cattle and fed a lot of cattle, with little mules and
wagons to haul that cottonseed cake out. Fed a lot of cattle.
Bulls and stuff. So I think they thought I belonged home. I
was too young.

I went to the eighth grade, but I didn't get through it.
Well, I wanted to cowboy too much. I wanted to be a wild boy
and I just couldn't stay in that schoolhouse. That schoolhouse
was getting to me. So they promised me everything if I'd go
ahead and finish. I just thought, well, I'd got a taste of making
some money, and I thought that was more important than
school. But I've decided after, and lately, that I wish I had went
on and went to school. I think everybody maybe regrets that,
that they didn't go ahead and finish their school. But there was
too much cowboy work and driving cattle. We drove lots of
cattle from the panhandle of our country, into Canadian,
Texas, and to Shamrock, Texas. They give me $6 a day to drive
cattle, and that would be a dollar for my horse and five for
myself. We'd have to stand guard at night, three hours at night.
We'd stand guard on cattle. We'd move 1,000 head of steers.
We'd take them about 80, 90 miles. Then we'd come back and
we'd get 1,000 to 1,200 head of cows and calves. We'd take
them down there. They was moving them out of that country
'cause it was droughted out and the grass was short. That
being the fall of the year when I should have been in school,
why, I could make me $400 or $500. One time I come back

with $335, and I thought I was rich, you know. I had a lot of money. But we would go to Canadian and cross the Canadian River. That was quicksand and we had a lot of trouble. It would take us several days to get them cattle across the river because they would bog down in that water in the river.

And sometimes it would be different outfits that had these steers on pasture and the cows on pasture. Some outfit might be a steer man and another outfit be cows and calves, see? We'd gather cattle for a week before we ever started. Right across the country. No fences, till we got down close to Canadian. Then there would be some fences cause there was some little places and farms out north of Canadian, Texas.

There was guys there to receive them, staggering them around. They'd put maybe 200 off in another place over here and take 200 or 300 over to another place, and another 100 over to another place. They'd stagger them around. Wherever they had their pastures leased, you know, where they had feed.

I think I was 15 years old when I went to Hitch Ranch. That was 35 miles west of us. I think I was 15. I thought that I was old enough to be a big cowboy, I guess, and I just went from there. Course there was things I could have done at home, but it wouldn't be a-making money, you see. And I bought all my clothes and bought all my boots and everything from then on, cause, that's what I wanted, boots and cowboy clothes. So I'd buy my clothes that way. Then I had two horses, later. I had two good saddle horses. I could go from place to place, or I could go anywhere and get a job, if I wanted a job. I stayed on the place when the folks moved from Oklahoma to Liberal, Kansas. I stayed there. They wanted me to go to Liberal and go to school, and I said, "No, I believe I'll stay here." Well, I had several head of horses at that time, and I had a good work team, and I had some saddle horses, and I had a mare that raised colts. So my mother cut out a good jersey heifer they had, that was going to have a calf. And she left me a bunch of chickens. I stayed right there on the place. But we leased out all the farmland to a neighbor east of us. He farmed it to wheat, for several years. But I could stay at the house and the corral and the pasture land. We had about 300 acres of pasture off south, there, that was leased. It was open, what little pasture we had. I could run my stock in that. Then I'd put up a lot of feed there for my stock, and I'd stay there during the winter and during the summer. I'd work. I'd take four head of horses and go work on the roads and stuff like that. Make a dollar and 15 cents an hour with four head of horses, and I boarded myself and fed my horses. We worked eight hours, so you'd say, a dollar and 15 cents an hour for four head of horses and you feed them and you feed yourself—it wouldn't be very much, but we got along all right. We made it all right. Saved some money.

We had a lot of hogs, you know. And we had volunteer wheat. Naturally, we didn't have much feed for the hogs, but the hogs were in pretty good shape, as I remember. And big sows. Us kids would have to take these hogs across the piece of pasture land and put them in the wheat and let them eat green wheat, you know. Well, you'd just leave them down there two or three hours, and they all filled up pretty good you know, and then they'd start back towards the house to get a drink of water or something. So we'd go through the fence, you know. They'd just go in under the fence. Barbed wire fence. Wasn't a very good fence in them days. So I got tired of walking, I suppose, and I just run and slipped up behind one of the old sows and jumped on her, and when we got to the corral she was just going "Uh-uh-uh."

My dad seen me, and he didn't go for that very much. He kind of give me a good straightening out on riding that hog to the house. But she never whimpered. That old sow kept a-running, and I just set up there and rode her to the house. But he said, "Don't you do that no more." I don't think I did, either. I don't think I done that.

The shift from a cowboy's life to show business was a matter of simple economics.

I was in Lubbock, Texas, and I was working on a ranch out there west of Lubbock, Texas, for a fellow by the name of

Goodwin. This show was in town, so I went to town. I went to
the show. They was giving $2.50 amount to any outsider to
come in and ride a bucking horse. In their show. So I said,
"Well, $2.50, why, that's a pretty good deal. I think I'll do that."
I told one of these boys, I said, "Say," I said. "How do you get
a horse?" I said, "You're advertising $2.50 a mount for an
outsider to come in and ride some of these horses." He says,
"Are you a bronc rider?" I said, "I don't know." I said, "I
would try some of your horses for $2.50 a mount." He said,
"Well, now listen, some of them are pretty tough." And I said,
'Well, I don't want a tough horse. I just want a bucking horse. I
don't want one I can't ride." He says, "Well, we've got some
here that you can't ride." I said, "Well, I don't want that horse."
He says, "I'll get you a good horse that'll just buck easy." So he
did. He got me a horse, and I rode one or two that night. Well,
they were going to be there for a week. They always stayed a
week in a place. So every night, I was there. For my horse. I'd
make $2.50 every night. They had a horse called Redwolf. They
said, "Now, if you want him, we'll give you $10 to ride him."
And I said, "Well, what does he do?" He says, "Well, he'll just
eat you up." I says, "Well, I don't want him." After that week,
some of the boys said, "Say, we're short of men. Why don't
you go with us? We're going to Post, Texas. Down below the
caprock." I said, "Oh, no," I said. "I don't want to do that. I'm
out here on a ranch," and I said, "I wouldn't know how to do
this." "Oh," he said, "nothing to it. It's kind of fun. We have a
lot of fun." So they just kept talking to me and talking to me,
and I decided: well, I might go down there with them. So I did.
I went. I stayed on that outfit two years.

I broke my leg twice in that two years. My left leg. A
horse fell with me, out of the chute. We had a portable bucking chute, and the horse fell with me. Then the second time,
why, we had a big steer in there. He'd weigh about 1200
pounds or more. We called him Gold Standard. He was in the
chute. He wanted out. You'd put your rig on him and put a
flank on him like they do to ride him. So I got on him. Instead
of the boy in front opening the gate, well, he didn't open the
gate. He let the gate slip. This steer got his head started out

through there, and he just went right on and caught my toe in
the gate like that. It was so tight agin' him and the gate, too, it
just twisted that and broke it again. Broke it again right above
where it was broke before. So that slowed me up for a while. I
was on crutches, you know. The fellow that we was working
for was a good guy, and he was an up-to-date man. Some of
those shows in them days wasn't too up-to-date. But he wanted
his stuff good. He kept his horses fat. He wanted his show
nice and clean and neat, and it was. He had some good boys.
Everybody, well most everyone that come along there and go
to work for him would stay a while. They wouldn't just stay a
short time. They'd stay right with him because he was good to
them, the pay was good. We got $25 a week. That was $100 a
month. And they boarded us. That was in '24, '25, '26, along in
there.

The first time I broke it, he paid me right straight on till
that leg got well. That was quite a while. But you know, after
you could walk on it good, why, you wrapped it up and went
right back to riding again. Then the last time I broke it, the
third time I broke it, I broke it in Baton Rouge, Louisiana. My
bulldogging horse turned over a steer and broke my left leg,
and the saddle horn hit me in the stomach and knocked me
out. I was in the hospital down there for a while. That was in
November, I broke it, the third time. Then we was supposed to
go to Sydney, Australia, in February. Well, I had a cast on my
leg and I was on crutches.

So I went to a doctor in Pueblo, Colorado, and he made
me a brace to go on. I told him what I wanted to do. I was
going to Australia, and I'd ride bucking horses and bulldog. He
said, "Well, I'll fix you up a brace. You lace it on, on your
boot." I cut my boot down and put ties in it so I could lace it
up. So I got on this boat in Los Angeles. I had my crutches but
I threw them off. I didn't take them on the boat. I had a
walking cane. So when I got over there, then, we had to break
some horses and train some horses in Sydney for a while. Then
the show was to come off. I could limp a little bit, but I could
wrap that leg up good and tight and it didn't bother me. I
wanted to bulldog over there in '39, in Sydney. My wife wanted

the bronc riding—what they called "buck jumping" over there. That's the Royal Agricultural Easter Show, at Sydney, Australia. So you do have some bumps and bruises in that line. We were lucky. I never was hurt seriously, I don't suppose. The most serious hurt I was, was in Baton Rouge when my horse turned over and the saddle horn hit me in the stomach and broke that leg. That was about the worst I had.

That first outfit that I met in Lubbock was Texas Kid's Wild West Show. He's gone, his wife's gone, and his son took that thing and run it for several years. I don't think they have a show anymore. It'd be just like the 101 Wild West Show. They don't have a show anymore. I spent a year on that in 1927. I was on the Miller Brothers' 101 Wild West Show. This wild west show traveled by country, in trucks. Drove his horses from town to town.

Sometimes people would put a rope around a horse to make it buck. What they call a flank strap. That does cause a horse to buck, I suppose, but they're used to it and it don't hurt the horse. They think it hurts the horse, but it don't. It just tickles him. 'Cause he don't like to have anything in his flanks, you know. Just like a lot of horses, good old gentle horses, you can get on him and get behind the saddle and put your heels in his flank and he'll kick up. Well, he just don't like that, you know. It don't hurt the horse. They use a flank strap, they call it.

Riders from the local area could compete if they wanted to. Everyone had to pay an entry fee for any event he wanted to enter. In those days the purse for each event was fairly standard— $50 first prize, $30 second, and $20 third. After awhile the contestants realized the show sponsors, local chamber of commerce, Elks Club, or the town's municipal government was making money not only by charging spectators but off the riders. If 20 entrants paid $15 each for an event, and only $100 came back as prize money, the sponsors would turn a neat profit. Shorty and the others finally organized into what they called the Turtle Association, because they realized they were so slow getting together. By group action, they were successful in getting all the entry fees added to the purse.

In 1939 Shorty and Gene branched out into a show of their own.

There was a man told me in Rocky Ford, "Shorty," he said, "you're running these shows and running the arenas, why don't you get your own stock, if you're going to do this, and furnish your own stock?" And I said, "Well, I never thought of that." But it was far better than the straight rodeo because we was beating our brains out on those bucking horses and bulldogging steers and chasing from town to town and driving all night to get to them. So the rodeo stock proved out better for us moneywise, than going and competing. You put up your entrance fees and you're putting up that a-betting that you can beat that other 20 guys. You got one chance out of 20. If there's 20 guys in that event, well, you're just pumping uphill. Well, you can win. We won. But you know it's hit and miss. You don't win all the time. So with the rodeo stock we knew what we were going to get. We had a contract. We knew we was going to get so much money.

When that show was over we got it. I did in 1939. We put rodeo stock together. We put a string of stuff together. We had a full line of bucking horses, bulls, and calves, and steers, and bulldogging steers and rodeo horses.

Quarter Circle LD. That was my brand: Quarter Circle LD. I produced, I run the shows, directed the shows. I directed several shows before I ever got any rodeo stock. It was still a hard life. It was hard. And we had to be careful. Now, some of the boys went and lived it up and played pool and played poker and laid out at night. Well, they didn't wind up with very much. But we didn't do that because it was a business. We made a business out of it. We didn't want to throw that money away. When we could sleep out in a bedroll and save $1.50, we would. We could get what they called cabins, those days, for $1.50. Well, we had a bedroll. We stayed out in a bedroll, to save our money. So I think maybe today, the man that's winning $60,000, $80,000, why, he don't wind up with any more than we did. Because it cost us less. We could buy a new car then for $1040. And we did. We bought several of them.

We'd drive them 18 months; we thought they was wore out. We put a lot of miles on them. And we didn't have the good roads we got today, either.

I did that for better than 20 years for myself and about 18 years for my wife. Yeah, that's all we did. 'Course I had other things to do in the wintertime. I had land and ranches. We put a little thing together. We was working at it with the little money that we had that we could come in with. A lot of the boys would go lay up for four or five months or three months and spend what they made. If they come in with any, why, they'd spend it. Some of the boys would have to borrow some money in the spring to get started.

We had some cattle when we was first married, at Rye, Colorado. We bought some cattle for 12 and 15 dollars a head. Cows and some heifers. We'd drive them about 40 miles and bring them home. We kept them two years, and it dried out in 1934 and 1935. Dried out. Dried out, and the water was dried up a whole lot, too. Grasshoppers was bad. So we kept them two years. I'd haul feed and I'd buy hay. We bought hay for $5 a ton, them days. I'd haul that hay 12 and 15 miles—if you can find it. It was hard to find, the hay was. So we had a bull, or two or three bulls, and then we had the cows. And we raised some calves. We kept them two years, and it looked like the prices wasn't going to come up to amount to anything so I shipped them to Blakely, in Denver, that commission company, and sold them. So we had it figured out. We had about $165 profit that we'd made off of that bunch of cattle in two years. My wife wanted a fur coat. So she went down to May Company or whatever company that store was there in Denver, and bought this fur coat. And I don't remember to this day. . . .

Mrs. Creed: "Eighty-five dollars."

Eighty-five dollars for this fur coat. Well, I said, "Get the fur coat." That's the profit in them cattle for two years. But we had our own place. We never did rent a place. When we first got married, we bought 640 acres in New Mexico, which was bad. It was bad roads in and out of there and too far from

town. Well, it was 135 miles north of Albuquerque, New
Mexico, and it was bad. The snow got deep in there so getting
in and out, getting to our rodeos. . . .Then we had to get out of
there and come to Rye, Colorado, and start from there. We
found a little house in town. We bought that. Very cheap. Four
hundred and fifty dollars, I think we give for it. We always had
our own house to live in. We never did rent. We kept that place
out south because it was pasture and water. We kept that for
the cattle and horses. We always lived in our own home. We
never did rent a place to live. I guess we did stay out there
about a year, on this place south of Rye. Then when we
bought that other place, we moved in there and we lived in our
own. Because I never did like to pay rent.

Shorty said he never got nervous before a ride.

Oh, no. You. . . . Eager beaver! You wanted him. Oh,
yeah. It'd be just like Ali getting in the ring, I guess. He wants
him, you know. You ride up to that chute and that steer, you
know, you want him. Or if you're going to get on that bucking
horse, you're standing there waiting for them to get the saddle
on him, why, you're ready. I think maybe your pulse would
come up a little. I think it'd have to. We had one fellow saying
one time, he said, "It don't bother you to get on a tough
bucking horse." Said, "After the first jump," he said, "you're
unconscious anyway."

In Australia, when I was bulldogging those steers, I threw
the fastest steer over there. I threw a steer in six seconds in
Australia —that's the fastest steer that they've had over
there—with my leg all wrapped up like that. They said, "Well,
ain't you afraid to set down on them things?" No, I wasn't. I
never thought of that leg. I never thought of it. Because I had
it bandaged good. I think you could run the car wheel over it,
and it wouldn't have hurt it too much. 'Cause I had it wrapped
and bandaged good. But I limped a little bit. It was a little sore,
but it had been time enough to heal up. It was healed up pretty
good. I didn't have to use a walking cane or anything like that,
you know.

When our interview was finished, Shorty wanted to show me some pictures from the old days. The earliest was from Lubbock, when he was a young boy working for the Texas Kid. Then we went out to take a photograph of him with his saddle, which he had thrown over a fence rail along the carport, in anticipation of my visit. I snapped a couple, then asked if he would sit in the saddle for one more. Easily and naturally he swung his leg over and sat there for a moment. Something changed in his eyes as I focused the camera, and I could see that he was somewhere back down on the plains. Back with some of his old mounts. Salty Dog, maybe, or Midnight or Black Diamond or High Roller. Or Crazy Dan, the one the Texas Kid said you really had to look out for. He'll kill you, the Kid said.

Ride the Buckin' Horses

In 1925, her mother put a 16-year-old girl aboard a train in Holly, Colorado, and waved her on her way to the New Mexico border to help another daughter who was having a baby. When the railroad forked at La Junta, instead of taking the train south, the girl rode north to Wyoming, and entered the women's rodeo division of the famous Cheyenne Frontier Days.

Three days later the young girl – Mary Geneva Krieg – had won the bronco-riding or "buckin' horse" contest, its $300 first prize, and a new hat. She had adopted a "rodeo name"– Gene Krieg– and had decided to join the rodeo life. Over the next 17 years, she and, after they married, her cowboy husband performed in rodeos all over North America, in Europe and Australia. She took in stride broken ribs, concussions and severe back injury. After professional rodeo dropped the women's event of bronco riding as too dangerous, she continued as a trick rider, until injury and the desire for a family life prompted retirement. Settling down to rural life in Pleasant Valley, she and her husband raised their son, savored their memories, and watched their old profession gentle down.

Mary Geneva's parents were used to the hard life. They had five children when they lived in Illinois, and they lost three of those. The mother developed tuberculosis, so she was sent to California, with her nine-months-old baby girl. She lived on the desert in a tent for nine months. Ever after she slept with a window wide open. The dry air cured her, but at a price. While she was out there, the baby took sick and died. So they brought it back to Illinois and buried it there. They left Illinois, seeking a drier climate, and settled near Jefferson City, Missouri, on a farm at Hamilton, where Gene was born on May 14, 1909. When a flood washed the farm away, the Kriegs moved on to Iowa, where they had another child, Gene's youngest sister. A couple of years later they moved on down to Brush,

*Colorado. By the end of World War I, Gene was nine, and she had
a brother two years older and another four years older. A grown
sister was married already. As in most families, the older kids set the
agenda for the younger ones.*

And they wanted to be cowboys. Well, they wanted to get
out on a ranch and raise cattle. They didn't like the farming. So
we bought a place east of Trinidad. I think it was 320 acres.
Then my father homesteaded on 640 acres of land. Well, you
had to improve it. In order to claim the land, you had to
improve this and live on it three years. Which he did. These
two other places were nine miles apart. Well, we'd be one place,
and then we'd be the other place, but he did prove up on the
land.

They were doing real good, and we had a blizzard. This
blizzard came in April, and I believe it was in 1921. Down
there they have canyons and caprocks. There was 50-some
head of these cattle drifted over fences, and when they came to
this caprock they went down the canyon. Well, 50-some head
went over this caprock. Well, of course that killed that many
of them. That was pretty much of a setback.

In fact there was a woman that died in this blizzard. And
my mother went over and set up with the family. She had just
one boy. They lived on this place about two or three miles
from us. She went to milk the cow that morning in this
blizzard. She wouldn't let him go along. She made him stay in
the house. She went down and she milked the cow, hung the
milk up on the post, and they found her a half a mile down
this fence, dead. She froze to death. She went the other way.

When we moved down east of Trinidad, why, the whole
family learned to ride. I can't even remember when I learned to
ride. And they couldn't either. We always rode, see? We always
had a horse, and we always rode.

When we lived down there in Branson, there was very
few cars, and you went with a wagon and a team. In fact, we
didn't even have a car. We'd had a car down here at Brush, but

when we left we sold it. When we went down there, we went
back to the wagon and team. Or horseback. I always loved to
ride, and whenever my brothers would go some place, why I
always wanted to go along. Well, they called me a tomboy.
Because I didn't care about housework, I just wanted to be out
and do what they did. On Sundays, they'd drive the calves in.
We had our own calves. And the neighbors' kids would come
over, and they'd drive in a bunch of calves and put them in the
corral, and then they was going to ride these calves. Well, if
they'd find a calf that none of them could ride, it would buck
them all off, then they'd always come and get me. They'd say,
"Well, we'll go and get . . . " instead of calling me Gene, then,
'cause my name is Mary Geneva, they always called me Neevy.
They'd say, "Well, we got to go get Neevy, 'cause she can ride
this calf." So they'd always come and get me, and usually I
could ride the calf. Once in a while it'd buck me off. But
usually I could ride the calf.

We used to go to dances. Well, I wasn't old enough—say
12 or 13 years old—to go to a dance. But my brothers, you see,
they were older, and there was nothing for them to do. So, like
on Saturday nights, why, at schoolhouses, they'd have dances.
So I'd always want to go with them. My brother just two years
older, he'd always say, "Well, sure, you can go along." But my
brother four years older, he didn't want me to go along. He
didn't want to have no part of me being along. He was too old,
and I was too young. But the other one, he'd always say, "Well,
sure, you can go." So, my mother—there was no place for me
to go—so she used to let me go with my brothers. And I'd go
to these dances, and we'd ride 20 miles a-horseback to a dance.
The people, most of them, would come in wagons, and they
had three or four in their family, and they'd bring the kids in
the wagon, and they stayed all night long. They'd bring their
lunch and at twelve o'clock, why they'd quit their dancing, and
for an hour they'd eat their lunch and have cake and coffee.
Then they'd dance again, and they'd dance till daylight. Then
the people would go home. And we'd still have that 20 miles to
ride until we'd get home. Well, one time, we got so tired and so
sleepy, we said, "Let's just stop and sleep a while, and then we'll

go on home." So we just got off of our horses, and tied the rein to our leg, and laid down on the ground and went to sleep. Slept awhile. The first one that woke up woke the others up and said, "Well, come on, let's go home." Well, my father, he never was much for any kind of entertainment. But he was a hard worker. He always felt, well you must work. So whenever the boys would get home from the dance, why they'd want to go to bed and sleep. But no way. They had to work all that day before they could get any sleep. He wouldn't let them sleep. They'd been out playing, and he wanted them to do their work.

This one brother, the one that was four years older than I am, he started breaking horses for other people—breaking them to ride. I had heard or read that if you tied a red handkerchief around your neck, a horse couldn't buck you off. Well, of course that's not true, but that's what I thought. So he'd maybe have two or three horses that he was breaking for some other people. I don't remember how much they would give him, but it seemed to me like, oh, maybe $10 or $15 or $20, or something like that, to break the horse. He had a horse, and it was pretty well broke, and I wanted to ride that horse. And he was gone. My mother was out hoeing in the garden. I went in the barn and I tied that red handkerchief around my neck and I saddled up that horse and I got on that horse, and got on him in the barn, and when he came out, boy, he just went down that lane. He was really flying when he went down there. My mother said, "I just liked to swallowed my tongue, I seen you going out down the road on that horse that wasn't broke." I said, "Well, he couldn't hurt me, I had my red handkerchief 'round my neck." So that's kind of how I got started riding and not being afraid of riding bucking horses or that sort of thing.

I never had no girl friends. They just wasn't any. They was just my family, see. I had a sister older than I was, and she was married. She was older than this brother that I was talking about. She was married, and her husband and her homesteaded on another piece of land in the same country. He had been in World War I. When he came back and we moved, why, they moved with us. And then he homesteaded.

Then we decided that we would leave Branson and go. We moved to Holly, Colorado, up on the Arkansas River, so that we could go to a better school and where there'd be churches. We just lived at Branson three years. But my father kept his land. He used to have a thrashing machine. He used to thrash his own. He used to raise lots of wheat. He was a farmer and he had the cattle but he couldn't get the farming out of his life. He still had to farm. So there was a lot of land that he broke up and put into wheat which other people hadn't done in that country. Well then, of course, he had to get him a thrashing machine to thrash this. Well, then the other people kind of caught on and they thought, well, maybe this is a better way to make money, see? So then they broke up land. But he was the only one that had the equipment to thrash the grain, so he kept this. After we moved to Holly, then, each summer he'd go back down. I think it was for three years he went back down there and he'd thrash his grain and then he'd thrash the other people's grain. So he'd be gone all summer. Then we started to school at Holly. My oldest sister was married—but the other four of us went to school there at Holly.

But the way I got started in the rodeos. . . . We used to take *The Denver Post*. I'd always read in there about the Cheyenne Frontier Days. That's one place I wanted to go. Wanted to go up there and ride. Well, 'course I never told my folks, but I'd talked to my brother about it. In 1924, we went to Rocky Ford for the Watermelon Days. It was the first Thursday in September. My two brothers and I had a Model T Ford. It was only about, oh, 60, 70 miles. We decided that we'd go up there to Watermelon Days. My folks let me go. They didn't go, because like I say, my father, he never went any place. He always stayed home and worked. I went with them up there, and my brother got in the bronc riding there. There was some prize money. It was a three-day affair. On the second day, which was Watermelon Day, why, there was a girl there, a cowgirl, and she was supposed to ride a bucking horse. Exhibition. Wasn't contest, it was just an exhibition. She came out on this horse, and this horse, it just what we call 'crow hopped.' It just never got its feet off the ground over about a foot. Well,

the grandstand booed her, you know, because they had built
her up so high that she was supposed to be such a famous
rider and could ride these bucking horses, and then she came
out on this horse and it didn't buck very much.

Well, my brother, he says, "Humpf. I got a sister that can
ride any horse you got in that corral down there." And, 'course
somebody said, "Well, if she's so good, where's she at?"
"Well," he said, "she's up there in the grandstand." "Well, why
don't she get down there and ride one of these horses, then?"

He came up and he got me, and he says, "You go down
town." It was only two blocks to the downtown stores in
Rocky Ford from the fairgrounds. I had on a dress. He said,
"Get you a pair of Levis, and come back," and he says, "I want
you to ride a horse for me." So I went down and I got these
Levis. I went to the restroom, put the Levis on. I came out
there. They said, "Which one of these horses you going to
ride?" My brother says, "It doesn't make a bit of difference.
Whatever one you want her to ride she'll ride."

So they picked out a horse and they saddled this horse
up, and I got on and I rode this horse. Well, it did buck, and
the crowd nearly tore that grandstand down when I rode that
buckin' horse down the race track right in front of the grandstand.

Well, that kind of gave me that idea that I'd like to ride in
the rodeos. Then, in 1925 I had been reading in *The Denver Post*
about the Cheyenne Frontier Days. I said, "I'd sure like to go
up there." They had $300 in prize money for first place, and a
$75 hat. Stetson's always had made a hat. This man worked for
Stetson, but he pulled away from Stetson, and he made this
other hat, and I can't remember the name of this hat. But
anyway it was supposed to be a $75 hat. In those days, why,
that was quite a prize.

So this sister of mine, she was still living down in
Branson where they homesteaded on their land. She was about
to have a baby. My mother says, "Now you must go down and

take care of her and help her with the baby." So they put me
on the train. I would have to come up to La Junta, and go
from La Junta to Trinidad and from Trinidad back to Branson
in order to get there. On the train, you know how they've got
the newspapers and everything. When I got to La Junta,
instead of going on to Trinidad, I just came on to Cheyenne.
When I got there, why, of course there was so many people
there, and I was so young. I was only 16 years old—and I
didn't know what to do. So I went to the Chamber of Com-
merce. They said that they had lots of rooms, and they could
get me a room in a private home. So I said, well, that would be
fine. So they got me a room. Her name was Nora Finnerty, and
she worked for a Dr. Savery in Cheyenne for years and years.
Just her and her father lived in this house. They had an extra
room, so she rented me this room. She knew I was just a kid,
you know? So she kind of looked after me. She kind of gave
me advice and she'd tell me, "Now don't stay out at night, and
don't do this and don't do that." Well, whatever she told me, I
thought well, she knew more about it than I did, and so I went
along with her.

Then I went down and entered in the bronc riding. There
was a fellow that I had met in 1924. Must have been at Rocky
Ford. I said, "Now I don't have a saddle. What am I going to
do for a saddle?" He said, "Well, you can ride my saddle." I
didn't have the clothes the other girls had. He was a jockey. He
rode race horses, and he owned race horses. He was from over
here at Gunnison, Colorado. He loaned me his jockey shirt,
and his jockey cap. See, I didn't have a hat. I guess I did have
some Levis. And I must of had boots, 'cause I don't remember
borrowing the boots.

We rode three horses up there. You snubbed them up.
You didn't ride them out of the chute. They just took them out
in the middle of the arena, and they snubbed them up to
another horse, and one man would get on the ears and ear 'em
down and the other would hang onto the rope. Then they'd
saddle it, and then I'd get on, and then they'd just turn it loose.
And, of course, they had a pickup man to pick it up. There was
five days, and we got three horses. On the fifth day when I was

to ride my horse, somebody stole my saddle. I didn't have any saddle to ride. Well, I felt bad because the saddle wasn't mine. But this fellow, he got one of the boy's saddles that they'd been riding. He fit my stirrups. Then there was another fellow from Rocky Ford by the name of Bussey, and he wanted to kind of help me out. See, these boys—they could see that I was green, and I needed some help. So, anyway, he snubbed down one horse. The last horse they took out on the racetrack right in front of the grandstand. The other two I had rode just in the arena—in the center. His name was Blue Dog. Just as they turned this horse loose, one of the judges hollered, "Don't turn that horse loose! That horse is one of the men's horses!" It was one of the worst horses they had. But they'd already turned it loose. And I was on it. And I rode it.

Well, there wasn't nothing else they could do but give me the championship for bronc riding. I never did know whoever stole the saddle. Never did find it. And I don't know who switched the horses. What I did, I rode what they call 'slick.' I rode like the cowboys. The other girls rode with their stirrups hobbled. That is a strap that they tie their stirrups with underneath their horse's stomach. They get their feet in them stirrups and turn their toes out, it's hard to buck them off. But I never even heard of a hobble. So I rode just like the cowboys did.

This Nora Finnerty, where I was staying, she says, "Have you wired your mother?" Back in those days you wired, you didn't call on the telephone. We had no telephone. But you could send a telegram, and they'd take it out on the mail next day. She says, "Have you wired your mother where you're at?" I said, "No." She says, "I'll take you down there. You go down there and you let her know where you're at." And she did. The rodeo was over on Saturday. Mother went to church on a Sunday. Well, here *The Denver Post* headline said, "She's Sweet 'Cause She Comes From the Land of Holly, Famous for Sugar." Holly, Colorado. Well, my mother, soon as church was over, why all the people was congratulating her on her daughter winning the bronc riding at Cheyenne. She said, "Well, I don't know what you're talking about." "Well," they said, "you better get the paper and read the newspaper." But I'd changed my name, from Geneva to Gene. G-E-N-E. I just left the V-A off. Because I thought, well, Geneva, that don't sound like a professional name. So I just changed it.

I didn't go home. Right then. I went from there to Monte Vista. Of course, I wrote home, see? Told them where I was going. But I never went home.   I never even asked them. I was just like you might say, runaway. Because I never asked them. I just told them that I was going to Monte Vista, and the dates that I would be there. Before I did go to Monte Vista, see, I had no clothes. Most of the girls made fun of me, because I looked like I did. So I went down to Denver. Somebody told me that there was a lady there that would make me some rodeo clothes. I had this $300 that I had won. Well, anyway, I went down there and had this lady make me two pairs of trousers and two blouses. Then I went on to Monte Vista. Well, then I didn't feel so bad because I was dressed about half as good as the other girls. I went down there and I won the bronc riding in Monte Vista. Then after Monte Vista, they were going to have a show in Denver. It was going to be held for a week, I believe. It was going to be in the stadium, but we had to wait for several days.

So when I got back there and I was waiting for this show, there was a man that furnished the stock: Ed McCarty of Chugwater, Wyoming. He had seen me ride in Cheyenne. And they were going from Cheyenne to Chicago. To Soldier's Field stadium in Chicago, for a nine day stand—nine days and nights—rodeo. So he sent Vern Elliot, who used to live here at Platteville, and he finally wound up with Ed McCarty's rodeo stock. because they finally went in partners and eventually then he bought him out and Ed McCarty died and he kept on.

But they sent Vern Elliott down to Denver and he says, I wish you'd come back to Chicago and ride relay for me." And I said, "Well, I never rode relay in my life. In fact," I said, "the only one relay I ever saw was in Cheyenne when I was there." He says, "Well, the way you rode bucking horses," he said, "we can teach you to ride relay in three days, and we'll have plenty of time." He said, "We'll give you $500 and your expenses to come back there and ride relay for us." Well, that sounded pretty big to a 16-year-old kid, so I said, "Well, okay."

So I never waited for this show to come off in Denver, because we had to go. So when I got off the train in Cheyenne, I was sick. I didn't know what in the world was wrong. My throat was sore. Nora Finnerty, she met me at the train, and she says, "Let's just take you over to Dr. Savery's, and just let him look at you." Took me over there and he says, "Well, you've got tonsillitis, and you've got to have your tonsils out." And I said, Well, I can't do that, I'm supposed to go to Chicago." And they was leaving the next day. And he says, "Well, you're going to have to have them out," and so I told Vern Elliott, "The doctor says I got to have my tonsils out, and I won't be able to go." And he says, "Well, you go ahead and have them out. As soon as you're able," which—I was able the next day. All I could drink was malted milk. My throat was so sore there was nothing else you could eat. But they went on. I had to have this operation, and just one or two days later, then I got on the train by myself and went to Chicago.

And when I got back there, well, then, this Ed McCarty, who owned the livestock, and had hired me to go back there and ride, he met me at the train and took me to the hotel and got me a room, and then him and his wife sort of looked after me. 'Cause they knew I just didn't know anything. I was just that green. I'd never been any place, how would I know? And I won them $1200 in the relay race back there. And then I entered the bronc riding. And it was a contest. And so he was very helpful. The horses belonged to him. He had to be real careful because if them girls thought he was helping me, then he'd be in trouble. But I didn't win the bronc riding back there because I think I got bucked off one time. But I drew a real bad horse and he turned to me and he says, "You know, I think it would be wise," he says, "if you'd put on a pair of hobbles on this horse 'cause I don't think you can ride this horse. He's a tough horse." And he says, "I don't think you can ride him." I said, "Well, I've never rode hobbles in my life. I don't even know what they feel like." He says, "Well, why don't you ride

them," he says, "in the grand parade?" We always had the
parade before the rodeo started. "And see how they feel."

And so he had one of the cowboys put this on this
gentle horse, and I rode those hobbles in the grand parade, in
the grand entry. And when we come back, I said, "No way
would I get on a bucking horse with my feet tied down. And if
the horse would fall, why, then, I'd be.... you know, I'd get
hurt." And I said, "I'll just take my chances, and I'll ride the
way I've always ridden."

And that's the way I did. There was one horse that
bucked me off, so I didn't win the bronc riding in Chicago. So
then when we came back, I was getting pretty homesick. And I
thought, "Gee, I'd like to go home." They wanted me to go on
to Pendleton, Oregon, with them. And we were going to lay
over in Cheyenne for about a week before we went on to
Pendleton, ' cause Pendleton is in September, in the latter part
of September. And so I said, "Well, I believe I'll go home, and
then I'll be back." So I got on the train and I went home. And
I stayed one night, and after that, you know, and then I never
was homesick after that. But I was so homesick, I had to go
home. Just felt like I had to go home. But after I just stayed
one night, I was ready to go back, and I never was homesick
after that. Oh, I liked to go home, but to be real homesick,
boy, you're sick, and you're really sick if you're homesick.

Well, my mother, she worried, and I know she worried a
lot. But my father he said, "She can take care of herself." He
says, "I'm not worried." He said, "She can take care of herself." And that's the way he always felt, that I could always take
care of myself. And so, he never worried, but of course she
always worried. She always worried about me. They never told
me I couldn't do it, and so I just went ahead.

And then I went on to Pendleton, Oregon, with this Ed
McCarty, and when I got up there, why, they needed another
trick rider. They were supposed to furnish like six trick riders,
and they was minus one. And he says, "I wish you'd trick ride,
'cause I need another trick rider." I said, "Well, I can't trick

ride. There's one trick I can do. I can stand up." I'd always been able to stand up on a horse, with him running. and so I said, "There's one trick I can do, but," I said, "I don't know nothing about the others." He says, "I'll have one of the girls show you how, and there's two or three easy tricks that you can do, and then you can fill in, because we've got to have another trick rider."

I had no saddle. I had no horse. I had nothing. And they got me the horse, they got me the saddle and a girl took me out and she showed me one or two other tricks that I could do. I think we had to do three tricks. Well, of course, I could do this one trick, see. And so I filled in for them, and I did the trick riding there and then I entered the contest for bucking horses. I think I rode, it was a five days show, and I think I rode three bucking horses. And one of them, this horse was a gray mare and her name was Miss Wyoming. And she started to. . . . Well, she, when they turned her loose . . . now they snubbed these up to other horses, see.

When they turned her loose, she went right straight to the grandstand. Well, the race track fence was about, oh, three, three and a half, four foot high, I'd say. And she just started to jump over this fence, and when she did she just fell right back on top of me. And when she did she broke two ribs. And so, then, course, that put me out of winning the bronc riding there, see, because I never had another chance.

They were going from there to Los Angeles, to the Shriner's convention. And they were having a rodeo there. They wanted me to go, and ride for them there. So I had made friends with two or three of the girls and one girl in particular; her and her husband, they kind of took me under their wing and kind of looked after me. So she was going to Fort Worth to pick up a new Buick car, and she was going to drive that out to California. And he was going from Pendleton on the train. They used to take the horses on the trains. And so we took the train. She says, "Why don't you go with me?" And that was a little more experience, so I went with her, so we rode the train to Fort Worth, we picked up this new Buick car, and then we drove it out to California.

And back in those days—this was in 1925—out there on the desert, all they had was boards that you drove on, on the sand. Because if you'd get off of them boards, you'd just go right down, you know, clear to your axle. And ever so often there'd be a turnout. And so her and I were driving at night. It was dark. And we seen the lights coming. Well, that car didn't stop for their turnout. So she was going to have to back up to the one where we could get out so he could get by.

So I said, "Well, let me get out, and I'll get out and I'll hold the flashlight so you can see to stay on the boards." 'Cause we didn't want to get off those boards. And when I stepped off in that sand, I had on my cowboy boots, and it went clear down in the top of my cowboy boots, that's how deep that sand was. But we finally backed up and let them people go by, and then we went on. It was really bad in those days. Now when you go across that desert, you don't even think of it.

But then I went out there, and I rode at the rodeo there. I rode bucking horses and relay races, 'cause they wanted me to ride the relay race. You ride three horses. And the first horse you ride, you ride a half a mile. And then you change over to the next horse, the second horse, and you ride another half a mile. Then you come in on the second horse, and you get over on the third horse and you ride another half a mile. And so that gives you a mile and a half. And the way you win is to quick change from one horse to the other. Three different horses. And the one that comes in first is the winner. With the best time. But what makes you win is how quick you change from one horse to the next horse. Lots of times I never touched the ground. I'd come in, and I'd stop that horse, and I'd just jump over on the other horse and they'd cut him loose, see? And I had what they called a holder, who held this horse, see, and then I had what they called a catcher, that caught the horse as I come in. They was two cowboys, and as I'd come in and pull up this horse, he'd catch it, and then I'd just jump over on the other horse, and then he'd turn the horse loose.

When I was out there in Los Angeles, why Tom Mix came to me, and he had a girl the same age as I was. And her name was Ruth Mix. And he said, "Would you take a room with my daughter?" He says, "I know you don't drink and you don't smoke. I don't want her associating with some of them that do. And I would like for her to get acquainted with you. I've heard so much about you." And he was so nice, and so Ruth and I, we roomed together there for about two weeks. And we got to be real good friends. Well, later on, she married a cowboy, but it didn't last. She didn't live with him very long. And after she divorced him and left, then I've never heard of her anymore. I don't know what ever happened to her. But, of course, I did run into quite a lot of celebrities. There was Gene Autry, and Roy Rogers, and, you see, they used to perform at the rodeos where we did.

When I went to this Watermelon Days in 1924, then's when I met Shorty. But then I never seen him anymore until 1929. He was rodeoing and I was rodeoing. But I rodeoed mostly in the north, and he rodeoed most in the south. And in 1929, I went to the Rocky Ford, because they just thought that I belonged to them at Rocky Ford. And I had to always go to that show. So I went to this show, and Shorty had a younger brother who is a year younger than I am. And how or why he was there, I'll never know. But anyway, he was at the Rocky Ford rodeo.

And I was riding a race. Now, it wasn't a relay race. It was just a flat race. This was a half a mile flat race. And one of the riders either couldn't handle his horse or he was going to cut me off. But anyway he ran me into the fence, and when my horse stopped it threw me over and all the horses ran over me. And so I was knocked unconscious, and they took me to the first aid tent. And I had my father up there with me. I'd took him up there with me to see the rodeo. 'Cause it was only 60 or 70 or so miles. And he had gotten to where he couldn't work any more. And I wanted him to go and see me ride. So I took him up there, and I had him up in the grandstand. And so we were staying at a private home.

Back in those days, so many places you'd go, they wouldn't have room in the hotels for you. And I liked to stay in a private home because I could get maybe my breakfast, in my room, and then if I needed to do a little laundry, I could do that. And it was more convenient than staying in a hotel. And then if I wanted to go to bed at nine o'clock, I could go to bed at nine o'clock. If it was in a hotel, why they'd probably keep you up till twelve. So I always looked for a private room. Well, I'm still good friends with this woman that I got this room in Rocky Ford back there in 1928. She lives in Denver, and she's close to, well, I think she's past 80. And well, she just thinks like, we're just family. You know. I've known her so long.

And so she was working in one of the booths underneath the grandstand, and she knew now my father he could walk, but he couldn't get up out of the chair. If I'd help him out of the chair, he could walk. She heard over the loudspeaker that I had been hurt. And so she went up in the grandstand. She thought she would go up there and help him get up and get down so he could see how I was getting along. And she went up there and he said, "No." He says, "There's not a thing I can do to help her." He says, "I guess I'll just sit here and finish watching the show." 'Cause he always thought I could take care of myself.

Well, where Shorty's brother came in, I didn't know that he was there, but after I got hurt, see, why, then he came down there to the First Aid station to see how bad I was hurt. So he came down there and . . . they took me out to this Ora Denny's house where I was living, or staying, and he stayed there and helped her put hot packs on me and I had a busted knee, and I was kind of busted up, and I had a black eye.

I was supposed to go to Eldorado, Kansas for the next show. By that time, I had gotten me a horse and a car and a trailer, see. And I had my own trick riding horse, and I had my own saddle. And so I was going to go to Eldorado, Kansas.

Well, Shorty was coming from some place down in Texas or
Oklahoma, and he was coming to Eldorado, Kansas, so we was
going to see each other there. So his brother says, "Well, I
think I better drive you there." He says, "I don't think you're in
very good shape." And so he drove me back to Eldorado, and
when we drove in, why Shorty was out there at the rodeo
grounds, and we pulled in there with my horse and the trailer
and I had on some colored glasses' cause I had this black eye,
and he just reached in through the door, and he just jerked my
glasses off, and he said . . . he'd already heard about the
accident, and he said, "What you got that there eye covered up
for?"

But then we went together for two years, and then we
was married in 1931. But I'd see him at some shows and he'd
go to some other show and maybe I'd go to some other show,
but along toward the last we'd try to make the same shows.
'Cause I know we went to Chicago in '29. I went with my
brother then that was four years older than I am, and he
rodeoed some. He never rodeoed as much as I did, but for two
or three years he rodeoed. One year he went to Madison
Square Garden. He bulldogged there. When he went to the
rodeos, he just bulldogged. He never rode the bucking horses.
He could do better in the bulldogging than he could the
bucking horses. However, when he started, he started on the
bucking horses.

The worst time I got hurt was in 1940, when we went to
New York. Well, in fact, I started to go to New York to
Madison Square Garden in 1937, and I rode there 1937, '38,
39, and '40. Well, in 1940, I was trick riding there. The bronc
riding was all contest, but the trick riding was contract. And I
had a contract to trick ride at Madison Square Garden, in 1940,
and the show was about, I'd say a third over, and one night as I
went in, why, I had made my first run and I think they was six
trick riders and I had made my first run and everything was
fine and the second time I went, in between the time I'd went
the first time and the time I went the second time, there was a
lady came in and she had on a white fur coat and she threw
this over the rail right. . . and I was running probably three feet

from the rail. My horse was running three feet from the rail.
He hadn't seen that when he went around there the first time.
When he went around the second time, he seen that white fur
coat and you know what he did? He just stopped, like a
calfroping horse, he just stopped. Well, I was standing up in
straps on the back of my saddle, and I would do this . . . this
trick I was doing, I would stand up on the back of my saddle,
halfway . . . well, down the full length of Madison Square
Garden. Then we'd go around the circle and as we went
around the circle, I would just fall over backwards and hang
with my feet around the circle. And then after we'd straighten
out, then I'd come up and get back up in the saddle. Well, as I
was going . . . as I was standing up in the straps, and when this
horse seen the white fur coat, he just stopped. And when he
did, it threw me off on the right hand side of the horse, which
is the wrong side of the horse, 'cause you get on on the left
hand side. And this scared him. Well, he turned around and he
didn't run off right then. He just kind of went to the back end
of the arena where the gate was that we had come in, and he
was just kind of trotting and I was talking to him, and I
thought, well, when he gets back there, he'll stop and then I'll
get loose, because I was helpless, just hanging on the wrong
side with one foot, and my head was just a-hanging down
almost to the ground.

They was three cowboys that would stand on each side to
keep the horses from cutting in. Sometimes the horses would
want to cut in and not go all the way around. So the one that
was closest to me, he thought . . . well, naturally it scared him
because he knew I was helpless and I'd have to have help. So
he ran at that horse instead of walking up to that horse and
taking a little time and talking to the horse. He could have went
up there and caught the horse, fine. Instead of that, he just ran
at the horse and grabbed at the rein and then he missed the
rein, and the horse swung around and hit my head into the
concrete wall and knocked me out. And here I was dangling.
And that sure did scare him, and then he ran off. Well, he ran
to the back end of the Coliseum, there was a hundred cowboys
down there. They all ran out there. They tried to catch him,

they couldn't catch him. And then they tried to close in on
him, and they couldn't ever catch him. He'd just whirl around
and he'd go first one way and then another. Finally they turned
in the pickup horses, two of them in on pickup horses and
they finally caught him. And then they cut me off, and I was
unconscious for—I don't know how long—but I was in the
hospital there for six weeks. And that's when I hurt my back.
And I think that's the reason I've had the back trouble in the
later years.

And then he stepped on my arm and I had a third degree
burn, like a third degree burn here on my arm, and while I was
in the hospital they'd put some kind of a . . . I called it medicine but it was something that made you grow a real thick scar
overnight, and then the nurse would come in every day and
pick that off and put some more on. And you know, I hardly
have a scar there left. That's how they kept it from making
such a scar on my arm. Otherwise, I'd have had a real bad scar.
But now that was the worst.

That was one of my feature tricks. Yeah, that was one of
my feature tricks. Now, I used to go under the horse's belly
when he was running, and then I'd go under his neck when he
was running. And . . . but this one . . . the people liked this one
better than they did. . . . They couldn't tell when I'd go under
the horse's belly for sure what I was doing. But this, you see,
whenever I'd stand up there and they thought, why, I'm just
standing up, and then I'd just fall over backwards, they'd all
gasp. They thought, why, sure, she fell off.

We wore tennis shoes. We wore tennis shoes, and you
didn't have them laced in there, it was just the strap on the
back of the saddle. You know where the strap is on the back
of the saddle, it's tied down to the ring—what do they call
that? The "D" ring. Just tied down to the "D" ring, which just
made a loop like that. Well, you'd just stand up in that loop.
Just slip your feet in there. Well, you see, when you want to get
out of there, all you've got to do is just slip your feet out of
there, and then I'd touch the ground on the back of the horse
and then I'd just vault up to my saddle and I'd be through.

After I got hurt back there, then Shorty he never wanted me to do that trick any more. In fact, they had to cut one of the strings off to get me out when I was hurt. So then he took his knife and took the other one off, and he never would let me have it re-laced. I always wanted to have it re-laced and have it put back on, but he never would let me have it re-laced.

I could tell in 1941 that I was kind of losing my balance. I didn't have a good balance that I had always had. And so I decided maybe it was about time to quit. And we had already been talking that we was thinking about quitting, because I'd put in 17 years and he'd put in 20, and that was long enough.

Despite the attraction the west had for the public, she never really tried to branch out, as so many western and rodeo stars had, into the movies. She took a small part in a picture Ken Maynard made in 1928 at the Cheynne Frontier Days. Called "Cheyenne," it dealt with trick riders, and she did her trick riding act. The movie was a novelty, but she never thought of trying for a career in films. What she loved was the riding itself.

Bronc riders are like bullfighters in that they are only half an act. The quality of the animal, the other half, is crucial. And, while it takes two to dance, the better the partner, the more dangerous the dance.

You might draw one that didn't buck very good. And then the next one you'd draw would be one of those horses that bucked real good. You'd always want one that would buck good—'cause you couldn't win if you didn't have a horse that would buck good. The same way with Shorty. He was always wanting to ride the worst horses he could get because if he could ride them, then he could win. But if he'd draw what we called a dog, one that didn't buck very much, why you couldn't win anything.

Bronc riders use a lottery to draw the horses they will ride in competition. But trick riders train their horses carefully.

Now this little black horse, his name was Tom Thumb, and I took him to London, England, in 1934. And we rode over there for 36 days and nights. And I had trained him. I bought him from a man in Garden City, Kansas, and he used him for bulldogging. He was a little bit too small, but he was fast. And he'd found him another horse. And he was a big man, he was probably bigger than Shorty. And this horse was a small horse, probably he'd weigh 850 or 900 pounds, see, and he was too small. So I bought him. Well, he knew something about rodeo, but he didn't know anything about the trick riding. And I trained him for trick riding. I took this horse and I worked twice a day, and it took about four or five months to train that horse so I could take him to a show and trick ride on him. And then I rode him for 10 years. And then I got me another horse, and I bought me a white horse. And this white horse was never as good as the black horse. He was a little bit bigger horse, and he was a little more flashy horse for the rodeos, but as far as being dependable, he never was as dependable, and he was the one I got hurt on in New York.

The British, as great horse lovers, enjoyed the rodeo stars.

We was supposed to work there 3 days, and they held it over six days longer because they enjoyed it so much. And, now, it was all contest over there. I had to contest in the bronc riding and contest in the trick riding. And I went 4th in the trick riding, and I would have went first in the bronc riding other than I rode 14 bucking horses and out of that 14, I won 13 first and bucked off of the 14th horse. . . . So then that lost me the finals. Course I got day money every time that I won a first day money I got money. Well, I made more money than any other girl there because I won all those first day money. But then if I could have rode that other horse, see, why? I could have won the finals, and I would have won the big prize.

And then we went to Australia in 1939, and we worked over there. In fact we were gone for four months, but actually we only worked for nine days and nights at the Royal Easter Show, because we didn't take any horses over there with us, we just took our saddles and equipment, and we broke the Australian horses and it was quite a job to break them in that length of time, so we had about like six weeks to break those horses and before, over here, maybe I'd work six months on a horse. But over there I had six weeks to break that horse so I could trick ride on him, and the same way with Shorty—he had to break his horse so he could bulldog off him in six weeks' time. And we rode on a train after we landed in Australia. They've got little trains over. . . . This, of course, is probably different now, but in those days, in 1939, they didn't have any doors on the train. It was just like a street car. And we went 250 miles in this train up from Sydney, Australia, up to a little town they called Meraw. And there was a station. It was a ranch but they call it a station, and this fella he had lots of horses, and they must have run in a hundred head of horses, and they let us pick out whatever horse that we wanted to see if we could train.

If we hadn't done the kind of work we done, we'd never have seen any of the world. Of course, we never could have afforded it.

When she died, in 1993, a few months after Shorty, Gene was sorely crippled by her back, which had bothered her ever since the Madison Square Garden accident more than 50 years before. Once in a while, the Cheyenne television station carries a rodeo. Whenever she managed to watch, she was likely to comment on the quality of the trick riders and, in particular, of the bronc busters. A crow-hopping horse would be sure to be remarked upon.

Would a friend or relative enjoy this book?

Bingham Hill Press would be pleased to send a copy inscribed by the editor to anyone of your choice. If you prefer, we will send the book(s) directly to you. Simply fill out this form and send it, along with a check for $18.95 (cost of the book plus $2 for postage and wrapping) for each book ordered to Bingham Hill Press, P.O. Box 87, Bellvue, CO 80512.

Your Name: _____

Your Mailing Address: _____

_____

If you wish inscription(s) signed by the editor, please tell us what to say:

_____

_____

_____

Send To: _____

Mailing Address: _____

_____

_____

Please allow at least three weeks for delivery.